Qualitative and Quantitative Mathematical Economics

ADVANCED STUDIES IN THEORETICAL AND APPLIED ECONOMETRICS
VOLUME 1

EDITORIAL BOARD

P. Balestra, Université De Genève, Switzerland
M.G. Dagenais, Université de Montréal, Canada
A.J. Hughes Hallett, Erasmus University Rotterdam, The Netherlands
J.H.P. Paelinck, Netherlands Economic Institute, The Netherlands
R.S. Pindyck, Sloane School of Management, Massachusetts Institute of Technology, Cambridge, United States

The Special Scope of the Series

The fortress of econometrics has often been laid siege to from one or a few sides only. According to their inspiration or inclination, authors have laid stress on model specification, parametrer estimation, testing and prediction or more generally the use of models (prediction in particular being a rare bird in econometric literature). Special topics, such as errors in the variables, missing observations, multi-dimensional data, time-series analysis, dynamic specification, spatial autocorrelation, were dealt with as and when the need arose.

No econometric exercises will ever be complete. Nevertheless, in setting up such an exercise as part of an operational economic investigation, one may reasonably be expected to try and encompass in it as many aspects of econometric modelling as may present themselves. This series is devoted to the publication of work which, as far as possible, addresses all aspects of a "complete econometric modelling" approach; for instance, spatial econometrics or policy optimisation studies which account explicitly for the specification, estimation or analysis of components of those models in the widest sense, including any complementary components from the environment in which the economic model must operate.

The very objective of the series may limit its extensions; but as André Gide put it (Les faux monnayeurs), "il est bon de suivre sa pente, pourvu que ce soit en montant".

All correspondence should be addressed to A.J. Hughes Hallet or to J.H.P. Paelinck at the Erasmus University, PO Box 1738, 3000 DR Rotterdam, The Netherlands.

Qualitative and Quantitative Mathematical Economics

edited by

J.H.P. Paelinck

1982

Martinus Nijhoff Publishers
The Hague / Boston / London

Distributors:

for the United States and Canada

Kluwer Boston, Inc.
190 Old Derby Street
Hingham, MA 02043
USA

for all other countries

Kluwer Academic Publishers Group
Distribution Center
P.O. Box 322
3300 AH Dordrecht
The Netherlands

Library of Congress Cataloging in Publication Data CIP

Main entry under title:

Qualitative and quantitative mathematical
economics.

(Advanced studies in theoretical and applied
econometrics ; v. 1)
Contents: Tribute to Luigi Solari / Richard
Stone -- The scientific work of Luigi Solari /
J.-N. Du Pasquier and E. Rossier -- Econometric
model building for the Common Market / A. Barten
-- A nonlinear expenditure system : qualitative
analysis and experiments with Canadian data /
F. Carlevaro -- [etc.]

1. Economics, Mathematical--Addresses, essays,
lectures. 2. Econometrics--Addresses, essays,
lectures. 3. Solari, Luigi. I. Solari, Luigi.
II. Paelinck, Jean H. P. III. Series.
HB135.Q33 1982 330'.028 82-7879
ISBN 90-247-2623-9 AACR2

ISBN 90-247-2623-9 (this volume)
ISBN 90-247-2622-0(series)

PRINTED IN THE NETHERLANDS

LUIGI SOLARI (1932-1977)

ESSAYS IN MEMORY OF LUIGI SOLARI

TABLE OF CONTENTS

The systematics of symbol use in this book:

- Lower-case letters (Latin or Greek) represent scalars
- Underlined lower-case letters represent vectors
- Matrices are represented by capital letters
- Gradients are noted as $\frac{\partial f}{\partial \underline{x}}$ or $\partial f/\partial \underline{x}$
- Jacobians are noted as $\frac{\partial \underline{f}}{\partial \underline{x}}$ or $\partial \underline{f}/\partial \underline{x}$

PRESENTATION OF THE VOLUME

J.H.P. Paelinck, Netherlands Economic Institute and
Erasmus University Rotterdam

Luigi Solari left us on November 12, 1977, at a moment of his life when he could have given many a contribution to the topics that are presented hereafter in memory of him.

Linearly logical, then mathematical economics preceding quantification, and sometimes leading up to more advanced "quantitative" (0-1, or combinatorial) problems, those were the subjects that had his permanent attention; how he worked out his ideas on epistemology is one moving chapter of this book, as it so vividly recalls the person Solari, to whom a well-deserved tribute has been given.

Specifying our relationships is a complex though indispensable step in our thinking. Probably no economist starts out in theoretical life by writing down complex equations, be it in terms of functional forms or of variables included. Non-linearities, discontinuities, asymptotes, they all result from previous - sometimes, during the gestation phase, sloppy - thinking. Two chapters are devoted to modelling, one being in a field Luigi liked very much, and to which he has contributed in an original way.

Estimating and testing these relationships is considered the econometrician's stronghold, which has to be permanently kept robust against missing data and specification biases; hence two contributions evaluating the cost of our ignorance or misbehaviour.

But what would it all be good for if no choices had to be guided by the results of the previous exercises? The volume is concluded by new results in the field of revealed-preference detection and multi-criteria decision processes, both exercises relying heavily on previous econometric results.

The final versions of the papers collected together in this volume were contributed in July 1980. The responsibility we unhesitatingly took in editing this volume was not only scientific, it had also a deep human dimension: would the volume as such reach the heights on which the person it remembers used to dwell and think? One thing is certain: all contributions have been prepared and written up as a token of lasting friendship and esteem for a colleague who honoured the profession, and this additional incentive could only bias them towards relatively more perfection.

But as the cartesian Nicolas de Malebranche once said, "il faut tendre à la perfection sans jamais y prétendre"; Luigi Solari, the humanist, would have wholeheartedly agreed with him.

While this volume was in press we heard of the tragic death of another colleague, Edouard Rossier, of the Department of Econometrics at the University of Geneva. We would like to evoke his memory together with that of Luigi Solari.

PART I

REFLECTING ON METHODOLOGY

CHAPTER 1

TRIBUTE TO LUIGI SOLARI*

Richard Stone, University of Cambridge, England

As most of you know, our friend and colleague Luigi Solari died unexpectedly less than a year ago. He was forty-five years old. It happened near Paris when he was returning to Geneva on 12 November 1977 shortly after giving a lecture there. As professor of econometrics at the University of Geneva, founder and director of its Department of Econometrics, he was the original chairman of the programme committee for this conference. Before we begin our scientific work I should like to say a few words in his memory.

Luigi Francesco Felice Solari was born on 28 August 1932 in Lugano. He went to school there and then attended the universities of Munich, Geneva and Paris where he read economics and statistics, learning his econometrics in Paris from René Roy and Edmond Malinvaud. He obtained his first degree in economics from Geneva in 1954 and a doctorate from that university in 1963. In the intervening period he received various certificates and diplomas in statistics from the University of Paris to which he remained attached throughout his life.

In 1958, five years before he received his doctorate, Solari was put in charge of research at the Research Centre of the Faculty of Economic and Social Sciences at Geneva. Shortly after receiving his doctorate he was appointed extraordinary professor of econometrics, the first chair in the subject in Switzerland, and in February 1965 he was promoted to an ordinary professorship. In 1966 he founded an Econometric Centre at the university and became its director, a post which he continued to hold when it became a department of the faculty in 1968. In this capacity he trained a number of able econometricians, including several who stayed on as his colleagues at the department. Thanks to him Geneva has acquired a wide reputation for econometrics and is now one of the most active centres in our field. Its development has taken place in an international atmosphere since Solari made a point of meeting many of the dis-

*) This tribute was presented at the European meeting of the Econometric Society, Geneva, Switzerland, 1978.

tinguished academics who for one reason or another gather in Geneva and usually persuaded them to talk at his seminar. As a consequence the centre has close connections not only with France, Italy and Canada, which he knew well, but also with Britain, Soviet Russia and elsewhere.

In 1968 Solari became vice-dean and in 1971 dean of the faculty at Geneva, thus adding administration to his other duties. During his last ten years he devoted a great deal of energy to university reform, seeking to adapt his university to his conception of the tasks and responsibilities of the times. This was a controversial undertaking which answered to the fiery side of his character and made him enemies as well as friends.

Geneva was not the only scene of Solari's academic activities. Apart from short-term assignments as visiting professor at the School for Advanced Commercial Studies in Montreal and at the Université Laval in Quebec, he held an extraordinary professorship of statistics and econometrics at the University of Lausanne since 1964 and, after undertaking postgraduate teaching at the University of Paris IX-Dauphine from 1970, was appointed associate professor there in 1974.

As a teacher and researcher Solari was characterised by his broad interests, his great knowledge, which he was always seeking to extend, and his inspiring personal example. If he expected much from others it was clear that he expected much from himself. He had a passion for economics and for making it a reliable, practical tool. He wanted his students and assistants to see his vision, discuss it with him and help in the task of improving and advancing it. But he distinguished between value judgements and logical argument and did not try to overpersuade those who saw economics differently. He took a democratic attitude in such matters and I think he was right to do so.

Solari's breadth of interest and his conception of economics are reflected in his writings. Beginning in 1956, his scientific works, written alone or jointly with others, number forty-six. His breadth of interest is shown by the range of subjects they cover: economic methodology, econometric models, production theory, systems of demand equations, regional economics and demography. His conception of economics, his persistent striving after a clarification of fundamentals, can be seen from his three main works which appeared in 1962, 1971 and 1977 and which alone I shall attempt to comment on here.

The first of these, which was in fact his doctoral thesis, was entitled Modèles et décisions économiques: sur les fondements de l'économie pure. It is largely concerned with the structure and classification of models, the nature of decisions and the methods of analysing them. It makes use of the tools of modern mathematics, set theory, topology, abstract spaces and so on, and is written in the spirit of much contemporary mathematical economics, being concerned with the precise conditions under which familiar statements can be considered correct. Some economists are impatient of this way of treating their subject but there can be no doubt that we ought to be as clear as possible about such distinctions as those between endogenous and exogenous variables, deterministic and stochastic models or statics and dynamics. And when we consider how obscure much economic writing is and the oceans of ink that have been devoted to attempts at clarifying what distinguished economists of the past really had in mind, we can see the importance of treating fundamentals.

Solari's second book, *Théorie des choix et fonctions de consommation semi-agrégées: modèles statiques*, is a truly econometric work in that it covers estimation problems and applications as well as economic theory. It begins with the theory of demand by an individual household and goes on to aggregation problems. It then takes up two demand systems: the linear expenditure system and the indirect addilog system. In discussing the first, Solari points out that the committed expenditures (the elements of the vector c in the usual notation) need not all be positive, though negative values of supernumerary income (often written as $\mu-\underline{p}'\underline{c}$) are not admissible, and goes on to work out the consequences of this generalisation. In discussing the second system he emphasises the concept of the hierarchy of goods, an idea which had always played an important part in René Roy's work on demand analysis.

After dealing with economic theory Solari turns to various methods of estimating the parameters of demand systems and of carrying out the calculations. He concludes with applications of the linear expenditure system to Britain, Denmark, France, Italy and its major regions, Norway and Switzerland and of the indirect addilog system to Switzerland alone.

In my introduction to that book I expressed the hope that Solari would turn his attention to the development of dynamic versions of these models as I had tried to do a decade earlier. Although he had this problem in mind in his later years I am not aware that he did much work on it. Instead he became greatly interested in another branch of demand analysis namely the study of what is sometimes referred to as the total or, as Solari termed it, 'enlarged' consumption of the population, which includes not only the goods and services bought by households but also such items as education, health services and so on which are provided for them by public authorities. As president of l'Association scientifique européenne d'économie appliquée (usually known as ASEPELT on account of its original title) he organised in Geneva at the end of 1974 a conference on consumption covering both private consumption and the analysis and modelling of enlarged consumption. Contributions from writers in both Eastern and Western Europe were published in a volume edited by Solari and J.-N. du Pasquier entitled Private and Enlarged Consumption, ASEPELT series, vol. V, North-Holland, Amsterdam, 1976.

In his last major work, De l'économie qualitative à l'économie quantitative: pour une méthodologie de l'approche formalisée en science économique, Solari returned to general theoretical issues. It is based on his lectures, which were turned into a book at the instigation of and with the collaboration of his colleague Edouard Rossier. As I see it, the general theme can be stated as follows. Our aim is to understand the world we live in as exactly as possible and this requires quantitative knowledge, such as the numerical values of demand or supply elasticities or of the dynamic multipliers of the system. But to obtain this quantitative knowledge we need an organising framework and organising principles and these are essentially qualitative, that is theoretical. Theory is therefore necessary to attain our aim but it is not sufficient. The acquisition of suitable data, and the elaboration of suitable methods for estimating parameters and for testing both the parameters and the theories in which they appear, give rise to separate problems. And so, in relation to our aim, a theory is incomplete unless these problems are also solved and applications of the theory are carried out. With this in mind, Solari discusses such issues as: the concept and identification of a structure; comparative statics; dynamics; and the treatment of optimality in production, in consumption and in the economy as a whole. The final chapter is devoted to estimation problems in economic models.

In addition to his main activities Solari played a role, often an active role, in a number of learned societies. I have mentioned his part in organising the present conference for the Econometric Society and his work for ASEPELT, whose president he was since 1971, in organising their conference on private and enlarged consumption. In 1974 he was elected a member of the International Statistical Institute and from 1972 to 1975 he was president of the Swiss Society for Statistics and Political Economy.

It is a matter of great surprise and regret to me that Solari never became a fellow of our Society. When I consider all he did for econometrics, both through his writings and through his establishment of the centre at the

University of Geneva, I can only think that there must be something defective in our methods of election. It is not that he was never proposed: I proposed him myself in 1970 and eventually his name was put forward by the nominating committee. But there the matter ended.

Solari's work was recognised by the French government in the last year of his life through the award of the title of Chevalier dans l'Ordre des Palmes académiques.

Let me end on a personal note. Luigi Solari and I first met at the beginning of 1968 at a time when he was working on the linear expenditure system. At first we had language difficulties, his English in those days being if anything worse than my French. However, we persevered and, as I have been a frequent visitor to Geneva for many years, we met often. As we were both busy, these meetings were usually hurried and I hoped that at some point we should be able to meet in more relaxed circumstances in Cambridge but his innumerable committments never allowed this to happen. He had hoped to take part in the Econometric Congress at Cambridge in 1970 and it was a great disappointment to me to receive his last-minute telegram announcing that he could not come.

I remember Luigi as a man full of latent fires, who threw himself wholeheartedly into everything he did whether it was delivering a lecture or arranging a party. He was highly amusing, fond of the good things of life and extremely generous. These characteristics made him an excellent host and when, in 1971, I had the good fortune to receive an honorary degree from the University of Geneva, Luigi's conception of the proper way to celebrate such an occasion added a new dimension to the usual organisation of academic festivities: after the degree ceremony my wife and I and about forty or fifty of his friends and colleagues were taken across the lake in an elegant motor yacht to a sumptuous and leisurely meal in a medieval French château and eventually returned to Geneva as we had come. It was a perfect culmination to the day.

I will leave you with this picture of a warm-hearted man, a passionate scholar and a good friend.

BIBLIOGRAPHY OF THE WORKS OF LUIGI SOLARI

1956

(1) Evolution récente de la fécondité en Suisse, Revue suisse d'Economie politique et de Statistique, vol. 92, no. 4, 1956, pp. 476-93.

(2) Un aspect de l'evolution du niveau de vie. Le progrès de l'automobilisme selon les milieux de 1900 environ à aujourd'hui. Le cas de Genève (with E. Breuer), Alliance Internationale de Tourisme, Geneva, 1956.

(3) Perspectives concernant le parc automobile à Genève en 1977 (with R. Girod), in Recueil des Exposés, Semaine Internationale d'Etude de la Technique de la Circulation Routière, O.T.A., London, 1956.

1957

(4) Salaires annuels dans un métier manuel: le bâtiment à Genève en 1955, Etudes et documents du Centre de Recherches Sociologiques de Genève, 1957.

(5) Essai d'application de la logique Keynésienne à l'étude du problème de l'Italie du sud, Bulletin annuel de la Fondation suisse, Cité Universitaire, Paris, vol. VI, 1957, pp. 33-43.

(6) Le niveau de vie de la population salariée. Salaires annuels comparés dans une profession manuell typique, le bâtiment (with R. Girod), Revue suisse d'Economie politique et de Statistique, vol. 93, no. 1, 1957, pp. 49-59.

1959

(7) Sur les attentes à l'entrée de différents services. Recherche opérationnelle (with L. Feraud), in L'aéroport de Genève et son developpement, Publications of the Faculty of Economic and Social Sciences, University of Geneva, vol. XIV, 1959, pp. 193-240, Georg, Geneva, 1959.

1960

(8) Note sur une étude de Mrs. Joan Robinson à propos de la théorie de la répartition (with L. Devaud), Revue d'économie politique, vol. 70, no. 3, 1960, pp. 419-28.

1962

(9) Modèles et décisions économiques. Sur les fondements de l'économie pure, Publication de l'Institut de Statistique de l'Université de Paris, vol. XI, no. 4, 1962, pp. 275-505. Droz, Geneva, 1963.

1963

(10) Sur les fondements logiques des modèles et décisions économiques, Cahiers Vilfredo Pareto, no. 2, 1963, pp. 37-63.

(11) Contenu et portée des modèles économètriques, Dialectica, vol. 17, no. 4, 1963, pp. 328-52.

(12) Histoire et élaboration statistique. L'exemple de la population de Genève au XVe siècle (with J.-Fr. Bergier), in Mélanges d'histoire économique et sociale en hommage au Professeur Antony Babel, Georg, Geneva, 1963, pp. 197-225.

1964

(13) A propos d'un traité d'économétrie, *Cahiers Vilfredo Pareto*, no. 3, 1964,pp. 245-46.
(14) Per un indirizzo attuale dell'econometrica, *Rassegna economica* (Banco di Napoli), no. 2, 1964, pp. 431-46.
(15) Sur l'enseignement de l'économétrie, *Bastions de Genève*, no. 13, 1964, pp. 56-59.

1965

(16) L'économétrie, recherche d'une synthèse entre expérience et théorie, in *Pour une méthodologie des sciences économiques*, Publications of the Faculty of Economic and Social Sciences, University of Geneva, vol. XVII, 1965, pp. 23-40, Georg, Geneva, 1965.
(17) Pour une généralisation de la théorie conventionelle de la production, in *Mélanges publiés par la faculté des sciences économiques et sociales de l'Université de Genève à l'occasion de son cinquantenaire*, Publications of the Faculty of Economic and Social Sciences, University of Geneva, vol. XVIII, 1965, pp. 91-107, Georg, Geneva, 1965.
(18) Comptabilité nationale. Revue et produit nationaux, in *Lexique de l'économie suisse*, Baconnière, Neuchâtel, 1965, pp. 186-96.
(19) Démographie, in *Lexique de l'économie suisse*, Baconnière, Neuchâtel, 1965, pp. 233-36.

1966

(20) La simulation dans la prévision et la programmation en économétrie, *Revue suisse d'Economie politique et de Statistique*, vol. 102, no. 3/4, 1966, pp. 391-408, reprinted in *Analyse et Provision, Futuribles*, S.E.D.E.I.S., No 4, 1968, pp. 653-64.

1967

(21) Contre-note au "Rapport Général", in *L'éfficacité des mesures de Politique Economique Régionale*, Facultés Universitaires N.-D. de la Paix, Namur, 1967, pp. 76-83.
(22) Structures économiques et modèles de politique économique quantitative, *Revue suisse d'Economie politique et de Statistique*, vol. 103, no. 3, 1967, pp. 331-52.

1968

(23) Modèles économiques et régulations, in *The Social Sciences: Problems and Orientations*, Moutôn/Unesco, The Hague, 1968, pp. 384-96.
(24) *Analyse de la consommation privée en Suisse. Modèle DL.I (48/64-S). Spécification, méthode d'estimation et analyse*, Centre d'Econométrie, Cahier FN/4007/1, University of Geneva, 1968 (mimeographed).
(25) Fonctions de consommation semi-agrégées pour la Suisse, 1948/66, *Revue suisse d'Economie politique et de Statistique*, vol. 104, no. 2, 1968, pp. 111-54.
(26) De quelques extensions de la théorie conventionelle de la production, in *Recherches récentes sur la Fonction de Production*, Facultés Universitaires N.-D. de la Paix, Namur, 1968, pp. 73-95.
(27) *Extensions conceptuelles et statistiques du système linéaire de dépense, Centre d'Econométrie, Cahier FN/4777.1/1, University of Geneva, 1968*

(mimeographed).
(28) Inhaltliche und statistische Erweiterungen des linearen Ausgabensystems Institute of Statistics and Econometrics, University of Mannheim, D.P.8, 1968.
(29) Analyse économétrique d'une micro-région, in Mélanges d'étude économique et sociales offerts à Claudius P. Terrier, Publications of the Faculty of Economic and Social Sciences, University of Geneva, vol. XIX, 1968, pp. 241-49, Georg, Geneva, 1968.
(30) Mouvements migratoires (intérieurs et internationaux) et mobilité sociale en Suisse (with R. Girod), in Exode rural et dépeuplement de la montagne en Suisse, University of Fribourg, 1968, pp. 67-78.

1969

(31) Extension et spécifications économétriques des fonctions de consommation "Indirect Addilog". Première application aux données suisses 1948/66, Centre d'Econométrie, Cahier FN/5243.1/2, University of Geneva, 1969, (mimeographed).
(32) Sur l'estimation du système linéaire de dépenses par la méthode du maximum de vraisemblance, Centre d'Econométrie, Cahier FN/5243.1/3, Université de Genève, 1969 (mimeographed).
(33) Expériences récentes sur l'estimation du système linéaire de dépenses, Centre d'Econométrie, Cahier FN/5243.1/4, Université de Genève, 1969 (mimeographed).
(34) Sur l'estimation des fonctins de consommation semi-agrégées. l'exemple du système linéaire de dépense, Publications économétrique, vol. III, no. 1, 1969, pp. 71-100.

1970

(35) Sur le contenu et la portée de l'approche économétrique, in Transactions of the Sixth World Congress of Sociology, vol. III, 1970, pp.153-65.

1971

(36) Théorie des choix et fonctions de consommation semi-agrégées. Modèles statistiques, Droz, Geneva, 1971.
(37) Le systeme linéaire de dépenses généralisé: spécification et estimation, Cahier du Séminaire d'Econométrie, no. 13, C.N.R.S., Paris, 1971, pp. 67-96.
(38) Expériences économétriques dans le domaine des fonctions de consommation semi-agrégées, Centre d'Econométrie, Université de Genève, 1971 (mimeographed).
(39) Contraintes de production, prix et valeurs ajoutées dans un système input-output (with E. Fontela and A. Duval), Publications économétriques, vol. IV, no. 2, 1971, pp. 333-56.

1972

(40) Production constraints and prices in an input-output system (with E. Fontela and A. Duval) in Input-Output Techniques (eds A. Brody and A.P. Carter), North-Holland, Amsterdam, 1972, pp. 242-60.

1973

(41) Recherche sur l'inflation. Résultats empiriques préliminaires (with G. Antille), Department of Economics, University of Geneva, July 1973.

1976

(42) Introduction (with J.-N. du Pasquier) in Private and Enlarged Consumption, (eds. L. Solari and J.-N. du Pasquier) ASEPELT, vol. V, North-Holland, Amsterdam, 1976, pp. 1-12.

1977

(43) De l'économie qualitative à l'économie quantitative. Pour une méthodologie de l'approche formalisée en science économique (with E. Rossier), Masson, Paris, 1977.

(44) Exposé introductif, in Epargne et nouvelle croissance (ed. J. Craps), Bruxelles, 1977.

1979

(45) Introduction à l'économie quantitative par les applications, Recueil d'exercises et d'applications (with F. Carlevaro and E. Rossier), Masson, Paris, 1979.

(46) European consumption patterns. An East-West comparison (with J.-N. du Pasquier) in Consumption Patterns in Eastern and Western Europe (eds. V. Cao-Pinna and S.S. Chataline), Pergamon, London, 1979.

CHAPTER 2

2. THE SCIENTIFIC WORK OF LUIGI SOLARI

J.-N. Du Pasquier and E. Rossier
Département d'économétrie, Université de Genève

There is an obvious risk in presenting(1) the work of one's master: partiality. We have not tried to avoid this difficulty in any way. Rather than making a pretence of objectivity, we have chosen here to give a presentation of what we consider the essentials of his work.

The first three sections retrace his work, situating it with respect to methodological architecture, from the fundamentals to experimentation. This presentation will be quite cursory in order to almost force the reader to consult its source, to read the work itself.

The last point concerns more personal reflections, quite often suggested by the direct contacts we had with Luigi Solari.

1. THE FUNDAMENTALS

When Luigi Solari published his first book Modèles et décisions économiques - Sur les fondements de l'économie pure in 1962, he was thirty years old. His previous studies had enabled him to grasp the state of current knowledge in economics up to the 1960's. But rather than reporting it in the form of an assessment, he deliberately chose to base his thinking on the antecedents of that knowledge; on what lies, for example, behind the Foundations of Economic Analysis by P.A. Samuelson. Thus, in Luigi Solari's first book, the fundamentals of what the economists of the time (and perhaps of our time as well) considered the fundamentals of economics are the target of his questions.

At this stage of his reflections, Solari was not yet concerned with the various contradictory economic theories, nor even with the various analytic techniques available at that time (Samuelson's book is devoted to precisely that question). First, Solari wanted to find the answer to a preliminary question: what is our basis for saying that economics is a science? what are the fundamentals and the logico-mathematical sequences of this science?

In order to answer these questions, Solari behaved somewhat like the researcher who dissects and classifies, and then catalogues the elements thus isolated and the relationships between them. His tools were propositional logic, and set theory in particular.

1.1 The model

First, Solari listed the steps an economist takes to analyse a phenomenon and synthesized them in the following diagrams.

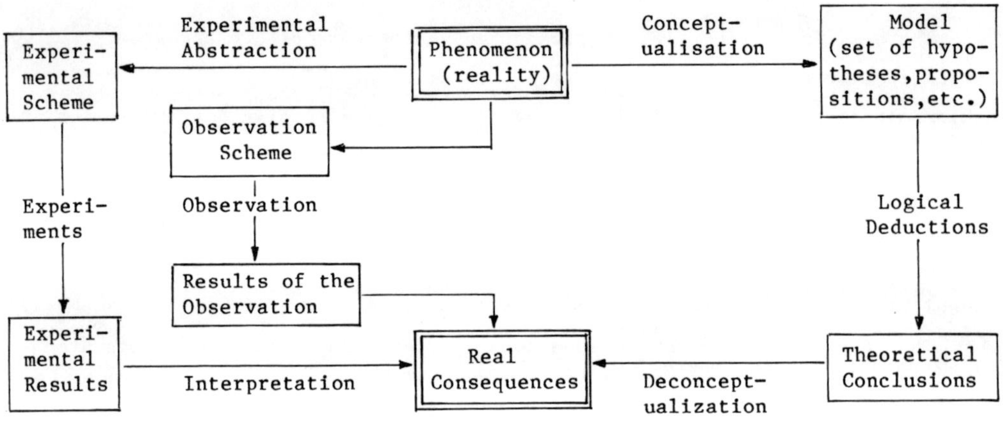

Diagram 1.

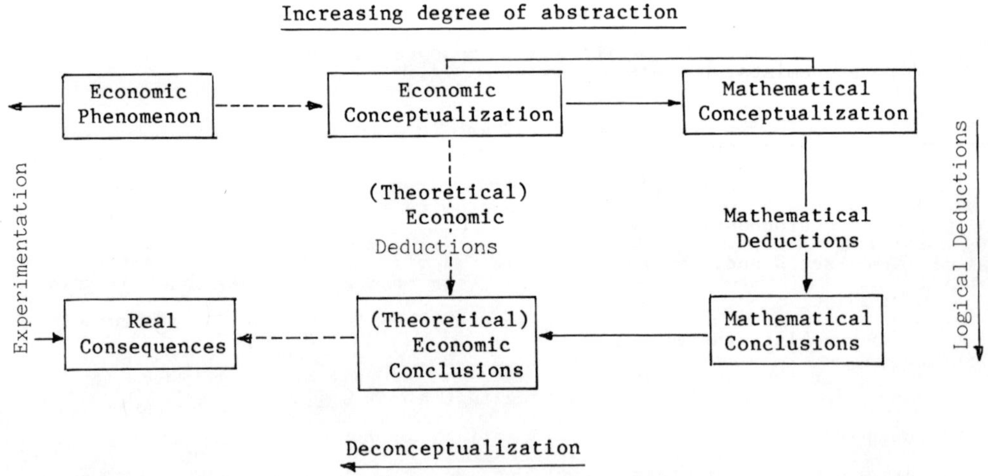

Diagram 2.

The dotted progressions in Diagram 2 correspond to what is sometimes called political economics (general economics in Solari's terms). The unbroken lines correspond to mathematical economics, which Solari called pure economics.

These diagrams might lead one to think that, according to Solari, theoretical elaboration and experimental verification might be dissociated and dealt with independently. That was not his opinion and he discussed the problem further in later publications[(2)].

Solari defines the model as a couple

$$M = (X,H)$$

where X is the class of concepts representing an economic phenomenon and H is the hypothesis[(3)] defined in X, i.e. a propositional form true for all elements of X.

After discussing the various properties of this couple (range, specification) and classifying the various kinds of variables (endogenous and exogenous) and of hypotheses, Solari gets down to analyzing different classes of models and their respective properties:

- separable models, where $M = (X,H) \Leftrightarrow \bigsqcup_i M_i = (X_i,H_i)$;
- deterministic or stochastic models, according to the relation that exists between the domain X and a reference set Ω, and according to the application that can be drawn from this distinction in the class of experimental models;
- the time-dependence models, where the reference set Ω is represented by a set V of functions of a temporal variable.

The simplicity and strength of the logico-mathematical language enabled Solari not only to establish a consistent list of the different kinds of models used by economists, but also to bring out the relative or contingent aspect of certain definitions or properties. Thus the distinction between an endogenous and an exogenous variable is based on a pragmatic decision derived from the phenomenon under observation. Thus, this other distinction between a deterministic and a stochastic model is the result, on the one hand, of choosing reference set Ω and, on the other hand, of choosing which function g(x) to map onto Ω .

Such a list, therefore, cannot be seen as a mere cookbook, but demonstrates that the way of looking at an observed phenomenon, and the way one intends to analyze it, interferes with the phase of conceptualization and theoretical elaboration. The classification of the various models is based on the nature of X, the phenomenon under observation, as defined by the economist.

1.2 The decision

By paying particular attention to the details of the conceptual and logical framework of the decision process in economics, Solari intended to mark the importance of the role the decision plays in the process of acquiring knowledge in the social sciences, as it is an absolutely indispensable complement to the theoretical construction of the model.

Thus we have to define the set of possible or admissable actions, with respect to the decision centres formed by economic agents. The choice of one of these actions is the decision.

Just as in the study of the model, Solari chose to go back to the sources of the intellectual process of the economist to define the logico-mathematical structure of the decision process in order to justify it. In doing so, he introduces the notion of a universe A of appreciations, whose elements represent a possible appreciation of the decision centre considered. A first necessary operation leading to a decision is to match each action of set X of possible actions to one and only one appreciation of set A. The meaning of an appreciation is therefore that of adequacy relative to the action to which it corresponds.

The structure of a set of appreciations obviously is much weaker than a numerical structure. In particular, the comparison of different appreciations, using their degree of adequacy, leads to the introduction of a binary relationship $\mathbf{R}_A$ such that, for example, $a_1 \ \mathbf{R}_A \ a_2$ is equivalent to the true proposition "the degree of adequacy of a_1 is less than or equal to that of a_2". Considering the conditions of consistency expressed by the reflexive and transitive properties, $\mathbf{R}_A$ provides set A with a total or partial quasi-ordering structure.

Solari then defined the extreme elements of A by introducing the distinction between maximum and minimum, and the maximal or minimal degree of adequacy. He finally came back to set X by making the distinction between situations corresponding to one or more optima and to one or more optimal actions.

Having defined the general conceptual framework of the decision, Solari also studies stronger structures in the universe of appreciations which can be suggested in order to emphasize the more or less elaborate character of comparisons between the different actions.

Lastly, he showed how structures introduced to characterize the universe of appreciations can be transported into numerical sets, so that each element of set A could be represented by a number, while still retaining the ordered structure of the set. Three classes of numerical indicators were proposed which respectively correspond to: the notion of ordinal magnitude defined within a steadily increasing transformation, the notion of locatable magnitude where the quasi-distance of appreciation retained is Euclidean, and the notion of measurable magnitude, usually defined within one (positive) multiplicative constant.

2. METHODOLOGICAL ARCHITECTURE

"An understanding of reality can arise only from clear and general thinking. Thus formalized in the sense that it must be today. But there must be a meeting between this general, clear and consistent thought and observable facts. That is to say, it must lead to an experiment"[(4)].

Thus Solari consisely defined the methodological programme of the scientific procedure in economics. From 1963 until he died, he never stopped working on this programme, devoting to it his teaching at the University of Geneva and ceaselessly searching, through constant dialogue with his students, to clarify and improve it. His last book[(5)], published in 1977, presents his reflections on the subject. In it, Solari performs the same sort of analysis that he did for the fundamentals of economics: he lists the problems, classifies them, enquires about their internal coherence, studies their properties. His analysis looks at the construction of the model, the variables that can be introduced and the functional relations that can be proposed. Thus it becomes an extension of the study of the fundamentals by making it more specific and by synthesizing it. This leads Solari to insist on the distinction between the qualitative aspect of a model, where the model is considered as a class of structures, and its quantitative aspect, whereby relations are specified, as well as to study what can be gained from this distinction.

In fact, there is nothing particularly new in the materials used, nothing which we cannot find traces of in the existing literature. The analytic methods are known. What, in our opinion, distinguishes the way Solari approached the matter is the systematic organization of these methods in view of the building of economic models: in other words, their architecture.

2.1 The variables

In general, economic variables refer to sets of observable situations which must then most often be ordered and compared. We have thereby to assume that there is a complete quasi-ordering structure for the set of observable situations. Very often the variables retained in the framework of a model are not directly observable, but can be expressed through other observable variables. In either case, there is generally a problem of aggregation of variables; that is to say, a study of the dimensions (or units of measurement) of the variables under consideration, so as to ensure the coherence of the aggregative operations.

Aggregation presents itself in the form of a correpondance

$$\bar{y} = g(\underline{y})$$

between the set $\underline{y}$ of individual variables and the aggregate $\bar{y}$ defined by the aggregation function g, which is an equivalence relation for the set of individual variables:

$$\underline{y}^1 \sim \underline{y}^2 \Leftrightarrow g(\underline{y}^1) = g(\underline{y}^2) \ .$$

2.2 Causality between variables

In a system of m functional relations written in implicit structural form:

$$\underline{h}(\underline{y}_t; \underline{y}_{t-1}, \ldots, \underline{y}_{t-\tau}, \underline{x}_t) = \underline{0}$$

where the endogenous variables $\underline{y}_t$ represent the state of the system as a function of endogenous lagged variables $\underline{y}_{t-i}$, $i=1,2, \ldots, \tau$, and of exogenous variables $\underline{x}_t$ describing the state of the environment, the variables $\underline{y}_{t-i}$ and $\underline{x}_t$ can be said to respectively exercise a role of temporal and strict causality on $\underline{y}_t$.

This is of help in discerning the impact not only of the choice of variables to be retained in a model, but also of the partition between endogenous and exogenous variables.

2.3 Separability of a sub-model

Let us first emphasize that the notion of the separability of a sub-model is weaker than that of a separable model such as Solari previously defined it.

In a system of n vector relations:

$$\left.\begin{array}{l} \underline{h}(\underline{y},\ \underline{x};\ \underline{z}) = \underline{0} \\ \underline{g}(\underline{y},\ \underline{x};\ \underline{z}) = \underline{0} \end{array}\right\}$$

the sub-model $\underline{h}$, with m < n relations, is said to be separable if:

$$\frac{\partial \underline{h}}{\partial \underline{x}'}\ \frac{\partial \underline{x}}{\partial \underline{z}'} \equiv \underline{0}$$

which yields
$$\frac{\partial \underline{h}}{\partial \underline{y}'}\ \frac{\partial \underline{y}}{\partial \underline{z}'} \equiv -\frac{\partial \underline{h}}{\partial \underline{z}'}\ .$$

The endogenous $\underline{x}$ variables can then be considered as exogenous in the relation defining $\underline{y}$ variables, and the sub-model $\underline{h}$ will be looked at independently of the complete model.

2.4 Qualitative economics

By discussing the various properties governing the variables and their interactions - such as independence, causality, separability - it is easier to grasp the implications of the procedure whereby a theoretical model is constructed, by simplifying the reality under observation in order to isolate a phenomenon and select the relevant variables with which to analyze it. From this point of view, the qualitative approach, which deals with the relations between variables in their general formalisation and attempts to appreciate the coherence of the hypotheses chosen, particularly in their logical implications, provides a valuable tool with which to better evaluate the nature of the model that one intends to use.

In a first elementary analysis of the model, a distinction is made between the endogenous variables that are present and those that are not in each of the relations $\underline{h}(\underline{y};\ \underline{z}) = \underline{0}$. Variables and relations are ordered according to the relation of "strict causality". Such an order is formally obtained by performing independent permutations on the rows and columns of the matrix $\partial\underline{h}/\partial\underline{y}'$, in order to write it in the form of a decomposable matrix:

$$\begin{Vmatrix} A_{11} & & & 0 \\ A_{21} & A_{22} & & \\ \vdots & \vdots & & \\ A_{k1} & A_{k2} & \cdots & A_{kk} \end{Vmatrix}$$

The endogenous variables defined by one of the A_{ii} blocks can then be considered exogenous with respect to the endogenous variables defined by blocks A_{jj}, $j > i$, and as such have an effect of strict causality.

Comparative static analysis in particular, where two states of equilibrium expressed by the structural relations of the model are compared, is simplified by this approach, which allows for many extensions. For instance, the identification of the structures of a model, to the extent that they overlap with the notion of the causal structures liable to be pointed out. Moreover, different conditions of agregation will result in the presence or absence of variables in structural relations.

A pre-requisite for such analysis is the stability of a state of equilibrium. Another is the overall unicity of the representation provided by the model's structural relations. Taken as a whole, the property of unicity of the representation $\underline{h}(\underline{y};\ \underline{z}) = \underline{0}$ is verified if and only if:

$$\underline{z} \in Z;\ \underline{h}(\underline{y}^1;\ \underline{z}) = \underline{0} \quad \text{and} \quad \underline{h}(\underline{y}^2;\ \underline{z}) = \underline{0} \Rightarrow \underline{y}^1 = \underline{y}^2 ,$$

where Z is the definition set of the endogenous variables. The domain of validity of the model is limited by the domain of validity of this property of overall unicity.

Thus, it is clear that from causality to overall unicity, or from dynamic stability to the necessary conditions for a preliminary optimum problem, there is no stage in the economist's conceptualizing process which cannot be clarified by qualitative analysis.

2.5 Model aggregation

When extended to include the notion of model, aggregation acquires a greater range than the aggregation of variables. It includes the set of problems created by the correspondance between two models M_0 and M in representing a given reality.

Often, M_0 will attempt a detailed representation of reality, while M will offer a more overall view, generally simplified. It is possible to limit oneself to a complete specification of the aggregate model, leaving the detailed model only qualitatively defined. The aggregated model may then not be deduced from the detailed one by a complete aggregative procedure.

It is also possible, by starting with the overall representation provided by the aggregated model, to orient oneself towards the disaggregated model by specifying the detailed variables as a function of aggregated variables. Using this procedure, attempts should be made to bring out relations stable enough to convey an explanatory content, as the stability of the aggregated model in this situation no longer necessarily depends on the stability of detailed relations.

A detailed model can also be seen as the reunion of several sub-models which function jointly. The size and complexity of the overall detailed model then makes it indispensable to use an aggregated model which will help us understand the former and clarify its logical sequences as well as its predictive capacities.

2.6 Quantitative economics

When quantifying the model, that is to say attempting to provide the reduced or structural form of the model with a particular structure, we have at our disposal basically two sources of information.

The first and most often non-stochastic source integrates technical knowledge with pragmatic considerations to fix certain coefficients or constraints between parameters, the value of which will characterize a particular structure.

The second source results from the principles of statistical induction, in which the formulation of the theoretical model is to be completed by a given probability law of the variables (generally a conditional probability law) for fixed values of the endogenous variables. The indentification problem in economics is concerned precisely with the study of conditions allowing this particular structure of the model to be determined.

The econometric specification of the model is then defined as an operation of completing the functional theoretical model by hypotheses which determine, at least in part, the probability law of the endogenous variables. Dealing with models with errors in equations of the structural or reduced form, the particular kind of structure adopted will result from the treatment intended for the random error vector.

These hypotheses facilitate the clarifying of the conditions under which the estimation of the model is made, both general conditions and conditions particular to each structure or class of models considered.

2.7 Remarks about the methodological architecture proposed by Solari

By reviewing several particularly meaningful steps in Solari's procedure for grasping economic method as we have done, we have tried to underline what we consider to be the originality of his contribution.

Taking into consideration the process which in economics leads from reflection and formalization (qualitative states) to statistical quantification (an econometric state), Solari attempted to construct an analysis defining each stage of our chain of reasoning, laying down the conditions for its existence, its characteristics and properties.

This attitude which, during the process of acquiring knowledge, emphasizes the antecedents of implementing econometric statistical methods, is designed to restore the latter to their true place in economics. They are indeed an indispensable technical tool but only when subordinated to qualitative thought whose absence renders them inoperative.

3. EXPERIMENTATION

Among the different applied econometric works which Solari undertook or directed, those dedicated to the analysis of household consumption were his favourite domain that, in fact, won him fame on an international level.

From the beginning of his teaching in Geneva in 1963, while simultaneously pursuing his quest for methodological clarification, Solari initiated his research into household consumption in Switzerland. This research, which he continued until his death, resulted in many articles over the years crowned by the publishing of a book in 1971 in which he summarized his findings in this field.

In simultaneously conducting theoretical and methodological reflection on the one hand, and experimentation on the other, Solari saw a necessary condition for his work as a man of science. Seen from this point of view ,the theoretical construction neither appears cut off from the operational extensions which validate it, nor is the experimental research confined to the mere application of statistical techniques to the observable manifestations of a phenomenon. On the contrary, the latter presupposes mastery of a theoretical and conceptual framework capable of ensuring the consistency of an experimentation.

It is this attempt at synthesizing theory and experimental research which is to be found in his 1971 book. We will try to retrace its main arguments.

3.1 The theoretical framework

The theoretical framework, which constitutes the underpinning for the specification of semi-aggregate consumption functions, is made up of individual demand functions $\underline{q} = \underline{q}(\underline{p},\underline{r})$ specified from choice theory.

The individual demand functions, by making possible the study of elasticities, allow goods to be classified according to the character of their necessity, as well as the analysis of substitutions and complementarities between them.

The choice theory endows these laws with a coherent and systematic structure. It emphasizes the structural hypotheses of the universe of consumer behaviour: a quasi-ordering structure leading to ordinal individual utility functions $u = u(\underline{q})$. With this structure, the individual laws then define an adapted complex of consumed goods, given prices $\underline{p}$ and an expenditure r. Moreover, the choice theory allows the definition, through a dual approach, of an indirect utility function $u^*(\underline{p},r) = u[\underline{q}(\underline{p},r)]$, which no longer evaluates the satisfaction level associated with $\underline{q}$ but that associated with the complex adapted to $\underline{p}$ and r.

Finally, the theoretical framework is completed by the study of aggregation problems occurring in the analysis of consumption phenomena. This refers to the aggregation of variables, where the variables originally retained are replaced by representative and operational aggregates. It also involves the aggregation of laws, where the connections between micro-economic relations expressing individual behaviours of consumption cells and aggregated relations supposed to synthetically represent the behaviour of a set of cells, are clarified.

3.2 Specification of the functional forms of the model

Two different particularizations of the general theoretical model are presented and, to some extent, dissected: the linear expenditure system, which assumes the linearity of expenditure functions and relies on a primal utility indicator, and the indirect addilog system which illustrates a dual approach in the context of the choice theory. A formal examination of their properties led Solari to propose hypotheses and formalisation of more general scope.

By way of an example, let us take the conceptual generalzation of the linear expenditure system introduced by Solari. In the past, most authors implicitly admitted that this system had a selection range adapted to goods characterized by a committed consumption. Taking his cue from the hierarchy of needs formalized by his teacher, René Roy, Solari extended the selection range of the linear expenditure system to include the idea of superior goods which do not give rise to obliged consumption, and he emphasized the theoretical fundamentals of the notion of a hierarchy of goods which is connected with the appearance of new consumptions, particularly of superior goods, in response to increasing levels of satisfaction.

3.3 Econometric specification and estimation

The analysis of the problems presented by econometric specification and the estimation of a complete system of demand functions can be viewed as the link between theory and experimentation. The statistical and numerical aspects connected with the estimation of these functions are described in a general fashion. In particular, the properties of the different estimators are presented systematically, as well as sundry numerical estimation methods suggested in the literature on the subject.

3.4 Experiments

Applications derived from these models are on two separate levels. First of all, Solari proceeded to estimate the linear expenditure system for seven European countries. By using two methods, the ordinary least squares method and the maximum likelihood method, to estimate series of data which vary in their degree of aggregation and their duration, it was possible to compare their operative behaviour. The quality of the results provided by the two numerical processes is also compared. Lastly, a simulation is performed to analyze the responsiveness and robustness of the estimators under consideration.

Secondly, Solari applied the two models under consideration, the linear expenditure system and the indirect addilog system, to the same set of data taken from private consumption in Switzerland. Thus it was possible to analyze the behaviour of a typical consumer in great detail; as much in terms of his reactions to the price structure and its evolution, as in terms of the hierarchical organisation of the categories of goods, together with the substitutions and complementaries that arise. This also makes it possible to compare the explanatory power of these two theoretical formulations.

3.5 Experimentation: a completely synthetic process

As Stone reminds us in his preface to Solari's book, "a full econometric study, such as is contained in this book, calls for the ability to put all these elements, data, economic theory, statistical methods and computing techniques, together; a causal attitude to any of them weakens the whole enterprise if, indeed, it does not render it impossible".

This remark is particularly apt when applied to Solari's attitude towards experimentation, that is to say the application of clear, coherent thought to observing reality, using strict analytical methods. A global, complete approach indeed; but each stage is presented and justified in detail and the logic of the sequences between these various components is always indicated.

It is noteworthy that, in a book devoted to presenting the results of an applied research, a good half of it is devoted to examining the conceptual and theoretical framework. This is an indication of the importance Solari attributed to this part of experimental procedure.

In the exposition, considerable space is also given to the problematics of econometric specification, estimation and numerical methods, which Solari discussed in detail. It should also be noted that, when this book was published in the beginning of the 1970's, there were very few econometric studies of complete demand systems, and even fewer experimental applications. In fact, Solari's book was among the first to present operational numerical methods of estimation and complete numerical results for such systems.

4. REFLECTIONS ON THE SCIENTIFIC WORK OF LUIGI SOLARI

In order to define the place occupied by the work of Luigi Solari in contemporary economic thought, it would be useful to pause briefly and remember two features of economics as a science: its age, or historical evolution; and its social status or, as it might be called, its political dimension.

Let us take the history first. Compared to mathematics, physics or biology, economics is a relative newcomer. For centuries, economcis was largely subordinated to philosophy and religion. It was less than a hundred years ago, beginning in particular with the Walras mathematical school, that this discipline assumed the task of breaking into the ranks of the sciences, at least in the modern meaning of the word. It must also be borne in mind that statistical data had largely been lacking and that the application of statistical methods in economics did not take place until nearly the end of the last century, to say nothing of the electronic techniques which originated after the Second

World War.

In its adolescence, as is normal for anyone who wants to prove himself and show his knowledge, economic science most often undertook to transpose existing trends of thought into a formal and operational language[7]. There was then a strong temptation to take advantage of the available methodological and technical arsenal to try to elicit confirmation of a postulate from observation of the facts, rather than to rigorously submit the theory to the test of experimentation. Solari was particularly conscious of this danger and sought to avoid it by weighting the scales in the other direction, concentrating most of his attention on the theoretical end of the theory-experimentation dialectical chain. It seemed to him to be fundamental to analyze the procedure leading up to the construction of the theoretical model and to endow it with a logic and coherence which would render irrefutable not the results it produces, of course, but its scientific character.

It is immediately clear, when referring to the social status of economics, that because of its goal and the implications of its results, it occupies a dangerous position since it is expected to provide information on the organization of social life. Thus it holds a political significance, in every sense of the word. The responsibility of the economist towards society, if it is not qualitatively different from that of other men of science, thus assumes a much more obvious and immediate political dimension. Moreover, social factors outside the scientific domain itself, and inherent in the evolution of industrial society since the end of the last century, have brought about a considerable growth in the importance of the economist's role. No longer is any decision made without the specialist passing judgement on it.

In such a context as this, for a man as convinced as Solari of the relative and fragile character of the conclusions reached by analyzing real facts, the scientific status of the economist's endeavour was the only guarantee of the honesty of the results obtained, the validity of which is never universal, always uncertain.

These remarks should help make Solari's attitude towards economics understandable, and clarify the progression of the reasoning behind his procedure which, taken in its simplest form, could be called an autonomous procedure and goes against all doctrines and ideologies.

At a time when the quantitative approach in economics is unanimously acknowledged to be <u>the</u> method of this experimental science, firmly established by reforms in university teaching in all corners of the world, crowned by

Nobel prize awards to the most famous theoretical and quantitative economists; at a time when one can find in the literaure a wealth of new models, applications or experiments, whose great technicality often vies with their great particularism; in short, at a time when this quantitative approach has become what T.S. Kuhn calls normal science[8], Solari rose up against it and, by asking himself, asked us all: do we really know what we are doing? have we forgotten that the quantitative experimental phase of our procedure, as with all scientific procedure, is necessarily proceeded by a stage, a qualitative stage, of theoretical conceptualization?

Pointing out the uncertainties of the validity of what we are doing, this questioning, whose latent epistomological character we will discuss later, led Solari to wipe the state clean. In other words, he went through the stages of the economist's process step by precise step in order to clearly demonstrate their good and bad points, to try to provide them with a justification and a foundation, before reintegrating them into a well-defined order.

4.1 The structural approach

His particular interest in practising the analysis of the scientific process in economics quite naturally compelled Solari to hold himself apart from what had been done before him, in order to master the necessary basic logical progression implied in the process of acquiring knowledge. He did not express this search for the fundamental by simply formulating some vague and general principles, whose originality would anyway be hard to perceive in the light of the great principles laid down by the whole of experimental science. On the contrary, Solari was seeking for characteristics which, if they are to be part of economic analysis, hint at methodological and conceptual hypotheses particular to this discipline. When studying the behaviour of economic agents, whether individual or collective, it is obligatory to particularize everything including the very foundations of the scientific approach in economics (models and decisions) and to trace these specific features through the subsequent stages of theoretical conceptualization, operational specification and experimentation. In this way Solari came to organize elements, variables and hypotheses, to regroup them in homogenous groups, and from the groups to deduce classes of models.

He conducted this systematic analysis in complete and detailed fashion for the field of consumption analysis, while merely sketching it out for other areas of study.

Thus, without even mentioning it explicitly, Solari brought together all the attributes of a structural approach in economics.

4.2 Theory and the theories

One would search in vain in Solari's work for references to existing economic theories, or research into new theoretical explanations for observed phenomena. On the other hand, his writings team with observations on theory, conceived as a structure of concepts.

This is no paradox if it is accepted that Solari chose to direct his attention towards the methodological and cognitive aspect of economic processes and to thus elucidate the general laws governing it. In this regard, it is natural for Solari to consider theory as a generic stage in the process of explaining a phenomenon, or as an outline of the conceptualization and construction of a model, rather than as an operational specification meant to solve an actual problem. The fact that, during his experimental work on consumer behaviour analysis, Solari had recourse to theoretic formulation tailored to the phenomenon under observation and thus used *a* specific theory, which was in this case the neoclassical consumer theory, in no way invalidates this observation since Solari only made use of the parts of the theory compatible with his methodological framework.

Such an orientation cannot be explained solely in terms of personal affinities or avocations, or by Solari's need to delve to the bottom of things in order to understand their ultimate nature. It is also motivated by what we have called the social status of economic science. Methodological uneasiness was combined in Solari's person with a still more radical political scepticism. Aware as he was that a man of science loses control over the results of his work as soon as they are published and can thus see the work he is responsible for put to uses he would not have desired, Solari always planned his work in such a way that it could not lead to extensions of too normative a political nature. To some extent, his dedication to science forbade any overt dedication to politics.

4.3 The position held by experimentation

We have already said that, for Solari, experimentation was the complement to theoretical conceptualization necessary to form a complete scientific process, and that it was not a mere quantified observation of reality. However, it is worth returning to his experimental research on household consumption, at which he worked for over ten years, many aspects of which help determine more closely his attitude towards the economist's profession.

First, the choice of this research project was not haphazard but corresponds to the fact that "consumption represents in a true sense the final state of any economic activity"(9) and that the only pertinent analysis of its nature and evolution is a structural one.

Here again we see his preoccupation with studying what is basic in economic activity, and undertaking the study in such a way as to detect its deepest mechanisms. Solari reacted with both suspicion and hostility to the short-term approach in economics. He thought it to be limited in nature to an analysis of the ephemeral aspects of phenomena, prossessing no real power to explain. His attitude compelled him on the contrary to seek out what was stable in the behaviour of economic agents, which explains the importance he attributed to distinguishing between the static and dynamic forms of analysis, and to the logical sequences between them.

This experimental research also allows us to make a better estimate of the place Solari reserved for statistical methods in econometrics: a necessary but insufficient tool. A tool, because the qualitative stage of theoretical conceptualization alone determines the orientation of an experiment and the significance of its conclusions. Necessary, because the quality of such conclusions can obviously only be attained through strict techniques. This may seem a trivial observation, but only if we fail to recognize the danger inherent in assigning a privileged status to statistical methods. Indeed, it is tempting to conceal, behind the glitter of sophisticated technique, deficiencies in theoretical formulations and logical incoherence of concepts on the one hand, and on the other, the limited explanatory power of restricted results.

It may also be added that Solari considered those developments of mathematical economics which result in non-operational theoretical formulations and which are therefore cut off from the experimental counterpart that could have been used to test their validity, to be no more satisfactory.

For the same reasons, he looked askance at contemporaneous trends in econometrics, in particular those oriented towards either empiricism or non-operational mathematical economics, and to feel some worry over the growing penetration of their influence on the European continent. In his opinion, ASEPELT was to be the rallying point for those who, aware of the limits of these trends, devote themselves to developing a complete scientific process in which theory and experimentation would co-exist simultaneously in their proper places, within a dynamic relationship. He saw this task as the original contribution which European economists, thanks to their historical and cultural heritage, could make to late twentieth century economics.

One last aspect of the experimental portion of Solari's work deserves to be mentioned; this time in the form of a question. Why had Solari, who quite rapidly evolved very satisfactory theoretical and operational formulations for representing consumer behaviour in Switzerland, not tried to extend the results he obtained? Here we are thinking of two fairly obvious extensions. First, the results could be exploited to improve our knowledge of the theoretical model used, and to perfect it by modifying it or by substituting other formulations. Second, while temporarily accepting this model as it stood, an attempt could be made at developing similar structural models for other sectors of the national economy, in order to obtain a formalized and operational representation of all the economic activities of the country.

Solari had indeed thought of both extensions in the 1970's as part of a research program which he had proposed should take place around him, leaving it to his students to bring it to a successful conclusion.

All in all, Solari implicitly assigned an unexpected position to the experimental side of his research work: that of an exercise in methodology, an example meant to prove to himself that the integrated scientific process he was aiming at, was feasible.

4.4 The epistomological aspect

Piaget has defined two distinct epistomological domains[10]: the internal epistomological domain, i.e. the activity of any science seeking through epistomological self-criticism to form a theory of knowledge for its own internal use, and the derived epistomological domain, where an attempt is made to bring to the fore the more general epistomological implications from the results obtained in a particular science especially when examining the problem of the relationship between observer and observed, and the modalities of the setting up of this relationship.

Considered from this angle, it immediately appears that the whole of Solari's scientific work corresponds to the definition given by Piaget of the internal epistomological domain. We have sufficiently discussed the stages of the scientific processes adopted by him, which can be considered as so many steps and logical sequences in the process of acquiring knowledge, for us not to go back into details about this.

At this point, it is possible to ask oneself if economic explanation, as Solari sees it, consists of discerning the existence of primary and irreducible theoretical structures of behaviour, of if it consists rather of a progressive construction of evolutive structures. In the first case, the object under study will be considered in a static fashion, as a being whose behaviour tends to conform to a state of equilibrium in aninfinite or original horizon. In the second, one does not consider the objects as entities but from the standpoint of the relationships which they reciprocally develop, in order to determine the laws of dynamic composition of these interactions. It is difficult to settle this question one way or another since Solari's work varies between these two poles. When he defined the quasi-ordering structure characterizing the universe of economic decisions or the existence domain of consumed goods, he used the first process. When, by his method, he implies an uninterrupted dialectical dialogue between theory and experiment, it is the second he follows.

Let us now consider the extensions of this cognitive approach to what Piaget called the derived epistomological domain, by studying Solari's position on the subject-object relationship, which raises a question basic to all sciences and even more so in the humanities: the problem of the degree of neutrality and objectivity in science.

However powerful the methods used by econometricians, said Solari, they do not stand as logically consistent on their own, and the results to which they lead cannot be labelled as scientific unless the theoretical framework into which they are to fit has been defined beforehand. To ignore this pre-requisite for all scientific activity menas that the conclusions arrived at will not be liable to interpretation, and that the experimental results will contribute no new actual knowledge whatsoever. Thus Solari considers that the intellectual act of theoretical conceptualization is pre-eminent compared to the act of experimental verification, in the dialectical relationship which unites them.

This affirmation brings up questions about the nature of the scientific procedure in economics, and on the role of the knowing subject in relation to the object to be known. Through the qualitative approach he proposed and defined, Solari questioned the objectivity of knowledge in the social sciences, contrary to the view held by those who are tempted to rely too much on the apparent irrefutability of the logico-mathematical instruments they use. He reminds us of the subjectivity governing experimental life and reintroduces the relative, temporary aspect of the conclusions reached.

Through this, he clarified his antagonism towards observing without a model or, it could be said, towards a loose description of reality. "There was and too often today still is a wide gap between the logical strictness of theoretical construction and the empiricism of experimental verification", wrote Solari(11). Now it is apparent that the presence of a theoretical model in the scientific procedure is not in itself a sufficient condition to guarantee the validity of this procedure, since it is quite possible that a badly chosen model, inappropriate or unspecified theoretical hypotheses, contribute to inconsistency rather than consistency. Any researcher who would take the easier path and pretend to ignore the implications of his choice and the criteria of his decisions, putting his confidence in the objectivity of the methods he used, would at the same time lose all hope of control over evaluating the results of his work. Although experimental, the scientific process is not neutral for all that. In the process of gathering knowledge, the subject is not a passive witness to the progress of the experiment. Results do not stem directly from the application of an analytic, objective method to the observable manifestations of a phenomenon. Nor is their elucidation provided for us directly from the facts themselves.

These, in our opinion, are some of the epistomological aspects of Solari's work which, at the same time, reveals itself as a critique of the modern trends of empiricism and neo-positivism.

4.5 The significance of the scientific work of Luigi Solari

Rarely, in the vast crowd of contemporary economists, does one encounter a person whose scientific work, taken as a whole, is primarily oriented towards self-interrogation in order to redefine its activity. It is much more natural to avail oneself of the accomplishments of great masters of the past in order to continue on the pathe they first trod. The first attitude demands great force of mind together with energy and endurance enough to bear the risk of isolation. It is quite significant, in this respect, that the only master in whom Solari saw something of himself, and whose thinking he was in sympathy with, was René Roy, the French econometrician.

As is evident, Solari's work occupies a special place. Even if it in no way claims to answer all the questions we could ask about the status and function of economics, even if it limits itself to an examination of the methodological content of the theories it implements, it still comes at an appropriate moment to remind us of the rigours of scientific honesty and of methodological lucidity, as well as the modesty of the man.

NOTES

(1) We wish to thank Professors V. Cao-Pinna, J.H.P. Paelinck and R. Stone, as well as our friends F. Carlevaro and D. Royer for their helpful comments and criticisms.

(2) In particular, Contenu et portée des modèles économétriques, Dialectica, 1963.

(3) Usually, it will be a set of hypotheses.

(4) De l'économie qualitative à l'économie quantitative, Masson, Paris, 1977, p. IX.

(5) Ibidem.

(6) Théorie des choix et fonctions de consommations semi-aggrégées - Moèles statistiques. Droz, Genève, 1971.

(7) It is significant, in this respect, to observe the extent of the intellectual debt contemporary economists owe to the great theorists of the 19th century and to see how slight is the advancement of today's prevailing theories compared to the large bodies of theory developed in the last century.

(8) T.S. Kuhn, The Structure of Scientific Revolution, The University of Chicago Press, Chicago, 1962.

(9) Cf. Solari, L. and Du Pasquier, J.-N., eds., Private and Enlarged Consumption, North-Holland Publishing Company, ASEPELT, vol. 5, Amsterdam, 1976.

(10) Cf. J. Piaget, Logique et connaissance scientifique, PUF, Paris, 1967.

(11) Cf. L'économétrie, recherche d'une synthèse entre expérience et théorie, Libraire de l'Université, Genève, 1965.

IN MEMORIAM

Edouard Rossier died in September 1981, while this book was in press. He was closely associated with Solari's research work since its beginning and, more particularly, with the qualitative approach in economics that Solari studied in the last years of his life. After Solari's death, he devoted his energy to developing this line of thought, which led Solari to the publication of a book (Economie Structurale, Economia, Paris, 1980) and of several articles.

In writing and rewriting this paper, which we did entirely together, a spontaneous division of labour occurred. Edouard was advocating a positive evaluation of Solari's work, while I was more critical. The result, as so often happens in such cases, was a compromise and both of us were left somehow unsatisfied with it. This paper stands only as a stage of an uncompleted reflection, as his death abruptly interrupted our dialogue on economics as a science.

This loss brings great sorrow to all who have enjoyed the companionship of this fine man.

JNDP

November 1981

PART II

MODELLING

CHAPTER 3
ECONOMETRIC MODEL BUILDING FOR THE COMMON MARKET

A.P. Barten, CORE and Catholic University of Leuven

1. INTRODUCTION

According to a very general definition a model is a representation of a set of empirical phenomena which enables one to answer, in a sufficiently realistic way, certain questions about the described reality. The type of questions asked has implications for the nature of the description, if only because of reasons of tractability. A road map contains less detail then an ordnance map, but is clearly more practical when traversing with some speed a particular area. Likewise, one can conceive of a whole variety of empirical economic models of the European Community, differing in purpose and consequently differing in emphasis and the type and amount of detail supplied.

A few examples may illustrate the variety of possibilities. If one's interest is in the relation of the E.E.C. with respect to other major economic blocks in the world, it may be sufficient to treat the E.E.C. economy as a whole, ignoring the specific contribution of each member country. One then complies with the rule of thumb (Occam's razor) never to specify more detail than is strictly necessary for the purpose at hand.

It is clear that if one is interested in the interdependence among member countries, the role of each member has to appear explicitly. Again here one has a considerable amount of choice. For example, if one is interested in the technological structure of the interdependence of production one will try to build an input-output model which links the industries domestically as well as internationally. It is useful to realize that if one distinguishes n industries such an input-output table contains $9n(9n-1)$ intermediate flows, entailing an enormous amount of work for already moderate values of n.

One can also concentrate on interdependence by trade, working with large aggregates like commodity imports and exports. One can be interested in the structure of the pattern of trade and build a gravity model. An example of this is part of the DESMOS model by Dramais (1974/75). Here all equations describing the imports by country of origin are basically identical, while the differences among countries express themselves by way of different values for the variables. This attempt to identify the "barriers" to trade is, however, not too much different from other trade flow models, like one which forms part of the COMET model constructed at the Center for Operations Research and Econometrics and the one which is a component of METEOR, the E.E.C. model made by the Dutch Central Planning Bureau, where differences in price sensitivity are allowed. Actually, such an import flows model already appears in the Resnick (1968) model, one of the earliest attempts to build a model for the Common Market. To avoid misunderstandings it is useful to point out that the trade interdependence is not studied and described in isolation, for its own sake. In the models just mentioned they provide the link between a set of sub-models, each describing the economy of a member country.

There are of course also financial and monetary channels by which the economies influence each other. If one's interest centers on financial and money markets, including those for foreign exchange, a different degree of refinement is indicated.

Not only the way interdependence is described can be different according to the purpose of the model. Also the domestic components can vary. For a short-run prediction model like METEOR one can consider expenditure by central government as an exogenous variable, i.e. one which takes its value independent of the other variables of the model. For a model like COMET which has a medium-term horizon such expenditure has to be predicted in conjunction with other variables measuring the performance of the economy. There are, of course, many other possibilities to differentiate the model according to its purpose.

In principle, differentiations are made because of pragmatic reasons not because one wants to present a different view of reality. Again in principle, differences between various approaches are differences in emphasis, in refinement and not in substance. However, in actual practice, there is no guarantee that the different types of models produce mutually consistent answers to policy questions. Would it then not be attractive to have one general purpose model, which can be used for short-run, medium-term and long-run purposes, for forecasting and policy design, for industry-wise analysis and as a description of macroeconomic interactions, reflecting expertise of the best talent to be found in Europe? Indeed, this sounds attractive but is it feasible? The construction, exploitation and maintenance of such a model require an enormous input of resources like data base, computer support, staff, coordination and, of course, ideas. Only a permanent and specialized institution, provided with a generous budget and a considerable amount of self-confidence and prestige could take care of such a mammoth project. As of now, this type of set-up seems to be still far off. Given the limited resources and the specialized interest of the model builders or of the organization for which they work, one can expect a continuation of the present state of affairs: the construction of special purpose models of limited scope by relatively small teams. With some luck the various models will complement, rather than contradict each other.

To illustrate and further elaborate these generalities about model building for the common market it is useful to discuss one particular model in some detail, namely the COMET model.

2. THE COMET MODEL, PURPOSE AND SCOPE

The European Economic Community started in 1958. Its main objective is the creation of a common market which requires more than a customs union. The E.E.C. can and does formulate a common economic policy to improve the efficiency of the common market. The authority of the E.E.C. is limited, however, and a considerable degree of autonomy in the field of economic policy remains with the member countries. In view of the increase in interdependence one would hope that the economic policies of the member countries complement and reinforce each other rather than the contrary. In the late sixties the desire for "coordination of economic policy in the medium run" was publicly expressed at regular intervals. It never was quite clear what was to be understood by the medium term. Moreover, the concept of "coordination" was never defined explicitly.

As long as coordination is still an ideal and not a fact, the least one can do is to check the mutual compatibility of the forecasts and plans of the member countries for, say, the coming five years. These predictions contain a "voluntaristic" element, i.e. they reflect intended policy measures and their assumed effectiveness. To be able to assess the degree of wishful thinking on the part of the economic authorities in the member countries, it is useful to have a macroeconomic model for that country. It is not necessary that this model can compete in every respect with the model used by the member countries themselves, its main role being to check the major features of the plans. At the same time one wants to have an instrument to analyze the impact of one country's performance on that of another, an aspect usually not covered by the typical national model. Since such mutual economic interdependencies are caused by movements of products, of production factors and of monetary and financial assets sets of relations are needed to describe such movements.

These considerations led early 1969 to the formulation of the project to build an interdependent medium-term model for the E.E.C.: a set of country models, one for each member country, reflecting "medium-term" aspects, linked together by a system of relations describing bilateral trade flows, and, if possible, other flows, between the member countries. The project was named COMET, for COmmon market MEdium Term model. It was started in 1969 but it got only seriously under way in the autumn of 1970. Work on it is still continuing. On average about one person is occupied full-time with its development.

Before turning to a discussion of the medium-term aspect and of the nature of the bilateral trade flows description two other topics will be briefly discussed: data base and the implementation of the model.

The ability to construct an empirical macroeconomic model is effectively constrained by the availability of data. When the project was started, there was no mutually compatible set of national account data of sufficient length available for all six member countries. Happily enough, there were annual data on total commodity imports broken down by country of origin and a set of price indices for commodity imports and exports per country. For this reason, the first part of the project to be completed was the import allocation model - see Barten (1971). As the project proceeded the availability of data improved. The more or less incidentally collected sets of data for the various countries could be replaced by O.E.C.D. statistics, when these were published. This, of course, required redoing part of the model. Next, as the consequence of a legitimate desire on the part of E.E.C. staff, the model data base was changed to the definitions and published time series of the Statistical Office of the European Communities. When the new system of national accounts was introduced another change had to be made. It is good to realize that the new data base begins really only in 1970. The period 1960-1969 has been "adjusted" according to the new definitions. For econometric purposes one would like longer time series, so another "adjustment" has been applied to obtain for most variables time series starting in 1953. As this story makes clear, "data" are not given once and for all. Another experience is worth quoting: the amount of time needed to collect the required data-sets and to bring them into the right condition before using them for estimation is usually underrated. Data search, treatment and management take at least one half of the total time needed for the construction of an empirical model.

Turning now to the aspect of implementation it should be realized that in most cases there are three echelons of people concerned with an actual model. The first echelon is the one of the model builders, the second one consists of the people who manipulate the model, who actually use it for various types of experiments, the third level is made up of the people who use the model results to formulate suggestions, predictions, policy measures and so on. The third echelon has to have some idea of the model and its credibility to be able to judge the reliability of the results produced by it. The second echelon needs a thorough knowledge of the inner working of the model and, of course, of computational procedures. Both levels are not indifferent with respect to the formulation of the model and want to influence it so that it better serves their needs. In general, there is a need for communication between the various echelons and a considerable, usually underestimated, part of the time of the model builders has to be devoted to explain what one has done and why and to discuss the feasibility and priority of further developments. Certainly in the initial stage the other parties have at regular intervals to be convinced that one is able to do the job as well as possible.

Once a first version of the model becomes operational the model builder has to hand it over to the second echelon. In the case of COMET this turned out to be a major difficulty in the early stage. The appropriate unit of the staff of the E.E.C. lacked adequate computer facilities, and knowledge about what a model is, its possibilities and limitations. After January 1973, when the staff was regrouped as the consequence of the entry of the three new members, this situation changed. By way of a series of seminars, the nature of the model was explained to a team of about six people of the staff, who were also instructed in its computer usage. Although at present only one person is charged with the manipulation of the model, it is of importance to have a larger group familiar with its operation.

For several reasons, and certainly because of understanding and explaining the model, the uniform specification has been useful. All country models employ basically the same specification for the various equations. The interdependencies follow the same pattern. The version of the model reported in Barten et al (1976) consists of a set of close to 500 equations. In fact, this set can be decomposed into 8 sets of 62 equations each, one for each member country, disregarding Luxemburg. Of these 62 equations, 32 are identities. Of the remaining 30 estimated equaitons, 7 explain imports from other member countries, all using a similar specification. Among the other equations the ones for prices follow the same pattern. To obtain intellectual command over the model requires therefore basically only the study of a relatively small number of elementary components which are simply replicated, of course with separately adjusted coefficients. This also applies to the current version of the model which involves some 1200 variables and 344 estimated equations.

3. MEDIUM-TERM MODELLING

A distinction is sometimes made between short-run and long-run models. In the short-run model the productive capacity is either fixed or changed trendwise. In this view a short-run model tries to analyze and describe primarily the way demand adjusts. In contrast, a long-run model is usually more concerned with supply conditions, assuming a full employment equilibrium path for demand. In the typical medium-term model productive capacity is not necessarily optimally utilised but also not exogenously given. The discrepancy between demand and supply for production, the degree of utilisation of capacity (DUC), plays a pivotal role as an endogenous variable in a medium-term model. A first operational example of such a model is presented by Van den Beld (1968).

In COMET the DUC variable has in the denominator maximum production and in the numerator actual gross national product. Maximum production is obtained from a production function in terms of total available labour in the economy and the past history of gross fixed investment. A high DUC will lead to increasing gross investment, employment, imports and domestic prices. A low DUC will result in the reverse tendencies. The increase in gross investment will increase the denominator of the DUC variable and hence reduce it. Higher imports and domestic prices will have a decreasing effect on gross national product and consequently also reduce DUC. This feedback mechanism does not work immediately but takes some time to materialize. One can expect an oscil-latory behaviour of the DUC around some equilibrium value.

As it turns out simulations with the COMET model indicate self-corrective behaviour of the DUC but with a very long delay. This is caused by the relatively weak impact DUC has on imports and prices on the one hand and on the other hand the fact that an increase in investment requires more capacity in the short run than it generates. In other words, in the short-run investment increases the numerator more than the denominator, causing a further increase in investment and so on, delaying a downturn in the development of the DUC. In part this may be due to the fact that GNP is an inappropriate concept, that at least the government sector should be excluded on the one hand and imports be included on the other hand. Anyway, at present research is under way to revise the part of the model which describes demand for inputs. It is too early to say whether the result will strengthen the typical medium-term aspect of the model.

The medium-term nature of a model also determines the extent in which one has to endogenize variables. As already mentioned: in the medium-run government budgets cannot be treated exogenously. They reflect fluctuations in economic activity. On the other hand demographic variables, endogenous in the long run, can still be treated as exogenous. However, labour participation rates, exogenous in the short run, are endogenous in the more intermediate future.

Another medium-term aspect of COMET is the reduced role of trends. In fact, only a technological trend is explicitly, but reluctantly, admitted. In general, every variable should be identified, because its representation by a trend, however valid for the past, cannot be taken for granted in the future. Unfortunately, scaling factors in dynamic adjustment processes appear to act sometimes as an undesired trend. Available estimation techniques lack the precision to avoid this. These pseudo-trends are to be eliminated in an ad hoc manner during the validation stage of the model construction: a tiresome and frustrating undertaking.

4. INTERDEPENDENCIES AND THE COMET MODEL

As is described in some detail in Barten and d'Alcantara (1976) the COMET model contains two types of structured interaction between member countries. One is by way of the explanation of the import and export prices. The other by way of bilateral import flows.

The price index of commodity imports for each country is explained as a weighted mean of the export prices of the other countries, corrected for exchange rate changes. The weights depend on the share in commodity imports by the exporting country. This is a standard type of explanation, but not without some shortcomings. It assumes, for example, that the composition of the export bundle is basically the same for all countries of destination. Anyway, in this manner a first price link across countries is established.

A second price link is provided by the way prices of commodity exports are explained. The export price index is a weighted mean of a domestic com-ponent and a competing export price level. The weights are estimated. It appears that apart from the United Kingdom, the weight for the competing export price level is high in the longer run. For small countries it turns out to be close to unity. The competing export price level is in itself again a weighted mean of export prices. The weights are calculated on the basis of the relative strength of the competing country on a third market, corrected for the importance of this market for the exporting country.

The importance of the competing export price level underlies the well-known absorption phenomenon. Absorption occurs when an exchange rate adjustment is only partially reflected in the export price, i.e. the adjustment is only in part handed on to the customer. A revaluation simply decreases the profits of the exporter, a devaluation results in the opposite. The large weight of the competing export price level also explains the loose ties which appear to exist between domestic cost components and international price levels: in the late fifties and in the sixties import and domestic prices in dollar terms moved up and down in a narrow band, while domestic prices moved steadily up.

On the basis of this type of price formation it can be expected that, for example, a devaluation will not necessarily result in an improvement of the trade balance. In Barten et al (1976) an experiment is reported which shows that devaluation of the Italian lira by 20 percent in 1975 increases exports. The long-run effects on prices in lira are: a more than 20 percent increase in the import price, a 16 percent increase in the export price, hence an absorption of 80 percent, and a 20 percent increase in the price index of private consumption. It has a slight expansionary effect on the other E.E.C. members but hardly any effect on their prices.

A more effective channel to transmit impulses is international trade. In a nutshell of a two-country theoretical world model, Metzler (1942) presents the essence of the idea to adjust the Keynesian multiplier because of the recovery of part of the import leak: the increase in imports by the country which in its turn increases its imports from the first country.

In COMET this line of reasoning is modelled as follows. First there is an equation for total commodity imports where the various types of final demand appear with positive coefficients. There is a rather weak elasticity of substitution associated with the ratio of import prices and domestic prices. Next, there is a relation which determines the part of imports coming from other E.E.C. countries. The imports from the rest of the world follow as a residual. Finally, there is a set of relations describing the country of origin of the imports from E.E.C. imports. Imports by country A from country B are a function of total imports by A from all other E.E.C. countries and of the relative price, i.e. the export index of B in dollars over the import price index of A, also in dollars. Moreover, the relative export capability of the country of origin plays a role as a non-price competition effect. The multi-level approach, namely, first determination of total imports and next its allocation by origin, reflects the assumption of separability of the pro-duction function in domestic inputs and imports. It is also pragmatically convenient. Work on the import allocation relations can be (and was) per-formed independently of the shape of the usual national model. At present, the bilateral trade flows model is being modified along the lines put forward in Barten and d'Alcantara (1977). It is the intention to also take into consider-ation export push elements and to introduce some inertia in the price reactions.

Imports from other member countries are, of course, exports for these countries, increasing their activity levels and so generating increased import demand, part of which originates in the member countries. In Table 8 of Barten et al (1976) one can find results of an experiment in which German fixed investments were autonomously increased by 10 percent. In the short run this causes an increase in German GNP and imports. Consequently, exports of France, Italy, The Netherlands, and Belgium increase by about 3 percent. Those of the U.K., Ireland and Denmark react less strongly. The short-run impact on GNP and employment of the other countries is very small. On the other hand, the medium-term effects are of considerable interest. First of all, German investment levels after the first year suffer from the overcapacity generated by the autonomous investment, but some net effect remains. Employment decreases in the long run because of its substitution by fixed capital. In the other countries, GNP levels and investment all increase slowly and steadily while employment stagnates. After 8 years Dutch GNP is 2.3 percent above its original time path while GNP for Germany has ultimately only increased by 2.1 percent. The picture that emerges is clear: an expansionary policy which generates growth and investment but unfortunately little or no extra employment.

Such simulation results reflect, of course, the assumption made for the structural relations and the numerical values assigned to unknown coefficients. One should keep in mind that some degree of arbitrariness is involved. Still, one can say that such experiments describe a possible course of events not devoid of realism. They also demonstrate that it is equally arbitrary to expect, like e.g. Peters (1974), that a devaluation (revaluation) will improve (reduce) the trade balance or that an expansionary policy will necessarily increase employment.

It has to be noted that the type of dependencies discussed until now reflect the rather traditional point of view of basically a multinational model. One can think of a development in the modelling effort where explicitly supranational elements are introduced. In the COMET model, but also in most other models, investment in fixed assets is made dependent on conditions within one country only. As the common market effectively proceeds the productive capacity of a certain country serves the whole community and its size and composition is more determined by the overall levels of activity in the community than the one in the country where it is physiclly located. One can think of a conceptual framework in which total investment and total employment is explained by variables pertaining to the E.E.C. as a whole while its distribution over countries depends on differential costs. Such a model displays then some of the characteristics which one usually associates with regional-national models - see for example, Thys-Clement et al (1973). It would be only natural that as the national economic boundaries are made lower and lower, that as the economic union proceeds, the models used to analyze and design policies for this union, follow in their structure this development.

5. CONCLUDING REMARKS

In the sales promotion jargon of the model building industry one speaks of a "total forecasting environment" rather than of a model. Indeed, model building is more than the specification of a set of structural relations. It means supplying a combination of computer hardware and software. The latter includes a data base (databank), treatment programs for estimation, simulation and display of results. It also includes a set of structural relations but with all kinds of options to include, change or delete equations and inequalities. The relative importance of the structural specification has decreased in the whole modelling package. The old-fashioned economist, educated in a tradition where one ponders carefully each structural equation, might feel somewhat lost in this more recent development, where larger and larger models are grinding out mountains and mountains of numbers. It is indeed almost impossible to digest the "content" of a structural form; one has to learn from the engineers to accept the idea of a model as a black box and to judge a model on the basis of its performance more than on a careful analysis of its structure. If on many accounts we are in agreement with Luigi Solari's views, we here take an opposite position for the reasons mentioned.

Still it will always be possible to take up one aspect of a model, study it in detail and comment on it. In a sense, this has been done here with COMET. The COMET project is still far from offering a "total forecasting environment" and those who really want can have a look inside its black box. One sometimes hears the paradoxal desire for greater simplicity of its relations and more detailed results. As it turns out the wish for more simpli-city is really an expression of the need for easier manipulation of the model, a matter more of adequate soft- and hardware than of economic specification. Also the amount of detail one can carry along is mostly a matter of computer programming. The role of the computer is clearly very important, and still growing as a powerful tool in the hands of the model builder. Indeed, the current renaissance in model building and model handling is to a large extent due to developments in the computer field more than to the development of economic, statistical and mathematical theory.

REFERENCES

(1) Barten, A.P., An Import Allocation Model for the Common Market, Cahiers Economiqus de Bruxelles, 1971,H CL 50, pp. 3-14.
(2) Barten, A.P. and d'Alcantara, G., The Linkage of Models of the E.E.C. Countries, in (ed.) H. Glejser, H., Quantitative Studies of International Economic Relations, North-Holland, Amsterdam, 1976.
(3) Barten, A.P. and d'Alcantara, Models of Bilateral Trade Flows, in (eds.) Albach, H. Helmstädter, E. and Henn, R, Quantitative Wirtschaftsforschung, Wilhelm Krelle zum 60. Geburtstag, Mohr, Tübingen, 1977.
(4) Barten, A.P., d'Alcantara, G. and Carrin, G., COMET, a Medium-Term Macroeconomic Model for the European Economic Community, European Economic Review, 7, 1976, pp. 63-115.
(5) Dramais, A., DESMOS III - Neuf Modèles Nationeaux liés pour l'Etude de la Diffusion des Fluctuations Conjoncturelles et des Effects des Mesures de Politique Economique entre les Pays Membres du Marché Commun, Cahiers Economiques de Bruxelles, 1974/75, 64, pp. 473-514; 65, pp. 53-108; 66, 201-260.
(6) Metzler, L.A., Underemployment Equilibrium in International Trade, Econometrica, 1942, 10, pp. 97-112.
(7) Peters, P.J.L.M., Interrelated Macro-economic Systems, Tilburg University Press, Tilburg, 1974.
(8) Resnick, S.A., An Empirical Study of Economic Policy in the Common Market, in (eds.) Ando, A., Brown, E.C. and Friedlaender, A.F., Studies in Economic Stabilization, The Brookings Institution, Washington, D.C., 1968, pp. 184-214.
(9) Thys-Clement, E., Van Rompuy, P. and De Corel, L., RENA, een Econometrisch Model voor het Plan 1976-1980, Planbureau, Brussel, 1973.
(10) Van den Beld, C.A., An Experimental Medium-Term Macro Model for the Dutch Economy, in Mathematical Model Building in Economics and Industry, Griffin, London, 1968, pp. 31-48.

CHAPTER 4

A NONLINEAR EXPENDITURE SYSTEM

Qualitative Analysis and Experiments with Canadian Data, 1947 - 1977

F. Carlevaro*, Department of Econometrics, University of Geneva

"Parfois les réponses que je trouve sont trop simples, et je doute de moi-même, car seul le compliqué impressionne, donne l'illusion du docte, du savant, c'est ainsi que dans le mystère de l'alchimie dont je ne peux vous dévoiler tous les secrets, les choses se passent".

Claude Paul Bruter, Sur la nature des mathématiques, (Paris, Gauthier-Villars, 1973), p.56

1. INTRODUCTION

The importance of quantitative analysis of household consumption in the development of econometrics no longer need to be stressed. This branch of economics, also known as demand analysis, is closely associated with the very origin of econometrics and has contributed to its expansion.

Trained in the field of demand analysis by René Roy, a leading figure in this discipline, Luigi Solari chose it from the beginning of his academic career as his favourite domain for his teaching and research work, the results of which were published in his book Théorie des choix et fonctions de consommation semi-agrégées. As pointed out by Du Pasquier and Rossier elsewhere in this book, his interest in consumption analysis may be explained by the fact that he saw, in this type of analysis more than in any other, the necessity to elaborate a complete econometric procedure, in accordance with his concept of econometrics. Solari stated that econometrics is an effort to "synthesize theory and experimentation with the joint help of mathematical economics and mathematical statistics, a synthesis that cannot be achieved separately by either of them"(1).

His research on systems of consumption functions occured at a historical turning point of demand analysis. In the immediate post-war years, Stone opened the path for empirical analysis with his linear expenditure system. Under the pressure of the post-war need for planning and forecasting, and with the help of the development of both statistical information and computer techniques, integrated systems of demand functions were developed in order to analyze the mechanisms which determine the private consumtion pattern. These models describe how household budgets are allocated among the various commodities, taking for granted that consumers have first decided upon the allocation of disposable income between saving and consumption.

Such systems of consumption functions are said to be "complete" because they combine, in just one expression, the totality of the demand functions that come into play on the markets of final goods and services. Up to that time, these various demand functions had been analyzed independently by means of separate functions defined mostly by pragmatic considerations. Well-known examples of these functions are the constant real price- and income-elasticity demand functions.

In this traditional and empiristic approach to demand analysis, reference to a theoretical background was only mentioned in order to enumerate the explanatory factors of demand. On the contrary, the complete system approach aims at a comprehensive view of all consumption functions, so as to throw light on their mutual dependence. This has been achieved by integrating demand functions into consumer choice theory. With the ordinal utility function, this theory indeed offers a powerful unifying principle for such an integration. It provides the consumption functions with a systematic structure capable of clarifying substitution and complementarity phenomena. Moreover, it enables us to enlarge the scope of these models to uses other than forecasting or simulation, and to give a coherent answer to the problem of measuring the variations, through time or space, of real living standards and of the cost of living of households.

Once this theoretical framework of mathematical economics has been chosen, the first task of the econometrician is to provide the model with a parametric specification(2). The question here is to select functions operating within the choice theory framework - characterized only by qualitative and local properties - by means of analytical expressions of which the only unknown elements are the "invariant" parameters that we intend to quantify through statistical procedures. This may seem trivial but in fact it is not. One has only to consider the ever growing amount of parametric forms proposed over two decades by those economists who based their analyses on the choice theory. Unfortunately, there exists no ideal parametric specification adapted to all purposes. Indeed, due to insufficient statistical information, such a model would be automatically overparameterized. We are then forced to select parametric forms orientated towards those empirical situations that we judge most important. In fact, models obtained in this way implicitly express a priori hypotheses.

Thus it is essential to bring the economic consequences of this a priori information to the fore, i.e. to define the limits we impose on the possible configurations of the phenomenon under observation. Such a clarification, by enabling a deeper knowledge of the adopted model, contributes as much to its scientific character as does the corroboration of the model through facts. This deeper inspection of the model requires a clear distinction of its implications, be it in terms of the type of analytical functions chosen, or in terms of their functional interrelationship as is the case when we adopt hypotheses of functional separability. In fact, we have to isolate the implication of each of the hypotheses that surreptitiously slipped into the model when we chose a particular specification.

We also have to evaluate the role of the unknown parameters, to bring out their economic meaning. Through this interpretation, we are able to delimit the domain of their admissible values as well as the type of information needed to quantify them. It thus permits us to test the model through "a simulation by parameters" when, for instance, in a long-term forecasting attempt, one is led to cast doubt on the values of the parameters yielded by statistical analysis.

It is precisely this attempt at clarification that Solari undertook when he applied two of the best known complete demand systems to the Swiss context: the linear expenditure system and the "indirect addilog" system. His attempt to bring out what he later called their qualitative content in no way prevented him devoting as much time and rigour to the quantification and empirical corroboration aspects of the research.

In that spirit I would like to propose here, by way of tribute, a complete system of demand functions that closely follows the path of the research work on the econometrics of consumption initiated by Solari at the Department of Econometrics of the University of Geneva.

The model I proposed under the heading "A nonlinear expenditure system" was originally designed for the modelling needs of the Projections and Programming Commission of the Economic Commission for Europe, in the context of developing general economic projections. It was built as a submodel of private consumption to be integrated into the SEM model[(3)] used by this organization for simulating growth scenarios for the market economies in Western Europe.

Designed for long-term perspectives, this sub-model of private consumption was conceived mainly for the identification and measurement through time series analysis, of the saturation or acceleration of consumption of certain groups of commodities, phenomena which have occurred in the past together with variations of the purchasing power of households. Our objective was to eliminate one of the principal limits of the linear expenditure system when applied to long-term analysis: the linearity of the Engel curves. We believe we have achieved our aim, while retaining the main characteristics which have brought success to this model: the simplicity of its economic interpretation, the ease with which it can be estimated and its simple extension to dynamic versions and for the introduction of environmental factors of demand.

The nonlinear expenditure system is described in section 2 below, as a generalization of the linear expenditure system. Sections 3 and 4 are then devoted to the qualitative analysis of the model and its economic meaning. We have mainly tried to explicit the functioning of the model in relation to the purchasing power of households. Finally, parametric specifications are proposed, leading to experiments with actual data. This is done in the last section of the chapter. Because of the difficulty in estimating large scale demand systems we give an outline of a hierarchical estimation procedure in an appendix, which allows for a relatively easy estimation of the model when a detailed disaggregation of consumption is adopted.

2. FROM THE LINEAR TO THE NONLINEAR EXPENDITURE SYSTEM

The model called linear expenditure system (LES) is based on the hypothesis of the linearity of expenditure functions with respect to its arguments, i.e. total expenditure and prices. It rests also on the hypotheses of the choice theory.

Its formal deterministic expression is[4]:

$$\underline{d} = \hat{\underline{p}}\underline{c} + \underline{b}(r - \underline{p}'\underline{c}) \ , \quad \text{with} \quad \underline{\iota}'\underline{b} = 1 \ , \tag{2.1}$$

where, in the unit of time chosen, $\underline{d} = \hat{\underline{p}}\underline{q}$ is the vector of expenditures necessary to buy, at prices $\underline{p}$, the quantities $\underline{q}$ of n goods; r is the budget allocated for this consumption, also denoted as total expenditure. In the static version of the model, $\underline{b}$ and $\underline{c}$ are the vectors of constant coefficients: the former are pure numbers whereas the latter have the dimension of the quantities $\underline{q}$.

With this system of demand functions is associated an ordinal direct utility function:

$$u = F(\underline{b}'\log(\underline{q}-\underline{c})) \tag{2.2}$$

as well as its dual (indirect utility function):

$$u = G(\log(r-\underline{p}'\underline{c}) - \underline{b}'\log \underline{p}) \tag{2.3}$$

where F and G are Pareto (monotone increasing) transformations.

The traditional economic interpretation of this model considers the $\underline{c}$ coefficients as minimum or "committed" purchases to which the purchasing power r is allocated in priority. For this, it is necessary to posit the hypothesis of a vector $\underline{c} \geqslant \underline{0}$. The discretionary or uncommitted budget $r - \underline{p}'\underline{c}$ left after this allocation, is devoted in constant proportions $\underline{b}$ to the purchase of other quantities of commodities. The $\underline{b}$ coefficients are thus allocation coefficients of the discretionary budget and are supposed to be positive.

This interpretation depicts clearly the role played by the prices in this model: they fix the committed expenditure but do not affect the allocation mechanism of the uncommitted expenditure. It follows that price changes have a limited impact on the structure of expenditure. Increases in the disposable budget are distributed according to the proportions $\underline{b}$, in the same way as the total discretionary budget. The $\underline{b}$ coefficients are thus identical with the marginal propensities to spend $\partial\underline{d}/\partial r$, sometimes called "marginal budget shares".

The evidence has nevertheless proved to contradict the hypothesis of a vector $\underline{c} \geqslant \underline{0}$(5). This contradiciton led Solari (1971) to propose a conceptual extension of the LES: as total expenditure increases beyond committed expenditure, thus revealing successive improvements in the standard of living, new or "superior" commodities will be purchased. Such goods and services are characterized by a negative $\underline{c}$. This reformulation of the LES broadens its practical scope: the demand functions are modified through a morphogenetic process every time a new commodity appears in the consumer basket. Moreover, this extension enables us to justify, within the framework of the choice theory, the notion of hierarchy of goods put forward by René Roy.

The nonlinear expenditure system (NLES) proposed in this chapter constitutes a generalization of the conventional LES, in a direction complementary to that explored by Solari. For the reasons stated in the introduction, we are mainly interested in more flexible Engel curves. Indeed, their linearity in the LES restricts the applicability of this model to situations of small variations in total expenditure. In this perpective it seems natural to relax the hypothesis of the invariance of the $\underline{b}$ coefficients with respect to total expenditure. On the other hand, such an alternative for the $\underline{c}$ coefficients would not seem appropriate, since their interpretation as committed consumptions independent from disposable purchasing power r, is very rich and liable to many possible uses. One of them is the measure of the minimum wage which ensures a socially justifiable minimum consumption. In another direction, they allow for dynamic versions of the model, as well as for taking into consideration economic variables other than prices and total expenditure and, also, environmental variables. One can, for instance, envisage the committed quantities as evolutive parameters whose evolution is determined, in one case, by habit formation processes through past consumption levels(6), or by physical or psychological stocks of accumulated goods(7) and, in another case, by environmental and exogenous factors.

In order to obtain flexible Engel curves without departing from the framework of the choice theory, we postulate a system of expenditure functions as in equation (2.1), with $\underline{b}$ coefficients as a function of

$$z = \frac{r - \underline{p}'\underline{c}}{P} ,$$

where $P=P(\underline{p})$ is a function of prices homogeneous of degree one. This homogeneity constraint ensures the absence of money illusion in our model, a feature required by the choice theory in any system of demand functions. We have chosen the uncommitted expenditure, rather than total expenditure, in view of the particular structure of the demand functions when the concept of committed quantities is introduced in the choice theory. The general form of demand functions with a two-stage allocation process, as supposed in the LES, shows that these functions depend on total expenditure only through uncommitted expenditure(8). Hence, giving the P function the role of a subjective consumer price index(9), the variable z may be considered as uncommitted real expenditure.

We have previously established(10) the structure imposed by the Slutsky conditions on the functions $\underline{b}(z)$ and $P(\underline{p})$. These conditions, necessary for the compatibility of the demand functions with the choice theory, restrict the admissable forms of $\underline{b}(z)$ and $P(\underline{p})$ to the following families:

$$\underline{b} = \underline{b}^0 + b^1\Phi(z) , \tag{2.4}$$

$$\text{with } \underline{\iota}'\underline{b}^0 = 1 \quad \text{and} \quad \underline{\iota}'\underline{b}^1 = 0,$$

$$\log P = \underline{b}^{0\prime} \log \underline{p} + \log \kappa(\underline{b}^{1\prime} \log \underline{p}) , \tag{2.5}$$

where $\underline{b}^0$ and $\underline{b}^1$ are constant vectors, Φ and κ arbitrary functions of only one argument.

These conditions, together with relation (2.1), define the NLES. Equation (2.4) constitutes a generalized linearity condition, i.e. the hypothesis of a linear (affine) dependency between the allocation coefficients of the uncommitted budget. Equation (2.5) posits the price index P as a product of a geometrical price index $\prod_i p_i^{b_i^0}$ by an arbitrary positive function κ whose argument is a function of prices homogeneous of degree zero.

In this broad family of demand function systems, the LES model features the particular case when $\underline{b}^1 = \underline{0}$ or, equivalently, when choosing a constant Φ function.

When analyzing long-time series of household private consumption with the LES, econometricians have always felt the inadequacy of the hypothesis of time invariant $\underline{b}$ coefficients. Stone was the first to point out this difficulty and he tried to overcome it by using cinematic versions of LES where the $\underline{b}$ coefficients vary gradually over time acording to an a priori given trend, most often a linear one(11). This procedure seems unsatisfactory to us as it cannot bring to the fore the factors responsible for the evolution of the $\underline{b}$ coefficients over time. We have here a first justification for building up a NLES in which their evolution is explained by changes in household standard of living, although it is fair to say that this explanation exists already, in an embryonic state, in Stone's works on the LES(12). The more original feature of our NLES model lies rather in the integration of this explicative hypothesis in the consumer choice theory framework. We can thus avoid the widely used, but theoretically unjustified, practice of grafting ad hoc hypotheses on a simple model considered as a prototype to be improved, without taking into consideration the coherence of such additions with the original conceptual framework.

Later on in this chapter we shall examine the empirical adequacy of the

NLES but it is worth noting here that we obtained a first corroboration of this specific hypothesis with a "sliding" estimation of the LES on Italian and German data[13]. That experiment was designed in order to give a time-series of estimates of LES parameters. The observation period was divided up into successive estimation periods of equal length. The principal conclusion was that the evolution of the parameters $\underline{b}$ could be related to that of the standard of living, as measured by total household consumption at constant prices.

Up to this point, our specification of the NLES is a non-parametric one as long as no analytical form is given to the functions Φ and κ. This would, however, be necessary before any attempt at econometric quantification. Under this general form of the model, no explicit expression can be given to the utility function associated with these demand functions. In its indirect version, this utility function can nevertheless be characterized in the following way:

$$u = F\big(f(\log x, \log y)\big) , \tag{2.6}$$
$$\text{with } \log x = \log(r-\underline{p}'\underline{c}) - \underline{b}^{0\prime} \log \underline{p}$$
$$\text{and } \log y = \underline{b}^{1\prime} \log \underline{p} ,$$

where F is a paretian transformation and f is one solution of the partial differential equation:

$$\Phi \left(\frac{x}{\kappa(\log y)}\right) \frac{\partial f}{\partial \log x} + \frac{\partial f}{\partial \log y} = 0 \quad (14) . \tag{2.7}$$

Under this transformation, we recognize the indirect utility function of the LES given in relation (2.3), either when $\underline{b}^1 = \underline{0}$ which yields $\log y = 0$ and thus a function f depending only on log x, or when Φ is a constant which yields the solution for (2.7):

$$f(\log x, \log y) = \log x - A \log y, \quad A \text{ being a constant.}$$

In writing the cost of living function which expresses, following (2.6), the minimum level of uncommitted expenditure which enables a given utility level to be reached:

$$r - \underline{p}'\underline{c} = \exp \{\underline{b}^{0\prime}\log \underline{p}\}\, g\big(G(u), \underline{b}^{1\prime}\log \underline{p}\big) ,$$

where G is the inverse of F and g the inverse of f with respect to log x, one can also observe that the NLES belongs to the family of demand functions with which Muellbauer (1976) builds up his theory of the aggregation of individual demands.

By the same token, Muellbauer's theory may justify the use of the NLES as the specification of collective demand functions. The aggregation, performed by Muellbauer over the space of total individual expenditures, should be conducted here over the space of uncommitted individual expenditures. This procedure would lead to a formulation of aggregated demand functions resulting from a NLES where the variable $(r-\underline{p}'\underline{c})$ would be an aggregate of the individual uncommitted demand distribution. A precise definition of this aggregate would of course require a knowledge of the distribution of total expenditures and of individual committed expenditures.

3. QUALITATIVE ANALYSIS OF ENGEL CURVES

Within the scope of qualitative hypotheses we shall examine here the possibilities offered by the NLES for describing the dependence between the expenditures on each commodity and the total expenditure, commonly called Engel curves. We shall do this in order to assess the potentialities of the model on this crucial point which led us to propose this system of demand functions.

The qualitative hypotheses to be formulated concern the values taken by the parameters $\underline{c}$, $\underline{b}^0$, $\underline{b}^1$ and the set of admissable forms of the function Φ. In this analysis, we can leave the form of the function κ totally undetermined since it does not depend on the total expenditure.

Concerning the parameters $\underline{c}$, we shall keep the conventional postulate of non-negativity and the related interpretation in terms of committed quantities. The principle reason for choosing this restriction comes from the mathematical difficulties of a complete analysis of the consumer behaviour in presence of negative $\underline{c}$'s within the scope of the NLES. Indeed, the procedure followed by Solari for the LES rests on the central role played by the direct utility function, which cannot be specified in the generalization treated here. Moreover, the non-negativity hypothesis will not be discarded in the estimation of the model presented hereafter.

With regard to the other unknown elements, let us adopt the following qualitative hypotheses:

$$
\begin{array}{llll}
\text{i)} & \underline{b}^0 > \underline{0} & \text{and} & \underline{b}^0 + \underline{b}^1 > \underline{0} \ , \\
\text{ii)} & \Phi(0) = 0 & \text{and} & \Phi(\infty) = 1 \ , \\
\text{iii)} & \Phi'(z) \geq 0 \ , & & \forall z \geq 0 \ , \\
\text{iv)} & \Phi''(z) \geq 0 \ , & & \forall\, 0 \leq z \leq z_0 \\
 & \Phi''(z) \leq 0 \ , & & \forall z > z_0 \ .
\end{array} \qquad (15)
$$

These hypotheses ensure the non-negativity of the allocation coefficients of uncommitted budget as well as a monotonic and smooth behaviour of these coefficients for all non-negative values of their argument. The non-negativity of the coefficients $\underline{b}(z)$ emerges as a logical condition as soon as we admit the conventional interpretation of committed quantities for the parameters $\underline{c}$. Indeed, for all $\underline{p} > \underline{0}$ and $r - \underline{p}'\underline{c} > 0$, it follows that $\underline{q} \geq \underline{c}$ and hence $\underline{b}(z) > 0$.

On the other hand, the hypothesis of monotonic functions $\underline{b}(z)$ stems from the empirical evidence brought by our experiment with "sliding" estimation of the LES which we referred to previously. This experiment has shown this monotonic behaviour at least for the largest expenditure item, that of food. But the restrictive condition of generalised linearity inherent to the NLES makes it necessary, if we wish to keep this hypothesis for one commodity, to extend it to all others.

These qualitative hypotheses guarantee that the domain of existence of the coefficients $\underline{b}$ is bounded by:

$$\underline{b}(0) = \underline{b}^0 \qquad \text{and} \qquad \underline{b}(\infty) = \underline{b}^0 + \underline{b}^1$$

when the real uncommitted expenditure increases from zero to infinity. This property clarifies the economic meaning of the parameters $\underline{b}^0$ and $\underline{b}^1$. $\underline{b}^0$ refers to the "subsistence" level of the allocation coefficients $\underline{b}(z)$, and $\underline{b}^1$ to the variation span between that level and the "affluence" level $\underline{b}^0 + \underline{b}^1$. It also clarifies the role of hypothesis ii) above which posits (in all generality) that these coefficients develop between finite bounds, and hence endows the NLES model with a globally applicable character.

Within these two limits, the $b_i(z)$ may vary in the same direction as the argument z when $b_i^1 > 0$, or in the opposite sense if $b_i^1 < 0$. Moreover, this variation will follow a sigmoid curve when $z_0 > 0$ and, in the extreme case where $z_o = 0$, a concave or convex curve if, respectively, $b_i^1 > 0$ or $b_i^1 < 0$. In short, the regularity condition of the function Φ, expressed by hypothesis iv), restricts the representation of the $b_i(z)$ to monotonic functions possessing one inflection point at the most.

The establishment of the admissible shapes of Engel curves within the NLES requires the analysis of the sign of the marginal budget shares

$$\frac{\partial \underline{d}}{\partial r} = \underline{b}^0 + \underline{b}^1\Psi(z) = \underline{\beta}(z) \tag{3.1}$$

and of their marginal variation rate

$$\frac{\partial \underline{\beta}}{\partial r} = \frac{\partial^2 \underline{d}}{\partial r^2} = b^1 \frac{\Psi'(z)}{P} , \tag{3.2}$$

with $\Psi(z) = \Phi(z) + z\Phi'(z)$. (3.3)

From hypotheses i) to iv), we have the following properties for Ψ:

v) $\Psi(0) = 0$ and $\Psi(\infty) = 1$

Indeed, $\Psi(0) = \Phi(0) = 0$.

And, using the development of Φ at the point $\frac{1}{z} = 0$, i.e.

$$\Psi(z) = 1 + \sum_{i=1}^{\infty} a_i z^{-i} ,$$

we get $\Psi(z) = 1 + \sum_{i=1}^{\infty} (1-i)a_i z^{-i} \to 1$ as $z\to\infty$.

vi) $\Psi(z) \geqslant \Phi(z)$,

for $\Psi - \Phi = z\Phi' \geqslant 0$.

vii) $\Psi'(z) \geqslant 0$, $\forall\ 0 \leqslant z \leqslant z_M$

$\Psi'(z) \leqslant 0$, $\forall\ z \geqslant z_M$

with $z_M > z_o$ solution of the equation

$$2\Phi'(z) + z\Phi''(z) = 0 \text{ (16)}. \tag{3.4}$$

Indeed, $\Psi' = 2\Phi' + z\Phi''$, and hence Ψ is decreasing as soon as $\Phi'' < -2\ \Phi'/z$ which, following iv), may occur when $z > z_0$, i.e. in the domain where Φ is concave.

In short, the Ψ function follows the shape of a function increasing from 0 to 1 when equation (3.4) has no solution, and otherwise the shape of an unimodal function with a maximum $\Psi_M = \Psi(z_M) > 1$.

From these results, the properties of the form of the marginal budget shares are readily established. As for the coefficients $\underline{b}(z)$, their extreme values are $\underline{\beta}(0) = \underline{b}^0$ and $\underline{\beta}(\infty) = \underline{b}^0 + \underline{b}^1$. However, the evolution between these two values will be monotonic if Ψ is increasing. In the alternative case where Ψ is unimodal, the $\beta_i(z)$ will have at the point z_M a maximum when $b_i^1 > 0$ or and a minimum when $b_i^1 < 0$. In the latter case, some $\beta_i(z)$ may prove to be negative in an interval containing z_M.

From this two different types of Engel curves result as shown in the two following charts.

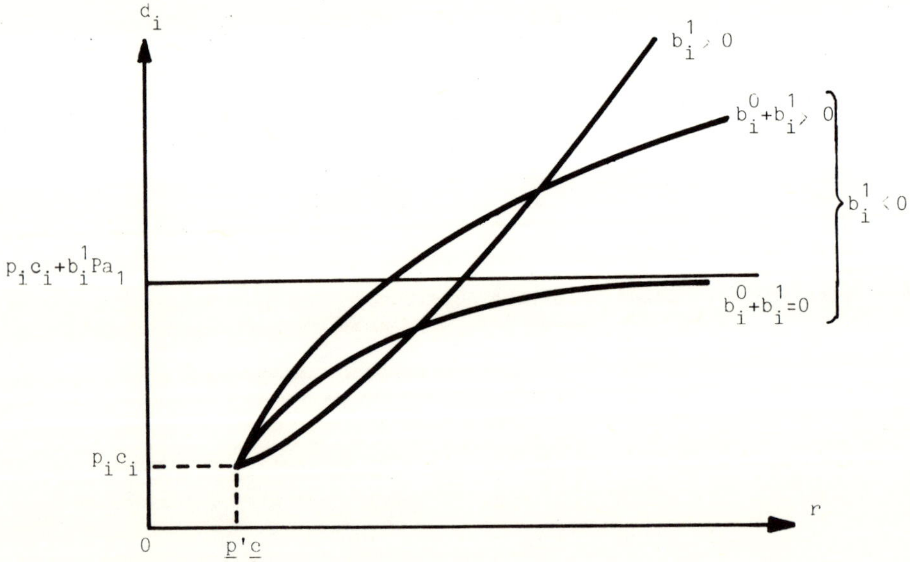

CHART 1. Engel curves of the NLES when $\Psi(z)$ is increasing

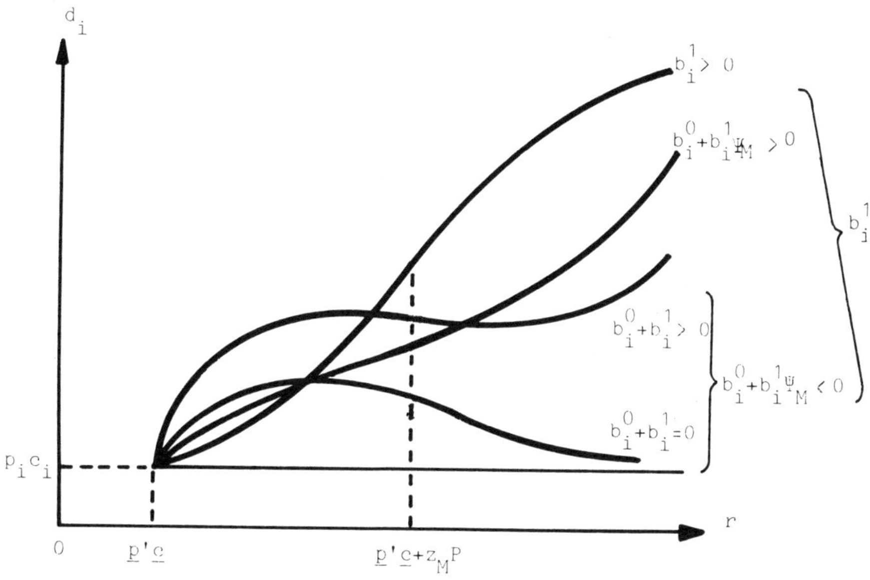

CHART 2. Engel curves of the NLES when $\Psi(z)$ is unimodal

When Ψ is increasing, the Engel curve of the commodity i is necessarily increasing. It is convex or concave if $b_i^1 > 0$ or $b_i^1 < 0$ respectively[(17)]. The first case illustrates the situation when the demand of the commodity under consideration will accelerate with an increase in the disposable purchasing power. Such a demand will characterise superior or luxury commodities. On the other hand, we observe the progressive saturation of demand when $b_i^1 < 0$, a phenomenon characteristic of the basic necessity commodities. For $b_i^0 + b_i^1 > 0$, this saturation is only <u>relative</u> in the sense that the demand rises indefinitely with the total expenditure. This saturation process becomes <u>absolute</u> in the special case when $b_i^0 + b_i^1 = 0$. Here, the marginal budget share equals zero when total expenditure tends towards infinity and we have an asymptote defining the saturation level for that demand, i.e.[(18)]:

$$\lim_{r \to \infty} d_i = p_i c_i + b_i^1 P a_1 = p_i c_i - b_i^0 P a_1 \ , \qquad (3.5)$$

with(19) $a_1 = \lim_{z\to\infty}[-z^2\Phi'(z)] < 0$. (3.6)

Consequently, the only shortcoming of the NLES when Ψ is increasing lies in its inability to represent the demand of the "inferior" commodities, the consumption of which decreases beyond a certain value of total expenditure.

As can be seen in chart 2, the choice of an unimodal function Ψ changes the range of the admissable Engel curves. This change is mainly due to the presence of an inflexion point corresponding to the level of the total expenditure when Ψ reaches its maximum.

In the interval where the function Ψ is increasing, i.e. for

$$\underline{p}'\underline{c} \leq r \leq \underline{p}'\underline{c} + z_M P ,$$

we find again the forms of Engel curves previously examined. However, for the goods with a parameter $b_i^1 < 0$ which satisfies the inequality $b_i^0 + b_i^1\Psi_M < 0$, the curve is unimodal and represents the demand for inferior commodities. Beyond the threshold $\underline{p}'\underline{c} + z_M P$, the decrease of the function Ψ produces a change in the curvature of Engel curves. We then observe, for the commodities for which the demand is accelerating before this threshold, a relative saturation phenomenon. On the other hand, for the commodities for which the demand reaches saturation, we have an acceleration phenomenon. Regarding the expenditure for inferior commodities, they keep decreasing towards the committed expenditure level $p_i c_i$ only in the particular case when $b_i^0 + b_i^1 = 0$. Otherwise, the Engel curve increases again after a minimum situated beyond $\underline{p}'\underline{c} + z_M P$.

This critical value of the total expenditure indicates a turning point in the standard of living where consumers change suddenly their appreciation of the utility of the purchased commodities.

Following these results of the qualitative analysis, we have to investigate the possible relationships between the two types of Engel curves that we have just examined. Do we face two alternative and separate models or not? In other words, is it possible to consider one of these models as the general case and the other one as an extreme case of the latter? This second question seems to have a positive answer if we look more closely at the threshold z_M. Let us consider a family of unimodal functions Ψ indexed by a continuous parameter, and let us choose a particular value of this parameter yielding an extreme and increasing function such that $z_M = \infty$ and $\Psi_M = 1$. The Engel curves of chart 1 are then a special case of those in chart 2.

4. PARAMETRIC SPECIFICATIONS OF THE MODEL

We envisage here two analytical specifications of the function Φ. Each contains only one unknown parameter and represents one of the two forms of Φ (sigmoid or concave) considered above. From a practical as well as theoretical point of view, it would have been preferable to work with a family of parametric functions Φ embracing the two forms considered in one single analytic expression. But we had to give up on that point because such a family may only be obtained at the cost of at least one supplementary unknown parameter[20]. This would have rendered the estimation problem considerably more cumbersome and it is already delicate enough when Φ has one parameter to be quantified.

Thus, our two parametric specifications define two separated families of functions. Their analytical expression is:

$$\text{exponential-sigmoid:} \quad \Phi(z) = \exp\{-\frac{a}{z}\} , \tag{4.1}$$

$$\text{exponential-concave:} \quad \Phi(z) = 1 - \exp\{-\frac{z}{a}\} , \tag{4.2}$$

where a is a positive parameter with the same dimension as the variable z, i.e. that of a real expenditure.

The graph of the first function is a sigmoid curve reaching an inflexion point at $z = z_0 = \frac{a}{2}$. From relations (3.3) and (4.1), we deduce a function:

$$\Psi(z) = (1 + \frac{a}{z}) \exp\{-\frac{a}{z}\} \tag{4.3}$$

which has also a sigmoid form, but with an inflexion point at $z_0 = \frac{a}{3}$. The exponential-sigmoid specification is thus related to the case illustrated in chart 1: inferior goods are excluded and, with the constraint $b_i^0 + b_i^1 = 0$, an absolute saturation level is reached with:

$$a_1 = \lim_{z \to \infty} \left(- a \exp\{-\frac{a}{z}\}\right) = -a .$$

The second specification of Φ entails a family of concave curves and a unimodal function

$$\Psi(z) = 1 - (1 - \frac{z}{a})\exp\{-\frac{z}{a}\} \tag{4.4}$$

reaching a maximum $\Psi_M = 1 - \exp\{-2\} = 1.1353$, for $z = z_M = 2a$. The exponential-concave specification is therefore identified with the case of chart 2, with a total expenditure threshold (when the curvature of the Engel curves is inverted) equal to $\underline{p}'\underline{c} + 2aP$[21].

The parameter a introduced in the two specifications of Φ plays a similar role in both cases. A variation of this parameter produces a network of curves of the same form but without any common point, except at both ends of their existence domain. In fact, each of these curves covers all the other curves defined with a superior value of a. In other words, the greater their coefficient a, the flatter these curves will be towards the z-axis.

In the extreme cases where $a \to 0$ or $a \to \infty$, the function degenerates over $0 < z < \infty$ in the constant 1 and 0 respectively. This nonlinearity parameter is thus a characteristic of the marginal variation rate of Φ, and hence of all the uncommitted budget allocation shares. Indeed, the derivatives of the exponential-sigmoid function does not exceed the maximum $\Phi'(2a) = 4\exp\{-2\}/a$, depending on the value of a, and the derivative of the exponential-concave function decreases exponentially towards zero from $\Phi'(0) = 1/a$.

An analogous qualitative discussion of the network of the curves Ψ generated by the admissable values of a brings out the role played by this parameter in establishing the form of the Engel curves. The nonlinearity of these curves, i.e. the phenomena of saturation or acceleration of the demand, approaches the level of committed expenditures as the parameter a approaches zero. Indeed, for indefinitely increasing total expenditure, the Engel curves of the NLES converge towards the linear curves of the LES with parameters $\underline{b} = \underline{b}^0 + \underline{b}^1$. Consequently, their nonlinearity is weaker in the region where the marginal budget shares converge towards their asymptotic value $\underline{\beta}(\infty) = \underline{b}^0 + \underline{b}^1$. This convergence, however, is regulated by that of the function Ψ towards its superior limit $\Psi(\infty) = 1$. The closer a is to zero, the faster this limit will be reached.

In order to complete the parametric specification of the NLES, we still have to specify the function κ operating in definition (2.5) of the "subjective" price index P. Here, the only restrictions imposed by the economic interpretation of the function P come from the desired properties of the index:

a) Non-negativity $\underline{p} > \underline{0} \Rightarrow \kappa > 0$

b) Monotonicity $\frac{\partial \log P}{\partial \log \underline{p}} = \underline{b}^0 + \frac{\kappa'}{\kappa}\underline{b}^1 \geqslant 0$

c) Index base $P(\underline{p}_0) = 1 \Rightarrow \log \kappa(\underline{b}^{1\prime} \log \underline{p}_0) = - \underline{b}^{0\prime} \log \underline{p}_0$

where $\underline{p}_0$ is the reference position to which any value of $\underline{p}$(22) will be compared. This position defines the unity in which the general price level P will be expressed.

In order to meet these constraints, we have limited our choice to functions entailing a price index with constant elasticity. These functions must satisfy the condition $\kappa'/\kappa = \alpha$, where α is a constant. This is a differential equation, whose solution gives, under condition c), the functions

$$\log \kappa = \alpha \underline{b}^{1\prime} \log \underline{p} - (\underline{b}^0 + \alpha \underline{b}^1)' \log \underline{p}_0 \ . \tag{4.5}$$

As desired, we end up with a price index of the geometric type:

$$P = \exp \{(\underline{b}^0 + \alpha \underline{b}^1)' (\log \underline{p} - \log \underline{p}_0)\} = \prod_i \left(\frac{p_i}{p_{i0}}\right)^{b_i^0 + \alpha b_i^1} \tag{4.6}$$

This choice ensures the monotonicity of P simply by restricting the values of the parameter α in the interval $0 \leqslant \alpha \leqslant 1$. This parameter will therefore fix the weighting of the index according to one of the admissable values of the coefficient vector $\underline{b}(z)$.

We still have to examine whether the values postulated for the unknown parameters of the NLES are compatible with the monotonicity and quasi-convexity hypotheses envisaged in the consumer choice theory for the indirect utility function. For this it is useful to specify more precisely the expression (2.6) of the indirect utility function. To do this, we have to restrict the possible forms of the function κ to those defined in the relation (4.5).

This leads us to look for the solution f(log x, log y) to the partial differential equation (2.7). In the case of an equation of the first order, linear and homogenous, it is known(23) that each of its solutions is also an integral of the associated ordinary differential equation, the so-called characteristic equation:

$$\frac{d \log x}{\Phi\left(\frac{x}{\kappa(\log y)}\right)} = d \log y \tag{4.7}$$

Thus, the equation

$$\log z = \log \frac{x}{\kappa(\log y)} = \log x - \alpha \log y + (\underline{b}^0 + \alpha\underline{b}^1)' \log \underline{p}_0$$

may be transformed into a differential equation with separated variables

$$\frac{d \log z}{\Phi(z) - \alpha} = d \log y$$

which admits as integral $\phi(z) - \log y = C$, where C is the integration constant and $\phi(z)$ a primitive of $1/z[\phi(z) - \alpha]$.

Hence, the solution f(log x, log y) we are looking for is represented by the function $\phi(z) - \log y$, expressed in terms of log x and log y. The indirect utility function (2.6) is then reduced to the following expression:

$$u = F\left[\phi\left(\frac{r-\underline{p}'\underline{c}}{P}\right) - \underline{b}^{1\prime} \log \underline{p}\right] , \tag{4.8}$$

where F is an arbitrary monotone transformation.

The monotonicity condition of u requires

$$\frac{\partial u}{\partial r} > 0 \quad \text{and} \quad \frac{\partial u}{\partial \underline{p}} = - \frac{\partial u}{\partial r}\underline{q} < \underline{0} \quad ^{(24)}.$$

But, in our model, $\underline{q} > \underline{0}$ as soon as $\underline{p} > \underline{0}$ and $r > \underline{p}'\underline{c}$, and we only have to check the sign restriction on $\frac{\partial u}{\partial r}$.

$$\frac{\partial u}{\partial r} = F' \frac{\phi'}{P} = \frac{F'}{(r-\underline{p}'\underline{c})(\Phi-\alpha)} . \tag{4.9}$$

Thus, extended to the whole definition domain of the NLES, the monotonicity of the utility function calls for the exclusion of the values $0 < \alpha < 1$ for which the function $\Phi(z) - \alpha$ changes the sign over its definition interval. The only economically admissible values for α are then $\alpha = 0$ and $\alpha = 1$.

Let us further impose the global quasi-convexity of function u. It is known that this condition is equivalent to a matrix of compensated marginal propensities expressing the pure price-effects. This matrix

$\delta\underline{q}/\delta\underline{p}' = \partial\underline{q}/\partial\underline{p}' + (\partial r)\underline{q}'$ is negative semi-definite over the whole domain of validity for the NLES. We have then for this model:

$$\frac{\delta\underline{q}}{\delta\underline{p}'} = -(r-\underline{p}'\underline{c})\hat{\underline{p}}^{-1}(\hat{\underline{b}}-\underline{bb}'-\xi\underline{b}^1\underline{b}^{1\prime})\hat{\underline{p}}^{-1} \qquad (4.10)$$

with $\xi = (\Psi-\Phi)(\Phi-\alpha)$.

The quadratic form

$$\underline{y}'\frac{\delta\underline{q}}{\delta\underline{p}'}\underline{y} = -(r-\underline{p}'\underline{c})\left[\underline{x}'(\hat{\underline{b}}-\underline{bb}')\underline{x} - \xi(\underline{b}^{1\prime}\underline{x})^2\right]$$

with $\underline{x} = \hat{\underline{p}}^{-1}\underline{y}$ is negative semi-definite whatever the values of the parameters $\underline{b}^0$ and $\underline{b}^1$ are when $\alpha = 1$, but not when $\alpha = 0$. Indeed the matrix $\hat{\underline{b}} - \underline{bb}'$ is positive semi-definite and the quantity ξ is positive or negative if $\alpha = 0$ or $\alpha = 1$ respectively.

In conclusion, it follows from this discussion of the theoretical constraints that the only admissible value for the parameter α is $\alpha = 1$. This value fixes the weighting of the geometric price index (4.6) at the "affluence" level of the uncommitted budget allocation coefficients: $\underline{b}(\infty) = \underline{b}_0 + \underline{b}^1$.

5. NLES EXPERIMENTS ON POST-WAR CANADIAN DATA

The data used in this experiment is taken from the time series of annual personal expenditures on consumer goods and services in current and in constant 1971 dollars, established by Statistics Canada for Canadian national accounts(25). In order to analyze the consumption behaviour of an average Canadian household, these series have been divided by the resident population at June 1 of each year, as published by the same institution(26).

The analyzed consumption functions reproduce, with two exceptions, the official breakdown of consumption expenditures in eight major groups of goods and services. The two modifications to this classification are, first, the merging of groups 3 (gross rents, fuel and power) and 4 (furniture, furnishings, household equipment and operation) into one category "housing", and second, the taking away of medical expenditures from group 5 (medical care and health services)(27), which we shall call hereafter "drugs and sundries".

The NLES has been estimated with annual data of the period 1947 to 1977. Each equation of the system expresses per capita expenditures in current dollars as a function of the per capita total expenditure in current dollars and the implicit price indices for the groups of commodities considered. From these expenditure functions in current dollars, or consumption function in value, we deduce by the simple transformation $\underline{q} = \hat{\underline{p}}^{-1}\underline{d}$ the consumption functions in constant 1971 dollars, or consumption functions in volume, as well as the budget shares functions $\omega = r^{-1}\underline{d}$.

The estimation of the parameters a, $\underline{b}^0$, $\underline{b}^1$ and $\underline{c}$ of the NLES has been performed with the maximum likelihood method. The likelihood function adopted is the function associated with the following econometric specification of the budget shares:

$$\underline{\omega}_t = \hat{\underline{\pi}}_t\underline{c} + [\underline{b}^0 + \underline{b}^1 \; \Phi \; (\frac{1-\underline{\pi}_t'\underline{c}}{\Pi_t})] \; (1-\underline{\pi}_t'\underline{c}) + \underline{u}_t \; , \tag{5.1}$$

with $\underline{\pi}_t = r_t^{-1}\underline{p}_t$ and $\Pi_t = \exp \{(\underline{b}^0 + \underline{b}^1)' \log \underline{\pi}_t\}$;

t is the year of observation and $\underline{u}_t$ a vector of random disturbances, assumed homoscedastic and with no autocorrelation. The additivity of the model requires that $\underline{\iota}'\underline{u}_t = 0$ and hence the singularity of the covariance matrix $\Omega(\underline{\iota}'\Omega=\underline{0}')$, with rank assumed to be n-1.

The singularity of the $\underline{u}_t$ distribution is a source of difficulty in establishing the likelihood function. The prevailing solution among specialists of this field consists in choosing a likelihood function based on the density of a sub-vector of $\underline{u}_t$ obtained by deleting one component of $\underline{u}_t$. This is equivalent to a likelihood function of a system of n-1 budget shares chosen among the n considered shares. We can then proceed with the method under the conventional hypotheses.

This procedure appears suitable inasmuch as the likelihood is the same irrespective of which component of the vector $\underline{u}_t$ is deleted, as has been demonstrated(28). We have proposed elsewhere(29) a more "natural" justification for this procedure. In fact, up to one multiplicative factor (independent of the parameters), the likelihood obtained in this way is equal to the likelihood based on the density associated with $\underline{u}_t$ in the linear sub-space embodying all the realisations of this disturbance vector, i.e. the hyperplane $\underline{\iota}'\underline{u}_t = 0$.

In order to facilitate the numerical calculations for the estimation of the parameters, the likelihood function is first analytically maximised with respect to the matrix Ω. This yields a "concentrated" likelihood independent of Ω, which is to be maximised with respect to the parameters a, $\underline{b}^0$, $\underline{b}^1$ and $\underline{c}$. This maximisation requires an iterative procedure, the NLES being nonlinear with respect to these parameters. For the calculations, we used a general program for the estimation of nonlinear regression systems elaborated by Snella (1979) in the Department of Econometrics of the University of Geneva. This program performs the maximisation of the concentrated likelihood of a system of additive demand functions with the help of a variant of the "scoring method" by Fisher-Rao.

An experiment using this procedure was made in starting the iterations with different initial values of the parameters to be estimated. This experiment has shown that the convergence is relatively rapid only if one chooses a "good" initial value. For this it has proved useful to proceed first to an estimation by the OLS method, the value of the parameter a being fixed arbitrarily. This was done by the same program and yielded good results.

Exploring the likelihood surface obtained through these estimations, we have not detected the existence of multiple local maxima. We may therefore suppose that these estimations do represent a global maximum of the likelihood.

Tables 1 and 2 on the following pages show the estimates obtained successively by the exponential-sigmoid specification (NLES.1 model) and by the exponential-concave specification (NLES.2 model) of the Φ function. In order to evaluate the concrete relevence of a nonlinear specification of the Engel curves, we have also estimated the LES by the same method. The results of this last estimation are given in table 3.

A global comparison of the empirical adequacy of the LES and NLES models may be performed with the likelihood ratio test, in which the LES is regarded as a special case of the NLES where $\underline{b}^1 = \underline{0}$. The NLES will be said to be more informative if the null hypothesis $\underline{b}^1 = \underline{0}$ is rejected.

The statistic $-2 \log \lambda$, where λ is the likelihood ratio of LES over NLES, yields the following values:

	NLES.1	NLES.2
$-2 \log \lambda$ =	80.3	109.5

This statistic follows asymptotically a χ^2 distribution with 6 degrees of freedom[30], of which critical values are $\chi^2 = 12.6$ and $\chi^2 = 16.8$ with level of significance of respectively 5% and 1%. As in both cases $\chi^2_{cal} > \chi^2$, we may clearly reject the null hypothesis.

The clear superiority of the NLES over the LES is confirmed when we compare in detail the estimates of tables 1 to 3. With the exception of the "Drugs and sundries" function, the share of which in the total expenditure is small

Table 1. NLES.1 for Canada, 1947/77: Maximum likelihood estimates for the parameters(1)

Functions	b^o	b^1	$b^o + b^1$	$c^{(2)}$	R^2	D.-W.
Food, beverages and tobacco	0.1291 (0.0364)	0.0118 (0.0438)	0.1409 (0.0089)	369.6 (10.4)	0.983	0.72
Clothing and footwear	-0.0454 (0.0389)	0.1297 (0.0447)	0.0843 (0.0086)	147.2 (8.1)	0.921	0.56
Housing	0.7339 (0.1201)	-0.4923 (0.1208)	0.2416 (0.0168)	184.4 (36.7)	0.884	1.51
Drugs and sundries	0.0266 (0.0051)	-0.0098 (0.0062)	0.0167 (0.0013)	7.2 (1.1)	0.124	0.84
Transportation and communication	0.4711 (0.0956)	-0.3257 (0.1029)	0.1455 (0.0167)	40.0 (27.9)	0.837	0.62
Recreation, education and cultural services	-0.2153 (0.1159)	0.4254 (0.1179)	0.2101 (0.0126)	145.2 (29.7)	0.988	0.39
Personal goods and services	-0.1000 (0.0623)	0.2609 (0.0595)	0.1609 (0.0093)	278.7 (17.9)	0.982	1.24
			$a = 541.3^{(2)}$ (89.5)			

(1) Numbers in brackets are estimated asymptotic standard errors.
(2) In dollars at 1971 prices.

Table 2. NLES.2 for Canada, 1947/77: Maximum likelihood estimates for the parameters(1)

Functions	b^o	b^1	$b^o + b^1$	$c^{(2)}$	R^2	D.-W.
Food, beverages and tobacco	0.1309 (0.0456)	0.0111 (0.0441)	0.1419 (0.0040)	348.0 (11.9)	0.984	0.71
Clothing and footwear	-0.0781 (0.0377)	0.1366 (0.0373)	0.0585 (0.0031)	148.3 (9.4)	0.918	0.53
Housing	0.9533 (0.0593)	-0.5991 (0.0553)	0.3543 (0.0063)	67.5 (28.6)	0.869	1.33
Drugs and sundries	0.0268 (0.0057)	-0.0085 (0.0059)	0.0183 (0.0004)	5.1 (1.2)	0.100	0.78
Transportation and communication	0.6395 (0.0821)	-0.4208 (0.0785)	0.2187 (0.0066)	-39.9 (29.9)	0.854	0.61
Recreation, education and cultural services	-0.4971 (0.0463)	0.6004 (0.0410)	0.1033 (0.0059)	227.0 (19.1)	0.990	0.56
Personal goods and services	-0.1753 (0.0327)	0.2803 (0.0273)	0.1050 (0.0060)	289.1 (14.6)	0.980	1.20
		$a = 787.2^{(2)}$ (33.7)				

(1) Numbers in brackets are estimated aymptotic standard errors.
(2) In dollars at 1971 prices.

Table 3. LES for Canada, 1947/77: Maximum likelihood estimates for the parameters(1)

Functions	b	c(2)	R^2	D.-W.
Food, beverages and tobacco	0.1251 (0.0035)	303.9 (9.8)	0.981	0.58
Clothing and footwear	0.0513 (0.0029)	98.4 (4.5)	0.887	0.27
Housing	0.2928 (0.0062)	137.6 (22.9)	0.449	0.21
Drugs and sundries	0.0154 (0.0005)	3.2 (0.7)	0.210	0.78
Transportation and communication	0.1808 (0.0055)	15.8 (14.9)	0.699	0.36
Recreation, education and cultural services	0.1583 (0.0032)	-87.3 (17.2)	0.957	0.25
Personal goods and services	0.1763 (0.0074)	18.1 (30.4)	0.913	0.34

(1) Numbers in brackets are estimated asymptotic standard errors.
(2) In dollars at 1971 prices.

with respect to the other functions, the determination coefficients R^2 are higher for the NLES models than for the LES. This improvement is especially clear in the case of "Housing" and "Transportation and communications". A similar conclusion may be drawn from the comparison of the values taken by the Durbin-Watson statistic[(31)]. One can indeed observe that, for all the groups of goods, the autocorrelation of the residuals is smaller in the NLES than in the LES. It is particularly noticeable for "Housing". These results suggest that the very strong temporal link between the residuals of the LES is not only attributable to the static form of the model, which does not allow for the consideration of short-term variations of the demand, but also to the specification error due to the choice of a too rigid analytical form of the Engel curves.

The results of the maximum likelihood ratio tests also point out that, amongst the two NLES versions studied, the NLES.2 gives the best fit to the Canadian data: the rejection of the null hypothesis $\underline{b}^1 = \underline{0}$ is the most clear-cut for the NLES.2. However, this conclusion is not confirmed by the comparison of the statistics R^2 and D-W. In fact, a difference between our two NLES versions only appears when we analyze their economic content.

The estimates obtained for the parameters $\underline{b}^0$ and $\underline{b}^1$ do not conform to the sign restriction indicated by the qualitative analysis of the model. We do have $b_i^0 + b_i^1 > 0$, but on the other hand b_i^0 is negative for the functions "Clothing and footwear", "Recreation, education, cultural services", "Personal goods and services". However, their asymptotic standard-error shows that the sign of these parameters is statistically defined only for the two latter functions and, moreover, only in the NLES.2 case.

In the estimation of NLES.1, the coefficients b_i^1 are negative for the functions "Housing", "Drugs and sundries", "Transportation and communication". For the remaining functions, we observe the acceleration of the demand phenomenon, which may seem surprising in the case of the function "Food, beverages and tobacco". For this group, however, b_i^1 is quite small and barely significant from the statistical point of view.

The inflexion point of the function Φ of the NLES.1 is reached for a real uncommitted expenditure of $a/2 = 227$ dollars at 1971 prices. Since this value is lower than all the corresponding estimated values over the period of observation, we may conclude that only the concave section of the exponential-sigmoid function is utilized in the estimation of the model.

In estimating NLES.2, we do not find any quantity $b_i^0 + b_i^1\Psi_M < 0$. All the

Engel curves are thus increasing functions, as in the NLES.1. The turning point in the real uncommitted expenditure where the curvature of Engel curves becomes inverted is estimated at $z_M = 2a = 1574$ dollars in 1971 prices.

During our period of observation, this threshold has been exceeded since 1972. Over the terminal period 1972/1977, the interpretation of the phenomena of relative saturation or acceleration of the demand is no longer coherent between the two models. This result offers strong support in favour of the NLES.2, in the framework of which functions like "Food, beverages and tobacco" and "Clothing and footwear" will be considered from 1972 onwards as first necessity expenditures. It is on that point that the two models proposed differ most clearly. We may expect analoguous discrepancies in their predictive behaviour.

We still have to look at the estimates of the parameters $\underline{c}$, interpreted as minimum or committed quantities of consumption in constant 1971 prices. These estimates are remarkably close to each other for the two versions of the NLES, whereas they are quite different from those of the LES. Such differences cannot be explained by the uncertainty lying in the estimation method used, which is measured by the asymptotic standard deviation of the c_i's.

In conformity with the economic interpretation, all the estimated $\underline{c}$'s are positive in the two versions of the NLES, except that of the function "Transportation and communication" in the NLES.2. Taking into account the uncertainty of this estimation, however, the sign of this particular parameter is not significantly determined and could be positive.

The interpretation of the parameters $\underline{c}$ as committed quantities requires not only the condition $\underline{c} > \underline{0}$, but also that the condition $E(\underline{q}_t | \underline{p}_t, r_t) \geq \underline{c}$ is satisfied over the whole observation period. In fact, this is only the case for the functions "Food, beverages, tobacco", "Housing", "Drugs and sundries" and "Transportation and communication". For the three remaining function, this inequality is violated during the first years of the observation period, more precisely during the years indicated below:

Functions	NLES. 1	NLES. 2
Clothing and footwear	1947/55	1947/55
Recreation, education, cultural services	1947/63	1947/70
Personal goods and services	1947/55	1947/60

For the first and third functions, this result can be explained by the statistical inaccuracy of the estimate. On the other hand, the negative c_i of the second function is not compatible with the committed quantity interpretation over a fairly long period. These results suggest that the hypothesis of a constant committed consumption over the entire period cannot be kept for all functions. For some of them, and especially for "Recreation, education, and cultural services", we should assume a committed consumption that changes as a function of environmental variables(32), or as a function of the level of consumption reached in the past, which imposes a "ratchet" effect on the demand and prevents its falling back(33).

In another perspective, we can also examine the elasticities of the NLES in order to see whether a nonlinear specification frees the model from the approximated link between the own-price elasticity and the total expenditure elasticity, called "Pigou's law" by Deaton (1974). Incidentally, Deaton's work has established how empirically groundless this law is. It is, however, a law inherent in the LES and more generally in all demand systems stemming from additively separable functions of direct utility.

Table 4 shows the values of these elasticities for the NLES and LES models, calculated with respect to total expenditure and prices, at average values over the observation period and, alternatively, at values of the terminal year 1977. Average total expenditure elasticities are almost identical for NLES.1 and NLES.2, in contrast to the results for 1977. The differences appearing in the terminal year show how the two models become differentiated from each other in 1972 with the crossing of the threshold so that the curvature of the Engel curves is suddenly modified in the NLES.2 case. On the other hand, own-price elasticities differ as much, or even more, for the average values as for 1977 values, between NLES.1 and NLES.2 estimates.

Nevertheless, as expected, even wider differences appear between these elasticities and those of the LES model. They are the consequences of the Pigou relationships, prevalent in the LES but not found in the NLES. This result is illustrated in Chart 3 below, where we draw (for the three estimated models) the scattered diagram of the couples (η_{ii}, ε_i) where η is the own-price elasticity and ε the total expenditure elasticity. Pigou's law is represented by the straight line

$$\eta_{ii} = -\left(\frac{r-\underline{p}'\underline{c}}{r}\right)\varepsilon_i \ .$$

The LES couples (η_{ii}, ε_i) will tend to lie along this line as the number of functions tends towards infinity.

Table 4. NLES and LES for Canada, 1947/77: total expenditure elasticities and own-price elasticities

Functions	Models	Total expenditure elasticities average(1)	Total expenditure elasticities 1977	Own-price elasticities average(1)	Own-price elasticities 1977
Food, beverages and tobacco	NLES.1	0.58	0.67	-0.37	-0.50
	NLES.2	0.59	0.68	-0.41	-0.53
	LES	0.52	0.61	-0.47	-0.57
Clothing and footwear	NLES.1	0.86	1.09	-0.26	-0.53
	NLES.2	0.88	1.01	-0.26	-0.51
	LES	0.60	0.74	-0.49	-0.64
Housing	NLES.1	0.98	0.90	-0.73	-0.79
	NLES.2	0.98	1.01	-0.79	-0.86
	LES	1.02	1.01	-0.84	-0.89
Drugs and sundries	N ES.1	1.30	1.23	-0.72	-0.87
	NLES.2	1.28	1.25	-0.80	-0.91
	LES	1.14	1.11	-0.87	-0.94
Transportation and communication	NLES.1	1.18	1.03	-0.85	-0.89
	NLES.2	1.15	1.13	-0.99	-0.99
	LES	1.24	1.15	-0.96	-0.98
Recreation, education and cultural services	NLES.1	2.14	1.74	-0.53	-0.80
	NLES.2	2.17	1.52	-0.13	-0.56
	LES	1.87	1.47	-1.36	-1.20
Personal goods and services	NLES.1	0.98	0.98	-0.34	-0.53
	NLES.2	0.98	0.88	-0.31	-0.49
	LES	1.24	1.14	-0.96	-0.97

(1) Caluculated on the basis of the average total expenditure and of the average prices over the period 1947/1977.

In this chart there is no observable pattern in the scattering of the NLES elasticities to suggest the existence of a functional link, not even a vague one between price and total expenditure elasticities. On the contrary, there is a systematic tendency for the own-price elasticities of the NLES to be lower than those of the LES. In comparison to the LES, the NLES thus seems to reduce the role of prices as explanatory factors of the demand, at least in the empirical application of this study. This result seems quite plausible at the aggregation level of the demand that we use here.

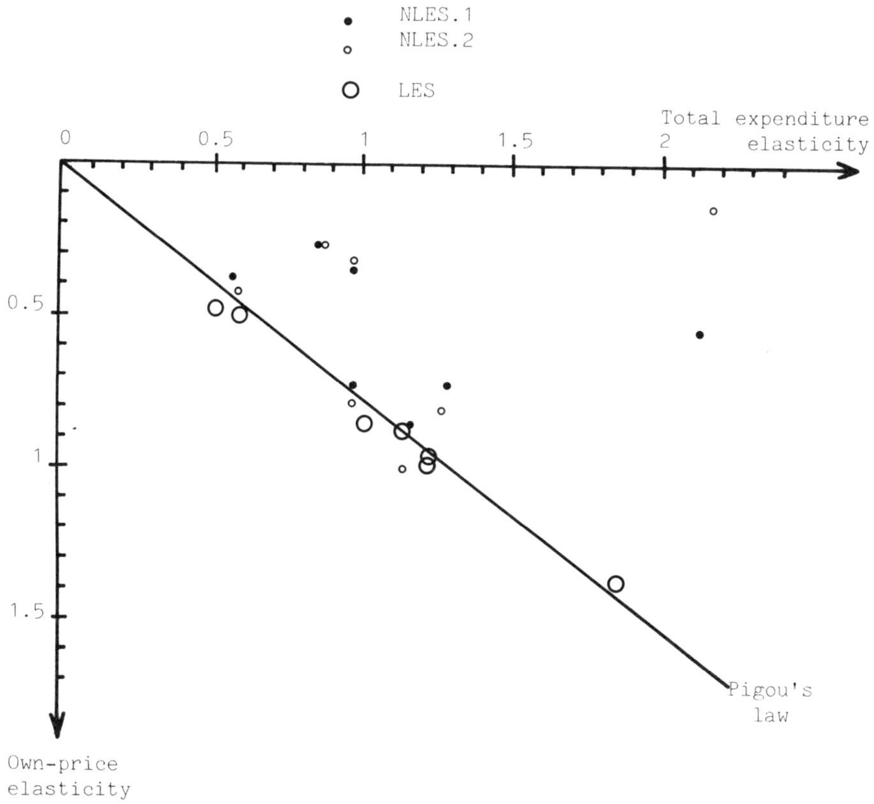

Chart 3. Own-price elasticities and total expenditure elasticities for Canada, average values 1947/1977

6. CONCLUSION

This experiment with the NLES on Canadian data seems to show in a particularly convincing way that nonlinear Engel curves are of significant interest for empirical studies of the private consumption patterns. In its present specification, however, the NLES should not be considered as wholly satisfying, as the analysis of its fit to the Canadian data has shown.

First, and because of its static definition, the model cannot reproduce short-term fluctuations. This probably explains the strong temporal link between the residuals for some functions and, in particular, for those where durable or semi-durable goods prevail or for which consumption habits are important. Secondly, the hypothesis of a constant committed consumption over such a long period of time as we have considered, does not suit all the consumption groups. More flexibility in the model is therefore desirable.

Yet the NLES model can be improved. It offers a sufficiently wide framework to allow for such modification. With no change in their economic interpretation, the parameters c_i can be assumed to be functions of predetermined factors, and that easily leads to dynamic versions of the NLES. This way, it is also possible to include economic or non-economic environmental variables.

By adapting Stone's suggestion(34) to replace the constants $\underline{c}$ by homogeneous price function of degree one and with a negative semi-definite Jacobian matrix(35), we could further ensure complete independence between price and total expenditure elasticities. As they are, these possible improvements of the NLES sho its interest and encourage further developments in this direction.

APPENDIX: Towards an appropriate procedure for the estimation of disaggregate consumption functions

Parallel to the improvement of the NLES suggested in the conclusion, we should also concentrate on the estimation problem of this model. The difficulties appear to be insuperable when the breakdown of the commodity groups is greater than that used in this study. In fact, if we wish to analyse consumption expenditures for twenty or more groups of goods and services, the estimation of the NLES can no longer be carried out by the procedure proposed above, at least in the present state of the art of computer technology. The nonlinearity of the NLES with respect to the parameters requires iterative procedures, of which the cost in calculation time increases exponentially with the number of functions, and thus rapidly becomes prohibitive.

We shall sketch out in this appendix a hierarchical procedure of estimation, less informative than the full information maximum likelihood method, but which should allow the estimation of disaggregated consumption functions at a reasonable cost. The procedure is based on the fact that the NLES offers the possibility of a quasi-aggregation of the model with respect to the commodities. With this property in mind, we can express the expenditure for one group of commodities as a function of only two price indices of the group, of the other "elementary" goods and of the total expenditure, the form of this function being similar to that of a NLES function[36].

Let us consider a partition of n commodities into N < n groups, G = 1,2,...,N.

Let $\underline{p}_G$ be the price vector of the commodities of group G, $\underline{d}_G$ the vector of the expenditures necessary to buy these commodities, $\underline{b}_G^0$, $\underline{b}_G^1$ and $\underline{c}_G$ the sub-vectors of the parameters $\underline{b}^0$, $\underline{b}^1$ and $\underline{c}$ related to these goods. With this notation, we can write the NLES:

$$\underline{d}_G = \hat{\underline{p}}_G \underline{c}_G + \left[\underline{b}_G^0 + \underline{b}_G^1 \Phi \left(\frac{r - \sum_G \underline{p}_G' \underline{c}_G}{P} \right) \right] (r - \sum_G \underline{p}_G' \underline{c}_G) \,, \tag{A1}$$

with $\log P = \sum_G (\underline{b}_G^0 + \underline{b}_G^1)' \log \underline{p}_G$.

Adding up the expenditures of each group, we get a system of inter-group functions expressing the total expenditure of a group, $\bar{d}_G = \underline{\iota}'\underline{d}_G$, as a function of the total expenditure, of two types of intra-group price indices:

$$\bar{p}_G = \frac{\underline{c}_G'\underline{p}_G}{\underline{\iota}'\underline{c}_G}, \qquad \log \bar{\bar{p}}_G = \frac{(\underline{b}_G^0 + \underline{b}_G^1)'\log \underline{p}_G}{\underline{\iota}'(\underline{b}_G^0 + \underline{b}_G^1)} \tag{A2}$$

and with the means of aggregated parameters:

$$\bar{b}_G^0 = \underline{\iota}'\underline{b}_G^0, \qquad \bar{b}_G^1 = \underline{\iota}'\underline{b}_G^1, \qquad \bar{c}_G = \underline{\iota}'\underline{c}_G, \tag{A3}$$

i.e.

$$\bar{d}_G = \bar{p}_G\bar{c}_G + \left[\bar{b}_G^0 + \bar{b}_G^1\Phi\left(\frac{r-\sum_G \bar{p}_G\bar{c}_G}{P}\right)\right](r-\sum_G \bar{p}_G\bar{c}_G) \tag{A4}$$

with $\log P = \sum_G(\bar{b}_G^0 + \bar{b}_G^1)\log \bar{\bar{p}}_G$.

This result suggests an iterative procedure of estimation in which each iteration can be split into two following hierarchical steps:

i) The parameters of the system of inter-group expenditure functions (A4) are estimated with a priori fixed intra-group price indices. If these indices were, for instance, equal to the group implicit price indices, $\bar{p}_G = \bar{\bar{p}}_G = \underline{\iota}'\underline{d}_G/\underline{\iota}'\underline{q}_G$, the estimation problem would be identical to that analysed previously in this study, and could be solved with the maximum likelihood method.

ii) For each group considered separately, the parameters $\underline{b}_G^0$, $\underline{b}_G^1$, $\underline{c}_G$ of the system of the intra-group expenditure function (A1) are estimated under the linear constraints (A3). The values of the coefficients $\bar{b}_G^0$, $\bar{b}_G^1$, $\bar{c}_G$ obtained in the preceeding step are introduced into these constraints(37). These estimates of the parameters $\underline{b}_G^0$, $\underline{b}_G^1$ and $\underline{c}_G$ allow for the calculation of the intra-group price indices. We are then able to proceed with the iterative procedure.

In the conventional empirical situations prices follow a strongly collinear pattern so the intra-group price indices $\bar{p}_G$ and $\bar{\bar{p}}_G$ will be approximately equal. One can thus expect a rapid convergence of the iterative procedure, which could even be stopped after the second iteration.

In order to speed up the convergence, it might also prove useful to divide each iteration into more than two steps. This is clearly possible since, by aggregation, we can generate from the system of intra-group expenditure functions (A4) a new system of expenditure functions, analogous to the former but of higher hierarchical order, mapped on a set of expenditure categories obtained by a further partition of the commodity groups $G = 1,2,\ldots,N$.

NOTES

* This chapter is a completely revised version of a paper presented at the 1978 European Meeting of the Econometric Society (cf. Carlevaro (978)). I would like to express my gratitude to D. Bachmann for his friendly collaboration when experimenting with the NLES, a research sponsored jointly by the Department of econometrics of the University of Geneva and by the Projections and Programming Division of the Economic Commission for Europe.

(1) Cf. Solari (1979), p.39.

(2) One should not forget the difficult problem of aggregating individual demand functions, the solution of which is essential to understanding what we mean by "representative" consumer, an abstract concept common to all estimation of complete demand systems on the basis of national accounts data. An important step towards a satisfactory solution of this problem has recently been made by Muellbauer (1976). We shall see later on in this chapter that our NLES model is compatible with the aggregation procedure proposed by Muellbauer.

(3) Cf. United Nations (1977a,b).

(4) The notations used in this chapter are standard: $\underline{a}$ is a column vector and $\underline{a}'$ its transpose; $\underline{\iota}$ and $\underline{0}$ are the unit zero vectors; $\underline{\hat{a}}$ is the diagonal matrix whose diagonal elements are those of the vector $\underline{a}$; log $\underline{a}$ is a vector whose elements are the natural logarithms of the corresponding elements in vector $\underline{a}$.

(5) Empirical results are given in Solari (1971).

(6) This hypothesis appears already in Stone (1964a), but is fully developed in Pollack and Wales (1969).

(7) This hypothesis made by Houthakker and Taylor (1966) was applied to the LES model by Philips (1972) and Rossier (1974).

(8) Cf. Carlevaro (1977), pp. 1644 ff. In this article, we have shown that the NLES may be linked with the work by Fourgeaud-Nataf on demand functions in real prices and income.

(9) The adjective "subjective" is used here in the sense that this index describes how consumers perceive changes in the general price level. The subjective perception may, of course, not correspond to the objective measures given by official statistics.

(10) Cf. Carlevaro (1976 and 1977).

(11) Cf. Stone, Brown and Rowe (1964) and Stone (1964a and 1964b). This procedure has more recently been used by Deaton (1975) in a detailed analysis of household consumption in Britain.

(12) Stone (1964a) suggests to relate the evolution of the parameters $\underline{b}$ with a moving average of the total expenditures during the three preceeding years.

(13) Cf. Carlevaro (1976), pp. 76-79.

(14) It can easily be checked that this expression of the utility indicator leads to the demand function of the NLES, using the Roy theorem formulated in terms of budget coefficients:

$$\underline{\omega} = r^{-1}\,\hat{\underline{p}}\underline{q} = -\left(\frac{\partial \log u}{\partial \log r}\right)^{-1} \frac{\partial \log u}{\partial \log \underline{p}} ,$$

and using equation (2.7) to write the u elasticities as follows:

$$\frac{\partial \log u}{\partial \log r} = \frac{\partial \log F}{\partial \log f}\;\frac{\partial \log f}{\partial \log x}\;\frac{r}{r-\underline{p}'\underline{c}} ,$$

$$\frac{\partial \log u}{\partial \log \underline{p}} = -\frac{\partial \log F}{\partial \log f}\;\frac{\partial \log f}{\partial \log x}\left[(r-\underline{p}'\underline{c})^{-1}\,\hat{\underline{p}}\underline{c} + \underline{b}^0 + \underline{b}^1\Phi\right.$$

(15) The first and second derivatives of Φ are supposed to be finite for all $z \geqslant 0$.

(16) If we admit that this equation has one solution at the most, we introduce implicitly new qualitative hypotheses concerning the form of the function Φ.

(17) For $b_i^1 = 0$, we get the linear Engel curve of the LES.

(18) This extreme value is established by using the expansion of Φ at the point $1/z = 0$.

(19) The monotonicity of Ψ rules out the case $a_1 = 0$.

(20) This is the case for the family of log-logistic curves:

$$\Phi(z) = \frac{1}{1+\exp\{-\gamma\log\frac{z}{a}\}} = \frac{1}{1+\left(\frac{z}{a}\right)^{-\gamma}} ,$$

sigmoid when $\gamma > 1$ and concave when $0 < \gamma \leqslant 1$.

(21) I have elsewhere (Carlevaro (1979)) studied a third specification for Φ, leading to an exponential-concave function Ψ:

$$\Phi(z) = \frac{1}{z}\int (1-\exp\{-\frac{z}{a}\})\,dz = 1 + \frac{a}{z}\,(1-\exp\{-\frac{z}{a}\}) .$$

While Φ is concave as the function Ψ from which it stems, this specification entails the same Engel curves as the exponential-sigmoid specification. It is therefore an intermediary case between the two specifications of Φ analyzed in this paper.

(22) In experiments with semi-aggregated data, the elements of $\underline{p}$ are already synthetic price indices for groups of goods. We then have to posit $\underline{p}_0 = \underline{1}$ in order to identify the base of P with that of its elements $\underline{p}$.

(23) Cf. Goursat (1942), § 393.

(24) Cf. Solari (1971), chap. III.

(25) Cf. Statistics Canada (1976a, 1978), Tables 53 and 54.

(26) Cf. Statistics Canada (1976b), Table 1, and (1978), Table A.

(27) This elimination was necessary since in the middle of the observation period (1961), the application of a "law on insurance for hospitalisation and diagnostic services" introduced a compulsory health insurance system in Canada. The taking into account of such an institutional change and its effects on the consumer behaviour would require, in our opinion, a new and more complex formulation of the NLES.

(28) Cf. Barten (1969), Solari (1971), Deaton (1975).

(29) Cf. Carlevaro (1978).

(30) The number of independent parameters eliminated by the null hypothesis is equal to the number of $\underline{b}^1$ minus one, as these parameters are subject to the constraint $\underline{\imath}'\underline{b}^1=0$.

(31) The classical test used for linear regression cannot be used here, since we are dealing with a system of nonlinear regressions. Even in this case, however, if there is no temporal link between the disturbances $\underline{u}_t$, this statistic converges in probability towards 2, provided that the estimtors considered are consistent.

(32) For the function "Recreation, education, cultural services", we could think of variables such as "Leisure time", "Degree of urbanisation" and "Educational level".

(33) See Pollack and Wales (1969).

(34) Cf. Stone (1964b).

(35) We have noted elsewhere (Carlevaro (1977), p. 1647), that the specification of functions $\underline{c}(\underline{p})$ verifying those constraints may easily be obtained from a function $Q(\underline{p})$, homogeneous of degree one, increasing and concave, by writing $\underline{c}(\underline{p}) = \partial Q/\partial \underline{p}$. In short, these "variable committed quantities" may be defined as "forces" derived from a "potential" Q defined over the price space. $\underline{c}(\underline{p})$ being a homogeneous function, Euler's theorem $\underline{p}'\underline{c}(\underline{p}) = Q(\underline{p})$ shows that this "potential" expresses the total committed expenditure in the price space.

(36) This procedure is inspired by that used by Deaton (1976) for the estimation of his SNAM model on a set of 37 groups of commodities.

(37) As well as the estimate for the function Φ .

REFERENCES

(1) Barten, A.P., Maximum Likelihood Estimation of a Complete System of Demand Equations, European Economic Review, vol. 1, no. 1, 1969, pp. 7-73.

(2) Carlevaro, F., A Generalisation of the Linear Expenditure System in Solari, L. and Du Pasquier, J.-N. (eds.), Private and Enlarged Consumption, Essays in Methodology and Empirical Analysis, North-Holland, Amsterdam, 1976, pp. 73-92.

(3) Carlevaro, F., Note sur les fonctions de consommation en prix et revenu réels de Fourgeaud et Nataf, Econometrica, vol. 45, no. 7, 1977,

pp. 1639-50.
(4) Carlevaro, F., Une méthodologie économétrique d'analyse du budget moyen intervenant dans le calcul des indices budgétaires des prix à la consommation, Cahier FN/1.367-0.76/2, Département d'économétrie, Université de Genève, December 1978.
(5) Carlevaro, F., A Nonlinear Expenditure System for Analysing and Forecasting the Structure of Private Consumption. Specification, Analysis and Experiments with Canadian Data, Cahier 79.11, Department of Econometrics, University of Geneva, July 1979.
(6) Deaton, A., A Reconsideration of the Empirical Implications of Additive Preferences, The Economic Journal, vol. 84, no. 334, 1974, pp. 338-48.
(7) Deaton, A., Models and Projections of Post-War Britain, Chapman and Hall, London, 1975.
(8) Deaton, A., A Simple Nonadditive Model of Demand, in Solari, L. and Du Pasquier, J.-N. (eds.), Private and Enlarged Consumption, Essays in Methodology and Empirical Analysis, North-Holland, Amsterdam, 1976, pp. 55-72.
(9) Du Pasquier, J.-N. and Rossier, E., L'oeuvre scientifique de Luigi Solari, Cahier 79.10, Département d'économétrie, Université de Genève, July 1979.
(10) Goursat, E., Cours d'analyse mathématique, sixième édition, tome II, Gauthier-Villars, Paris, 1942.
(11) Houthakker, H.S. and Taylor, L.D., Consumer Demand in the United States, 1929-1970, Analyses and Projections, Harvard University Press, Cambridge, Mass., 1966.
(12) Muellbauer, J., Economics and the Representative Consumer, in Solari, L. and Du Pasquier (eds.), J.-N. Private and Enlarged Consumption, Essays in Methodology and Empirical Analysis, North-Holland, Amsterdam, 1976, pp. 29-53.
(13) United Nations, Poursuite de l'élaboration du modèle SEM: version élargie (SEM.3), Note du secrétariat, EC.AD. (XIV)/R.6/add.1., Geneva, Economic Commision for Europe, February 1977a.
(14) United Nations, Analyse de l'évolution à moyen et long terme de la consommation privée dans les pays européens d'économie de marché par un système non linéaire de dépenses, Note du secrétariat, EC.AD./SEM.5/10, Geneva, Economic Commission for Europe, July 1977, paper presented to the séminaire sur l'emploi, la distribution du revenu et la consommation: objectifs et changements de structure à long terme, Saint-Maximin-la Sainte-Daume, (France), 6-13, September 1977b.
(15) Philips, L., A Dynamic Version of the Linear Expenditure Model, The Review of Economics and Statistics, vol. LIV, no. 4, 1972, pp. 450-58.
(16) Pollack, R.A. and Wales, T.J., Estimation of the Linear Expenditure System, Econometrica, vol. 37, no. 4, 1969, pp. 611-28.
(17) Rossier, E., Contributions aux explications dynamiques de la consommation semi-agrégée, H. Lang, Berne, 1964.
(18) Solari, L. Théorie des choix et fonctions de consommation semi-agrégées, Modèles statiques, Droz, Geneva-Paris, 1971.
(19) Solari, L., Essais de méthode et analyses économétriques. Pour une utilisation combinée de la théorie et de l'expérimentation en économie, edited by F. Carlevaro, Droz, Geneva, 1979.
(20) Statistics Canada, National Income and Expenditure Accounts. The Annual Estimates 1926-1974, catalogue 13-531 occasional, Ottawa, March 1976, 1976a.
(21) Statistics Canada, catalogue 91-201 annual, Ottawa, August 1976, 1976b.
(22) Statistics Canada, National Income and Expenditure Accounts. The Annual Estimates 1963-1977, catalogue 13-201 annual, Ottawa, November 1978.

(23) Snella, J.-J., A Fortran Program for Multivariate Nonlinear Regression - GCM, Cahier 79.05, Department of Econometrics, University of Geneva, January 1979.
(24) Stone, R., Linear Expenditure Systems and Demand Analysis: An Application to the Pattern of British Demand, The Economic Journal, vol. LXIV, 1954, pp. 511-27.
(25) Stone, R., The Changing Pattern of Consumption, in Problems of Economic Dynamics and Planning, (in honour of Michael Kalecki), Warsaw, Polish Scientific Publishers, reprinted in R. Stone, Mathematics in the Social Sciences and Other Essays, Chapter XIV, Chapman and Hall, London, 1966.
(26) Stone, R., Models for Demand Projections, in Essays on Econometrics and Planning, (in honour of P.C.Mahalanobis), Pergamon Press, Oxford, 1964b, reprinted in R. Stone, Mathematical Models of the Economy and Other Essays, Chapter VII, Chapman and Hall, London, 1970.
(27) Stone, R., Brown, A. and Rowe, D.A., Demand Analysis and Projections for Britain: 1900-1970, Chapter 8, in (ed.) J. Sandee, Europe's Future Consumption, North-Holland, Amsterdam, 1964.

PART III

ESTIMATING

CHAPTER 5

A GENERAL APPROACH FOR ESTIMATING ECONOMETRIC MODELS WITH INCOMPLETE OBSERVATIONS

M.G. Dagenais, Université de Montréal and
D.L. Dagenais, Ecole des Hautes Etudes Commerciales

1. INTRODUCTION

Applied quantitative economics relies heavily on statistical methods to estimate the parameters of its models. In many situations, data is relatively scarce and it is therefore important to use all available observations, even those that are incomplete or for which some pieces of data are missing. The purpose of the present paper is to suggest a general estimation technique that can be applied when there are incomplete observations.

In most estimation techniques generally used to estimate the parameters of linear econometric models, the observed dependent and independent variables enter only in the form of average cross-products. This is the case, for example, of full information maximum likelihood estimators, three-stage least squares (3SLS) estimators, two-stage least squares estimators of simultaneous-equation models, of ordinary least squares (OLS) and instrumental variables estimators used in regression models involving serial correlation of disturbances and of other types of generalized least squares estimators.

When data is missing among the dependent or independent variables, the above estimators may be replaced by estimators in which the missing cross-products are evaluated by close consistent approximations. Under very broad distributional assumptions and under minimal assumptions concerning the missing data generating process, the suggested estimators will converge in probability to the corresponding complete data estimators. Analytical comparisons with other missing data estimators for simple cases suggest that our proposed estimators are asymptotically relatively quite efficient; Monte Carlo studies lead to similar conclusions for small sample situations.

Furthermore, the estimation technique suggested in the present paper is relatively simple and cheap to compute since it does not involve special iterative procedures. In most cases, the analytical expressions of the asymptotic covariance matrices of the parameter estimators can be derived by straightforward, although lengthy and tedious, algebraic procedures. Moreover, it appears that satisfactory approximations of these covariance matrices can be obtained readily.

The following section of the paper describes the basic general idea of replacing missing cross-products by close consistent approximations. Then, Section 3 discusses the implications of the requirement that the missing data pattern be random, within the context of the proposed approach. Section 4 compares the relative asymptotic efficiency of our estimator to that of alternative estimators in a simple model. Section 5 gives reports of Monte Carlo studies where the mean squared errors (MSE) of our estimators are compared to the MSE of other estimators, in small sample situations. Then, Section 6 illustrates how the covariance matrices of our estimators can be approximated in certain cases: the cases considered concern the OLS estimator of the multiple regression model and the 3SLS estimator.

2. THE BASIC PRINCIPLE

Let us assume that we have a sample of N observations, some of which are incomplete, and that for computing a given estimator, average cross-products of the form $\sum_{t=1}^{N} y_{jt}x_{it}/N$ have to be computed, where y_j and x_i are two stochastic or fixed variables appearing in the model. Now, if some observations are missing on y_{jt} or x_{it}, the above expression cannot be computed as such. It is therefore suggested to replace it by the estimate described below.

The above sum may be broken down as follows:

$$\sum_{t=1}^{N} y_{jt}x_{it}/N = \sum_{g=1}^{c} (N_g/N) \sum_{t\varepsilon S_g} y_{jt}x_{it}/N_g \tag{2.1}$$

where N_g is the number of elements in Subset S_g and c is the total number of disjoint subsets. Each subset S_g is characterized simultaneously by the following attributes:

- whether x_{it} or y_{jt} are available;
- how the missing variables are approximated.

For each subset, one may then write:

$$\sum_{t\varepsilon S_g} y_{jt}x_{it}/N_g = \sum_{t\varepsilon S_g} (y^a_{jt} + w^a_{jt})(x^a_{it} + v^a_{it})/N_g \tag{2.2}$$

$$= \sum_{t\varepsilon S_g} (y^a_{jt}x^a_{it})/N_g + \sum_{t\varepsilon S_g} w^a_{jt}\, x^a_{it}/N_g$$
$$+ \sum_{t\varepsilon S_g} y^a_{jt}v^a_{it}/N_g + \sum_{t\varepsilon S_g} w^a_{jt}v^a_{it}/N_g \qquad (2.3)$$

where y^a_{jt} and x^a_{it} correspond respectively to approximations of y_{jt} and x_{it}, $w^a_{jt} = y_{jt} - y^a_{jt}$ and $v^a_{it} = x_{it} - x^a_{it}$.

If, for a given subset, y_j and x_i are both observable, then $y^a_{jt} = y_{jt}$ and $x^a_{it} = x_{it}$ and the last three terms appearing on the RHS of (2.3) vanish. If only y_j is observable, then the second and last terms would be zero, while if only x_i is available the third and fourth terms would be equal to zero.

In order to approximate the missing y_j's and x_i's, proxy variables must be used. For example, if y_{jt} is not available for the observations of a given subset $S_{g'}$, but the associated proxy variables, say z_1, z_2 and z_3, are available for these observations and if furthermore, y_t and the z's are all available for another set of observations contained in $S_{pg'}$, then an auxiliary regression of y_j on the z's based on the observations contained in $S_{pg'}$ may be used to derive estimated values for the missing y's in $S_{g'}$.

The proxy variables used to approximate the missing data may be variables already appearing in the econometric model considered or they may be extraneous variables. Similarly, the auxiliary set $S_{pg'}$ may be a subset of the original sample or it may contain extraneous observations.

Note also that it could happen that more than one of the different subsets S_g (g = 1, ..., m) be characterized by the same missing data pattern (say y_j and x_i both missing) but that these subsets differ only by the fact that the missing y_j's or x_i's are not approximated with the same proxy variables.

Once the y_j's and x_i's have been expressed in terms of an observable part and a residual error, as in (2.2), the term $\sum_{t\varepsilon S_g} y^a_{jt}x^a_{it}/N_g$ appearing in (2.3) becomes always observable and directly computable. However, the three other terms contained on the RHS of (2.3) are not observable and must be estimated, unless they are known to be zero.

Suppose, as mentioned earlier, that for a given subset $S_{g'}$, y_{jt} is missing and can be predicted from proxy variables z_1, z_2, z_3, using an auxiliary regression based on a set of observations $S_{pg'}$; suppose furthermore that x_t is also missing and can be predicted from other proxy variables using an auxiliary regression based on a different set of observations $S_{qg'}$ and that a <u>sub-set of observations</u> is common to both $S_{pg'}$ and $S_{qg'}$, namely the subset $S_{pqg'} = S_{pg'} \cap S_{pg'}$; then the unobservable expressions contained in (2.3) may be approximated as follows:

$$\sum_{t\varepsilon S_{g'}} w^a_{jt} x^a_{it}/N_{g'} \doteq \sum_{t\varepsilon S_{pqg'}} w^a_{jt} x^a_{it}/N_{pqg'} \tag{2.4}$$

$$\sum_{t\varepsilon S_{g'}} y^a_{jt} v^a_{it}/N_{g'} \doteq \sum_{t\varepsilon S_{pqg'}} y^a_{jt} v^a_{it}/N_{pqg'} \tag{2.5}$$

$$\sum_{t\varepsilon S_{g'}} w^a_{jt} v^a_{it}/N_{g'} \doteq \sum_{t\varepsilon S_{pqg'}} w^a_{jt} v^a_{it}/N_{pqg'} \tag{2.6}$$

where $N_{pqg'}$ designates the number of elements in $S_{pqg'}$ and $\doteq$ means "approximately equal to". The general principle is that the average cross-product involving the unobservable w^a_j's and v^a_i's of subset $S_{g'}$ are replaced by the corresponding average cross-products of subset $S_{pqg'}$ for which the w^a_j's and v^a_i's can be computed.

Therefore, the unobservable expression $\sum_{t\varepsilon S_{g'}} y_{jt} x_{it}/N_{g'}$ may be estimated by:

$$\sum_{t\varepsilon S_{g'}} y_{jt} x_{it}/N_{g'} \doteq \sum_{t\varepsilon S_{g'}} y^a_{jt} x^a_{it}/N_{g'} + \sum_{t\varepsilon S_{pqg'}} w^a_{jt} x^a_{it}/N_{pqg'} + \sum_{t\varepsilon S_{pgq'}} y^a_{jt} v^a_{it}/N_{pqg'} + \sum_{t\varepsilon S_{pqg'}} w^a_{jt} v^a_{it}/N_{pqg'} \tag{2.7}$$

Clearly, the closer are the approximations y^a_t and x^a_t to the true values, the better will be the estimate of the LHS of (2.7). Given the well known property of convergence in probability of a continuous function of stochastic processes (Wilks, 1962, p. 103), the RHS of (2.7) will be a consistent estimate of the LHS if the last three terms of (2.7) are consistent estimates of the last three terms in (2.3). This will be the case if the missing data pattern is random, as discussed in the next section.

If for all cross-products involved in the econometric estimation under concern, unobservable average cross-products over relevant subsets can be replaced by consistent estimates as shown in equation (2.7), the resulting missing data estimator will clearly be a consistent estimator of the uncomputable complete data estimator.

To sum up, the basic idea of our reasoning is that the use of incomplete observations involves in general a relative loss of efficiency; this loss may, however, be reduced if the approximations obtained from the proxy variables for the missing data are very close. In economics, it is often possible to find very good proxies for the variables contained in our models.

3. THE RANDOMNESS OF THE MISSING DATA PATTERNS

Rubin (1976) has shown that one of the conditions that makes it appropriate to ignore the process causing the missing data for sampling distribution inference, is that the probability of the missing data pattern, in the sense to be explained below, be the same for all values of the variables concerned.

In our case, the variables of interest are the v's and w's. If, for example, the probability that y_{jt} be missing, given y^a_{jt} , is the same for all w^a_{jt} , and similarly the probability that x_{it} be missing, given x^a_{it} is the same for all v^a_{it} , then the RHS of (2.3) will be a consistent estimator of the LHS.

To take an example, let us assume that in a household survey, y_j designates household income and the z's designate such variables as age, schooling, occupation of head, net value of real estate owned, ..., etc., one could say that y_{jt} is missing at random if the probalitity that a household refuses to reveal its income is the same for all households with the same z-characteristics. However, if one believes for example, that for households with the same z-characteristics, those with a higher income have a greater tendency to refuse to reveal it, one would definitely have a case where the probability of the missing data pattern, given y^a_{jt} , would be larger for larger values of w^a_{jt} . In this case, the approximations obtained from the auxiliary regressions run with the observed data would be systematically biased on the low side and, correlatively, the unobserved w^a_{jt}'s pertaining to the missing values would be systematically higher, with a positive mean, instead of a zero mean. In this example, using the cross-products of residuals derived from the auxiliary regressions based on subsets of observations in which all data are observable, as estimators of the needed unobservable cross-products, would therefore entail systematic biases that would not vanish asymptotically.

In such a case, we would have to conclude that, for our purpose, the data is not missing at random. This suggests that great care should be exercised when using estimation techniques assuming randomly missing data. In the above example, the danger of systematic biases would probably be lower if the three variables included in the auxiliary regressions involve economic variables closely related to income, such as household expenses, savings, net real assets, ..., etc. than if they involve only more remotely correlated socio-economic characteristics such as schooling, age or occupation.

4. SOME ASYMPTOTIC RESULTS

In this section, the asymptotic efficiency of our missing data estimator is compared to that of alternative estimators described in the literature for the case of the multiple regression model with two independent non-stochastic variables. The model may be expressed as:

$$y_t = \beta_1 + \beta_2 x_{2t} + \beta_3 x_{3t} + u_t \qquad (t = 1, \ldots, N) \tag{4.1}$$

where y_t is the dependent variable, x_{2t} and x_{3t} are the independent variables, u_t is a stochastic error term with zero mean and finite variance σ^2. The sample size is N; y_t is available for all observations; x_{2t} and x_{3t} are also both available in N_c observations. In the remaining observations, either x_{2t} or x_{3t} is missing. It is further assumed, without loss of generality, that $\lim \sum_{t=1}^{N} x_{it}/N = 0$, $\lim \sum_{t=1}^{N} x_{it}^2/N = 1$ $(i=2,3)$. Furthermore, in order to approximate the missing values of x_{2t}, a linear regression of x_{2t} on x_{3t} is run with the N_c complete observations and the missing x_{2t}'s are then obtained as predicted values, given the values of the x_{3t}'s for the corresponding observations. Similarly, approximations of the missing x_{3t}'s are derived by running a linear regression of x_{3t} on x_{2t} using N_c complete observations.

For that special case, the asymptotic variance of our estimator of β_2 is(1) (provided $r^2 \neq 1$):

$$\tilde{V}(\hat{\beta}_2) = \sigma^2[1 - \bar{P}_3(1+\bar{P}_2)(1-r^2)]/[N_c(1-r^2)] \tag{4.2}$$

where $r = \sum_{t=1}^{N} x_{2t}x_{3t}/N$, $P_c = N_c/N$, $\bar{P}_i = 1 - P_i$ $(i=2,3)$, $P_i = N_i/N$ and N_i is the number of observations in which x_i is available.

If all incomplete observations are discarded, one can use the OLS estimator based on the complete observations. The asymptotic variance of this estimator is:

$$\tilde{V}(\beta_2^c) = \sigma^2/[N_c(1-r^2)] \tag{4.3}$$

It is readily seen that: $\tilde{V}(\hat{\beta}_2) \leqslant \tilde{V}(\beta_2^c)$ (2) .

Another alternative estimator is Glasser's (1964) estimator which is essentially obtained by replacing the required average cross-products of the form $\sum_{t=1}^{N} x_{jt}x_{it}/N$ by the average cross-products computed from the pairs of observable values, namely $\sum_{t \in S_c} x_{jt}x_{it}/N_c$. In the case under consideration, the asymptotic variance of Glasser's estimator for β_2 is:

$$\tilde{V}(\beta_2^g) = \sigma^2\{1/P_2 + r^2[1/P_3 - 2P_c/P_2P_3]\}/[N(1-r^2)^2] \tag{4.4}$$

The ratios of $\tilde{V}(\hat{\beta}_2)$ to $\tilde{V}(\beta_2^g)$ are shown in table 1 for different values of P_c, $\bar{P}_2$, $\bar{P}_3$ and r^2; $\tilde{V}(\hat{\beta}_2)$ is smaller than $\tilde{V}(\beta_2^g)$, except when r^2 is close to zero or when the proportion of complete observations is very small.

Another alternative estimator is the generalized least squares estimator derived by Dagenais (1973). It can be shown that for the case under study, the asymptotic variance of this latter estimator for β_2, is:

$$\tilde{V}(\beta_2^d) = (\sigma^2/N)[P_c + \bar{P}_2^* + \bar{P}_3^* r^2]/[(\bar{P}_c + \bar{P}_2^* r^2 + \bar{P}_3^*)(P_c + \bar{P}_2^* + \bar{P}_3^* r^2) - r^2(P_c + \bar{P}_2^* + \bar{P}_3^*)^2] \tag{4.5}$$

where $\bar{P}_2^* = \bar{P}_2/[1 + \beta_2^2(1-r^2)/\sigma^2]$ and $\bar{P}_3^* = \bar{P}_3/[1 + \beta_3^2(1-r^2)/\sigma^2]$.

For given values of P_c, $\bar{P}_2$, $\bar{P}_3$ and r^2 this expression attains its maximum value when $\beta_2^2 \to \infty$ and $\beta_3^2 \to \infty$. Then, $\tilde{V}(\beta_2^d) = \tilde{V}(\beta_2^c) \geqslant \tilde{V}(\hat{\beta}_2)$. This same expression attains its minimum value when $\beta_2 = \beta_3 = 0$. For this most favourable case, it can be proved that $\tilde{V}(\beta_2^d) \leqslant \tilde{V}(\hat{\beta}_2)$. In order to further illustrate the relationship between $\tilde{V}(\hat{\beta}_2)$ and $\tilde{V}(\beta_2^d)$, we may also examine the very special case where $\beta_2 = \beta$

It can be shown that, in this particular case, the relationship between $\tilde{V}(\hat{\beta}_2)$ and $\tilde{V}(\beta_2^d)$ depends, for given values of P_c, $\bar{P}_2$, $\bar{P}_3$ and r^2 on the value of the asymptotic multiple correlation coefficient (R^2) (3). Table 2 gives the critical values of R^2 for which $\tilde{V}(\hat{\beta}_2) = \tilde{V}(\beta_2^d)$; when R^2 is smaller than its corresponding critical value, we have $\tilde{V}(\hat{\beta}_2) > \tilde{V}(\beta_2^d)$; when R^2 is larger, then $\tilde{V}(\hat{\beta}_2) < \tilde{V}(\beta_2^d)$.

Table 1. Ratios of $\tilde{V}(\hat{\beta}_2)$ to $\tilde{V}(\beta_2^g)$

P_c	$\bar{P}_2$	$\bar{P}_3$	$r^2 =$ 0.	.2	.4	.6	.8	.99
1.0	0.0	0.0	1.00	1.00	1.00	1.00	1.00	1.00
0.9		0.1	1.00	.99	.97	.91	.75	.09
0.8		0.2	1.00	.99	.94	.84	.60	.05
0.6		0.4	1.00	.97	.88	.70	.42	.02
0.4		0.6	1.00	.95	.80	.58	.31	.02
0.2		0.8	1.00	.90	.71	.49	.25	.01
0.9	0.1	0.0	1.00	.98	.94	.87	.71	.09
0.8		0.1	1.00	.97	.92	.81	.58	.05
0.7		0.2	1.00	.97	.89	.75	.49	.03
0.5		0.4	1.01	.97	.85	.66	.38	.02
0.3		0.6	1.02	.99	.84	.61	.33	.02
0.1		0.8	1.08	1.25	1.06	.75	.39	.02
0.8	0.2	0.0	1.00	.95	.88	.77	.56	.05
0.7		0.1	1.01	.95	.87	.73	.48	.03
0.6		0.2	1.01	.96	.86	.69	.42	.03
0.4		0.4	1.04	.99	.85	.65	.36	.02
0.2		0.6	1.12	1.13	.97	.71	.38	.02
0.6	0.4	0.0	1.00	.91	.79	.63	.38	.02
0.5		0.1	1.03	.94	.80	.62	.36	.02
0.4		0.2	1.08	.98	.83	.63	.35	.02
0.2		0.4	1.32	1.24	1.05	.78	.42	.02
0.4	0.6	0.0	1.00	.87	.71	.53	.29	.02
0.3		0.1	1.12	.97	.79	.58	.31	.02
0.2		0.2	1.36	1.19	.97	.70	.37	.02
0.2	0.8	0.0	1.00	.83	.65	.45	.24	.01
0.1		0.1	1.64	1.37	1.07	.74	.39	.02

Table 2. Critical values of R^2 for which $\tilde{V}(\hat{\beta}_2) = \tilde{V}(\beta_2^d)$, when $\beta_2 = \beta_3$

P_c	$\bar{P}_2$	$\bar{P}_3$	$r^2 =$ 0.	.2	.4	.6	.8	.99
1.0	0.0	0.0	*	*	*	*	*	*
0.9		0.1	0.00	0.00	0.00	0.00	0.00	0.00
0.8		0.2	0.00	0.00	0.00	0.00	0.00	0.00
0.6		0.4	0.00	0.00	0.00	0.00	0.00	0.00
0.4		0.6	0.00	0.00	0.00	0.00	0.00	0.00
0.2		0.8	0.00	0.00	0.00	0.00	0.00	0.00
0.9	0.1	0.0	*	*	*	*	*	*
0.8		0.1	.02	.05	.08	.15	.30	.91
0.7		0.2	.03	.07	.13	.23	.43	.95
0.5		0.4	.04	.14	.27	.45	.69	.98
0.3		0.6	.06	.31	.53	.71	.87	.99
0.1		0.8	.15	.71	.86	.93	.97	1.00
0.8	0.2	0.0	*	*	*	*	*	*
0.7		0.1	.09	.16	.25	.37	.58	.97
0.6		0.2	.10	.21	.32	.48	.69	.98
0.4		0.4	.14	.34	.52	.69	.85	.99
0.2		0.6	.25	.60	.77	.88	.95	1.00
0.6	0.4	0.0	*	*	*	*	*	*
0.5		0.1	.31	.47	.59	.71	.85	.99
0.4		0.2	.36	.54	.67	.78	.89	.99
0.2		0.4	.53	.74	.84	.91	.96	1.00
0.4	0.6	0.0	*	*	*	*	*	*
0.3		0.1	.60	.74	.82	.88	.94	1.00
0.2		0.2	.69	.82	.88	.93	.97	1.00
0.2	0.8	0.0	*	*	*	*	*	*
0.1		0.1	.88	.93	.95	.97	.99	1.00

* $\tilde{V}(\hat{\beta}_2) = \tilde{V}(\beta_2^d)$ for all values of R^2.

5. MONTE CARLO STUDIES

Four sets of Monte Carlo experiments have been performed. The first three sets involve multiple regression models, while the fourth set involves three-stage least squares (3SLS) estimators of a two simultaneous-equations model.

5.1 The first set of experiments

In this first set of experiments, the regression models contained either three or five independent variables. Missing values affected only the independent variables, no more than one missing value was allowed per observation and the number of complete observations was always greater than the number of independent variables plus two.

Five estimators were compared, using the mean squared error (MSE) as the performance criterion. The five estimators are:

1) OLS applied to the subset of complete observations (OLSC);
2) the iterative generalized least squares estimator (IGLS) described in Dagenais (1973) and already mentioned in Section IV;
3) a single iterative version of IGLS (SIGLS);
4) the general econometric estimator for incomplete observations (GIO) described in this paper; in the specific case considered here, the GIO estimator corresponds to the OLS estimator applied to all observations, with the missing cross-products approximated as shown in equation (2.7);
5) a simplified version of GIO (SGIO) in which all terms involving cross-products of residuals, such as the three last terms on the RHS of (2.3) are ignored(4).

For each experiment, 1000 different random samples were drawn. Two hundred and sixteen different experiments were run corresponding to all possible combinations of the following situations, both for the three- and the five-variable case. The independent variables were alternatively considered as fixed or stochastic. Two sample sizes (N=20 and 40) were used, three different proportions of missing data (P_c=.35, .60 and .85), three different population coefficients of determination (R^2=.30, .60 and .90) and three different patterns of collinearity (pair-wise correlation coefficient among independent variables: r=.3, .5 and .8).

The values of the parameters used to generate the samples were:

	constant term	β_2	β_3	β_4	β_5	β_6
3 variables case	0.	-10.	1.	25.		
5 variables case	0.	-10.	1.	25.	14.	-18.2

The results were calculated under the assumption that it was not known a priori that the true constant terms were equal to zero.

The missing values are approximated in each case as predicted values based on auxiliary regressions using the subset of complete observations. In these auxiliary regressions, the dependent variable is the variable to be predicted and the explanatory variables are the other independent variables of the main regression equation.

As mentioned earlier, the independent variables were considered as fixed in a first group of experiments; then, the same experiments were repeated with stochastic independent variables. Even when the independent variables were considered as fixed, they were generated from a standardized joint normal distribution but in that case, the same set of values was retained for all samples within a given experiment. For the experiments where the x's were considered as stochastic, new sets of values were drawn for each sample.

The mean squared error (MSE) was used as a measure of performance. Since all results pertaining to each parameter and each experiment yielded virtually the same rankings for the five estimators studied, only very general average results are reported in figures I to XVI. For example, in figure I, the results correspond to the case of three fixed independent variables; MSE's are averaged over the three parameters, the three different proportions of complete observations, the three R^2 and the three patterns of multicollinearity. Distinct averages are given for the two different sizes.

In figure II, in turn, the results are averaged over the sample sizes but given separately for the different determination coefficients. To illustrate how more detailed results may compare to the average results of figures I to XVI, figure IVa gives the average MSE for the three parameters and the two sample sizes when K=3, R^2=.9 and r=.8, for different values of P_c.

As mentioned earlier, all results point consistently in the same direction[(5)]. It appears first that using appropriate methods to incorporate the incomplete observations is worthwhile. Also, as expected, the MSE are larger in the cases of stochastic x than in the case of fixed x.

FIXED X CASE (K=3)(6)

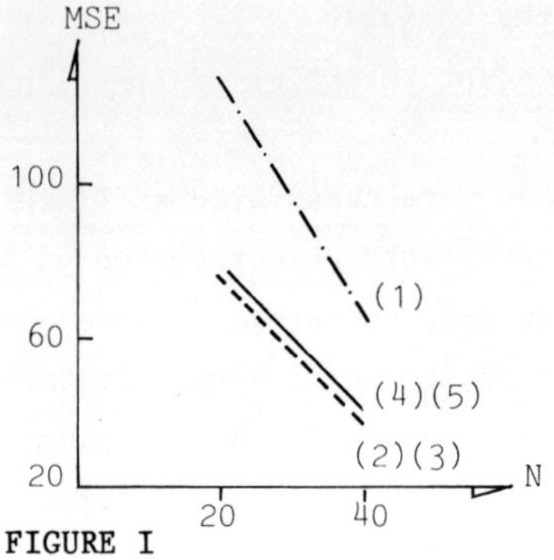

FIGURE I

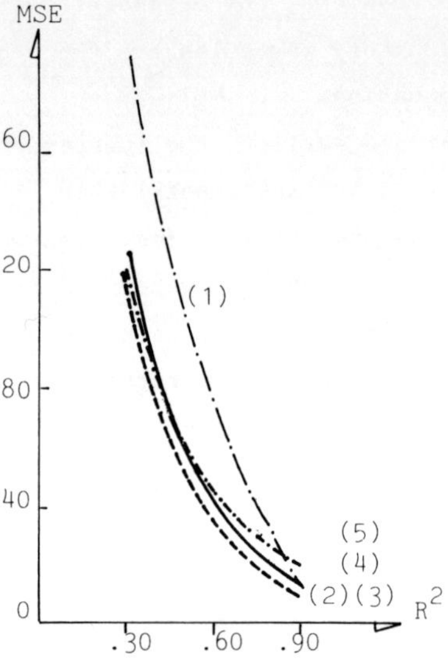

FIGURE II

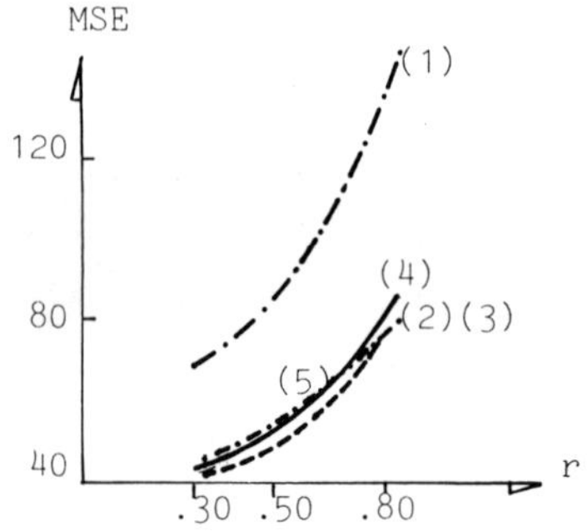

FIGURE III

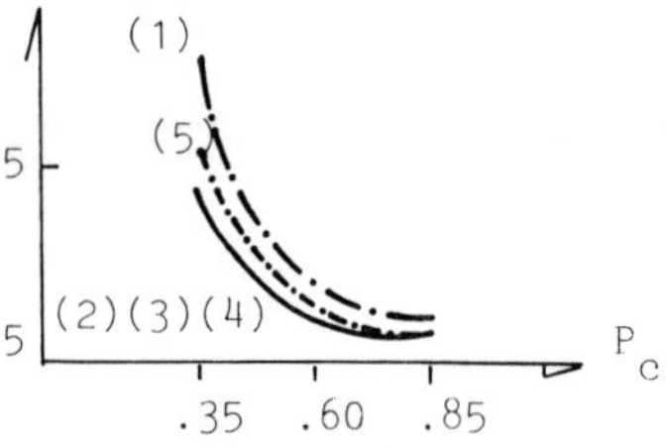

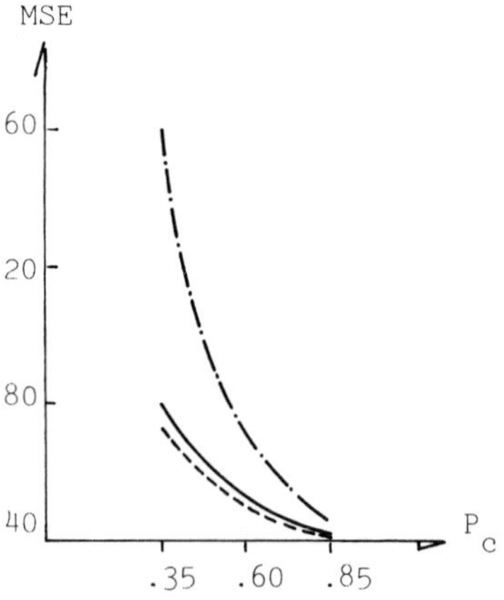

FIGURE IVA (R^2=.90, r=.80)

FIGURE IV

(1) OLSC: — . — , —
(2) IGLS: ---------
(3) SIGLS: ....
(4) GIO : ————————
(6) SGIO: -.-.-.-.-

STOCHASTIC X CASE (K=3)

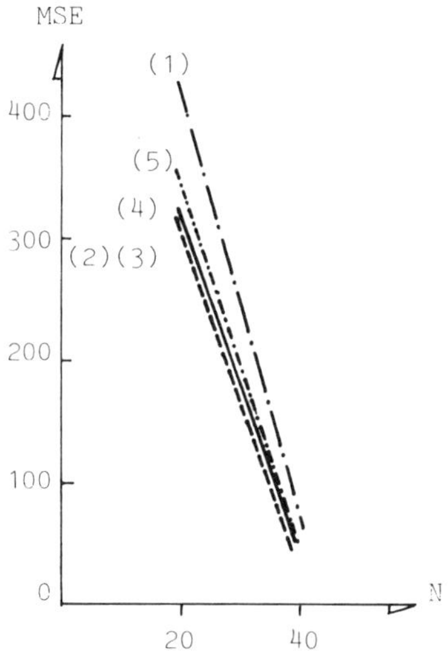

FIGURE V

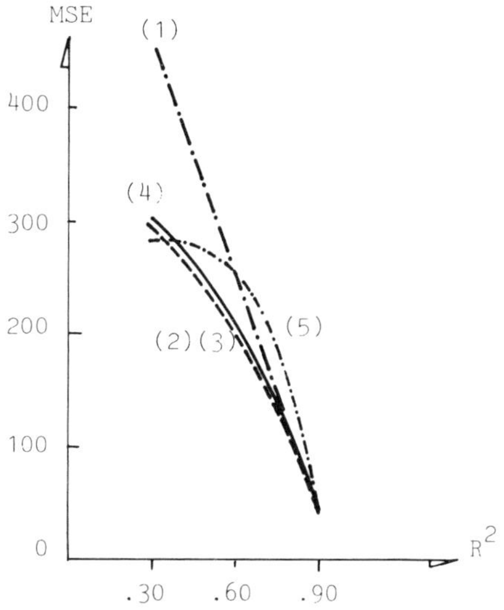

FIGURE VI

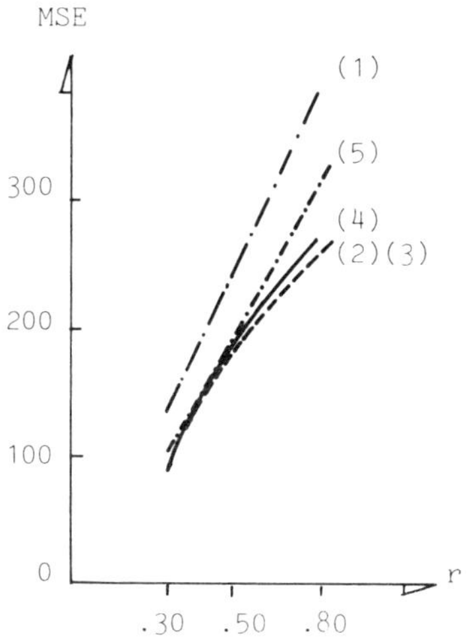

FIGURE VII

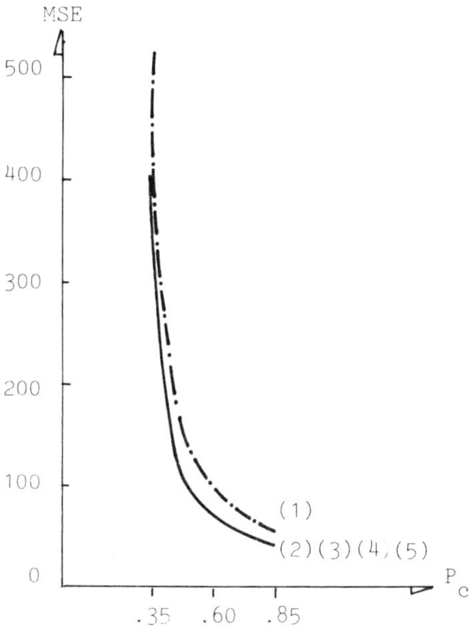

FIGURE VIII

FIXED X CASE (K=5)

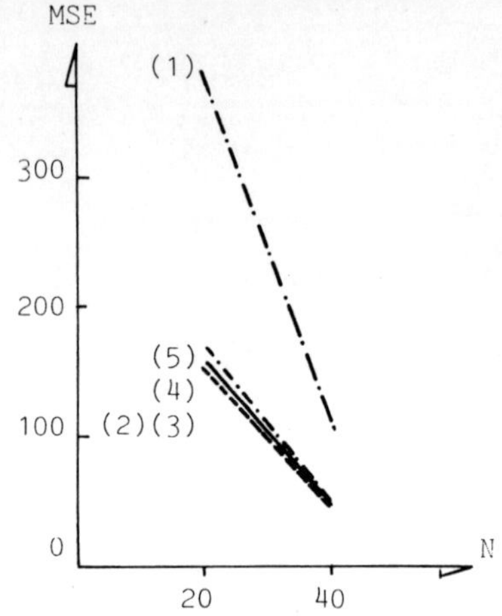

FIGURE IX

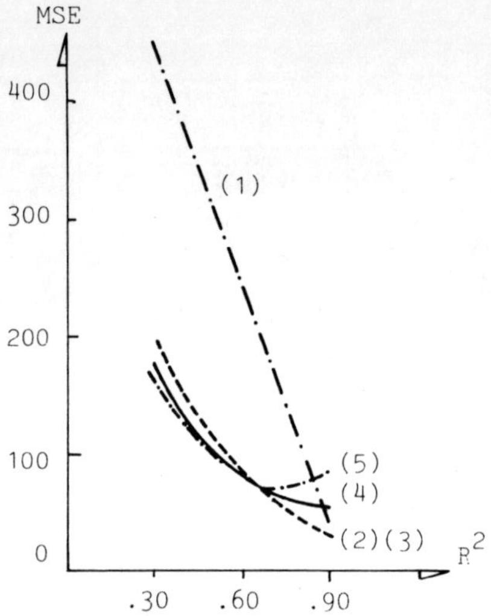

FIGURE X

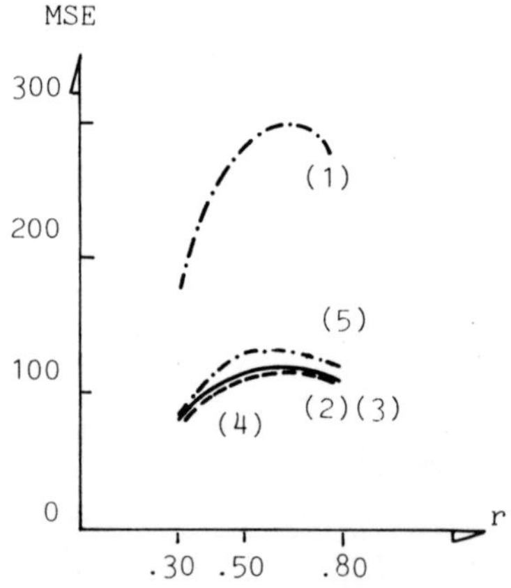

FIGURE XI

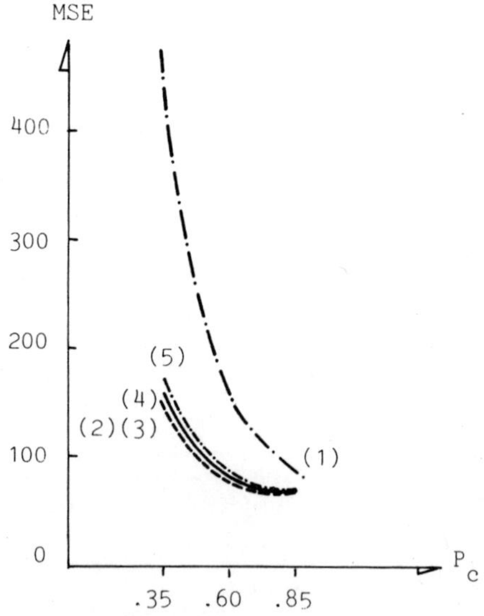

FIGURE XII

STOCHASTIC X CASE (K=5)

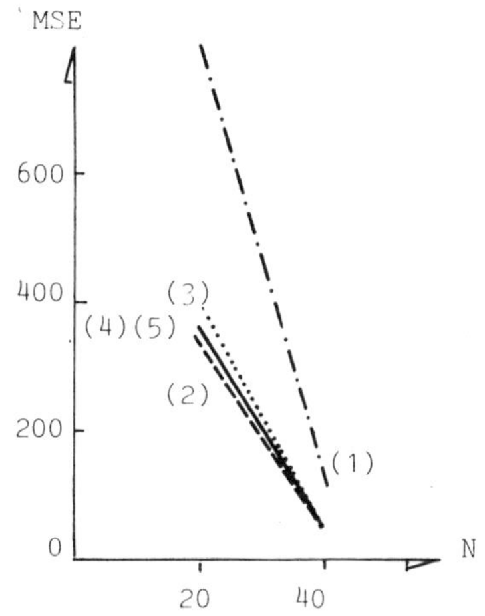

FIGURE XIII

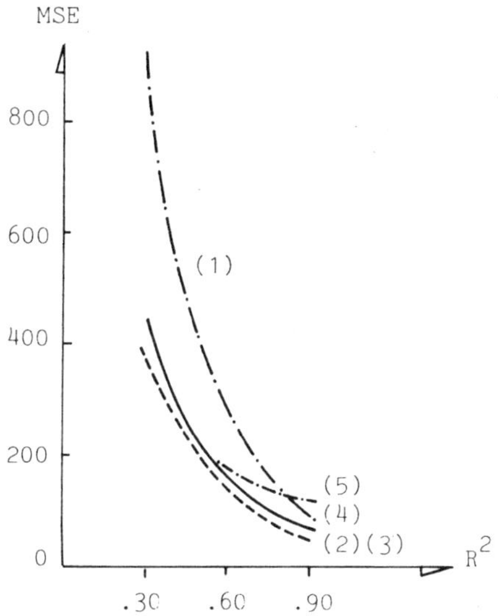

FIGURE XIV

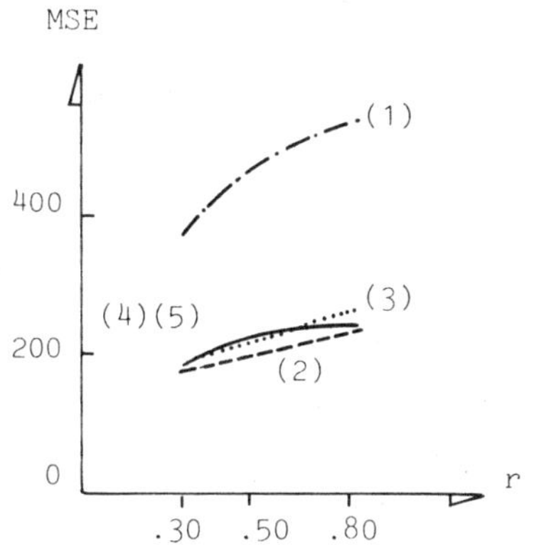

FIGURE XV

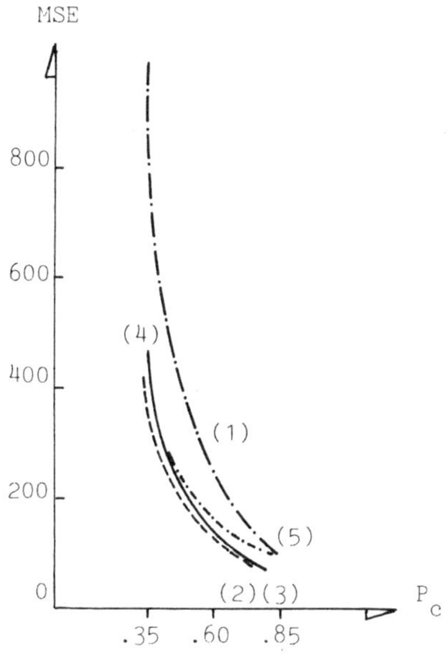

FIGURE XVI

The OLSC estimator yields markedly larger MSE than all other estimators considered. Therefore, as we already mentioned, it seems definitely useful[7] to use an estimator that takes account of the incomplete observations, even if the adopted approach consists simply in replacing the missing values by appropriate approximatons and applying OLS to the completed sample, as in the case of the SGIO estimator.

The MSE obtained with the four other estimators considered are so similar that any of these four incomplete observations (IO) estimators would be almost equally acceptable, in the particular type of situation examined in this first set of experiments. It must be pointed out, however, that in these experiments the auxiliary regressions used for all GIO estimators were purposely defined identically. Since the GIO estimator has the advantage of remaining consistent even if the dependent variable Y is included in the auxiliary regressions among the explanatory variables, while this is not the case for the other IO estimators examined here, a further comparison will be made below, in subsection 5.3, with the alternative GIO estimator obtained by including Y in the auxiliary regressions.

Figures I - XVI suggest that estimators that take account of the incomplete observations are particularly helpful when the sample size and the proportion of complete observations are fairly small. The effect of multicollinearity is not as clearcut; this is further discussed in subsection 5.2, below. Finally, the advantage of using these estimators seems to decrease as R^2 increases. Yet, figure IVa suggests that in small samples such as those considered in our experiments, when multicollinearity is high, a situation often encountered with economic times series, IO estimators are definitely superior to the OLSC estimator, even when R^2 is high; and, the superiority of IO estimators becomes more marked as the proportion of incomplete observations increases.

The results obtained in this first set of experiments suggest that IGLS performs systematically slightly better than GIO in small samples, for the type of situations considered here.

5.2 The second set of experiments

Among the factors affecting the MSE of the estimators studied in the first set of experiments are the precision of the approximations used for the missing data and also the collinearity among the independent variables. However, since in the previous experiments the missing data were approximated by auxiliary regressions on the other independent variables, the greater was the collinearity between the independent variables, the better were the approximations. Because of this interdependence between the collinearity of the independent variables and the quality of the approximations, it was not possible to evaluate the specific effects of these two factors. In a second set of experiments involving three fixed independent variables, the GIO estimators were computed with the missing data for each x approximated from extraneous proxy variables: the proxy variable for x_1 was z_1, that for x_2 is z_2, etc. ... Therefore, for a fixed pattern of collinearity between the x's, it is posssible to vary the quality of the approximations for the missing data by using z variables that are more or less correlated with the corresponding x variable.

Table 3 shows the sums of MSE for the three $\hat{\beta}$, averaged over different experiments. The results are broken down, in turn, according to the values of r, R^2, P_c and A where A corresponds to the square of the correlation coefficients between each x_i (i=1,2,3) and the corresponding z_i (i=1,2,3). The sample size used for these experiments was equal to 30. There, it is readily seen that MSE increases as r increases, as anticipated. Table 3 shows also the MSE of OLSC and the ratio of the MSE of OLSC over that of GIO. It is remarkable that there is considerable gain to be obtained from using incomplete observations methods even when the correlation between the missing variables and the proxies are relatively low. This finding supports Aigner's (1974) conclusions.

Table 3. Ratios of the MSE of OLSC estimators to the MSE of GIO estimators, for the second set of experiments

		MSE		MSE of OLSC / MSE of GIO
		GIO	OLSC	
r	.3	.17781	.75937	4.271
	.5	.29194	.68076	2.332
	.8	.93218	3.1261	3.354
A	.5	.55903	1.4533	2.600
	.7	.41756	1.4720	3.525
	.9	.42533	1.6409	3.858
R^2	.7	.74383	2.4621	3.310
	.9	.19079	.58207	3.051
P_c	10/30	.60454	2.9927	4.950
	18/30	.38120	.96892	2.542
	25/30	.41619	.60457	1.453

5.3 The third set of experiments

Since one of the advantages of GIO is that the dependent variable can be used as an additional proxy for any of the x without impairing the consistency of the estimator[8], the GIO estimators of the previous experiments were recomputed with the variable Y added to the proxy variables z_i (i=1,2,3) to approximate the missing data. Surprisingly, the introduction of Y among the proxy variables does not seem, in general, to improve matters, as can be verified from table 4. However, when A is low, the introductions of Y among the proxy variables does make a slight difference.

Table 4. Ratios of the MSE of GIO estimators to the MSE of the same estimators, with Y added to the proxy variables

		(1) GIO	(2) GIO with Y added to the proxy variables	(1) ÷ (2)
r	.3	.17064	.16935	1.0076
	.5	.29508	.29943	.9855
	.8	.96409	.98187	.9819
A	.5	.5027	.48546	1.0355
	.7	.47905	.49898	.9601
	.9	.44805	.46621	.9611
R^2	.7	.75175	.76119	.9876
	.9	.20145	.20591	.9783
P_c	10/30	.51276	.50805	1.0093
	18/30	.45790	.47499	.9640
	25/30	.45915	.46761	.9819

5.4 The fourth set of experiments

This set of Monte Carlo experiments used a model similar to Haavelmo's (1947) model which, after elimination of the identity, may be expressed as follows:

$$c_t = \alpha y_t + \beta + u_t \tag{5.4.1}$$

$$y_t = (1-\mu)(c_t+x_t) - \upsilon - w_t \tag{5.4.2}$$

where c_t = consumers' expenditures (endogenous),

y_t = disposable income (endogenous),

x_t = gross private capital formation plus government net deficit (exogenous).

All variables are expressed per capita in constant dollars. It was assumed that, just as for the actual data used be Haavelmo, the sample size contained 20 observations but that x_t was missing for the first 7 observations. An auxiliary regression relating x_t to the following three variables was also used (see Dagenais, 1976):

z_{1t} = total value of new private construction,

z_{2t} = expenditures by non-farm producers on main types of durable goods,

z_{2t} = federal government saving.

In order that the model be overidentified, the value of β was assumed to be known a priori. The three remaining parameters, namely α, μ and υ were estimated by the 3SLS method in three different ways:

a) the usual 3SLS method was first applied to all 20 observations, under the assumption that there was no missing data (3SLS-20);

b) then, assuming that x_t is missing in the first 7 observations, the same method was applied to the remaining 13 "complete" observations (3SLS-13);

c) the 3SLS - GIO estimator was finally computed, using both the 13 complete and the 7 incomplete observations.

Clearly, in actual situations the estimator defined in a) could not be used since it utilizes data which in practice would be unobservable.

One hundred random samples were drawn. The results are reported in table 5 below. These results confirm the usefulness of the GIO approach.

Table 5. Results of the fourth set of experiments

	mean estimator	mean squared error	bias	variance
parameter: α (true value set to .70494)				
3SLS-20	.70464	$.10554 \times 10^{-4}$	$-.29428 \times 10^{-3}$	$.10468 \times 10^{-4}$
3SLS-13	.70475	$.19280 \times 10^{-4}$	$-.18519 \times 10^{-3}$	$.19246 \times 10^{-4}$
3SLS-GIO	.70463	$.10570 \times 10^{-4}$	$-.30238 \times 10^{-3}$	$.10478 \times 10^{-4}$
parameter: μ (true value set to .20040)				
3SLS-20	.20343	$.10031 \times 10^{-2}$	$.30233 \times 10^{-2}$	$.99400 \times 10^{-3}$
3SLS-13	.20326	$.12058 \times 10^{-2}$	$.28532 \times 10^{-2}$	$.11976 \times 10^{-2}$
3SLS-GIO	.19640	$.10054 \times 10^{-2}$	$-.40037 \times 10^{-2}$	$.98940 \times 10^{-3}$
parameter: υ (true value set to -52.49)				
3SLS-20	-54.038	300.40	-1.5501	298.00
3SLS-13	-54.107	340.19	-1.6186	337.57
3SLS-GIO	-50.862	297.79	1.6258	295.15

6. THE COVARINCE MATRICES

The asymptotic covariance matrices of the parameter estimators obtained by the method suggested in this paper can be derived by straightforward procedures similar to those described in Theil (1971, pp. 497-99) for complete samples. The derivations may, however, become tedious and notationally complicated, when expressions are sought for fairly general cases. The asymptotic covariance matrix for the multiple regression model when missing data affect only the independent variables can be found in Dagenais and Dagenais (1979); the derivation is made under the assumption that the sample contains a subset of complete observations and that the missing values are approximated in the same manner as in the experiments reported in subsection 5.1.

The asymptotic covariance matrix of the 3SLS-GIO estimator is also given in Dagenais and Dagenais (1979) for the case where: 1) the missing values of both endogenous and exogenous variables, in any given observation, are approximated by linear combinations of the available exogenous variables in the same observation, and 2) the coefficients of the linear combinatons are computed from auxiliary regressions based on the subset of complete observations.

Monte Carlo experiments suggest, on the other hand, that for the multiple regression and the 3SLS-GIO estimators, the formulas given below yield very good approximations of the covariance matrices.

For the multiple regresssion case, $\tilde{V}(\hat{\underline{\beta}})$ may be approximated by(9):

$$\tilde{V}(\hat{\underline{\beta}}) \doteq \{ \sum_{t=1}^{N} [\hat{\underline{x}}_{it} \hat{\underline{x}}_{\ell t}]\}^{-1} \sum_{t \in S_c} (y_t - \sum_{k=1}^{K} \hat{\underline{\beta}}_k x_{kt})^2 / (N_c - K) \tag{6.1}$$

where $[\hat{\underline{x}}_{it} \hat{\underline{x}}_{\ell t}]$, $(i, \ell = 1, \ldots, K)$ is a (KxK) matrix for a given observation t; $\hat{\underline{\beta}}$ is the (Kx1) vector of GIO regression parameter estimators and the $\hat{\beta}_k$ are the parameter estimates obtained by applying OLS to the N_c complete observations.

For the 3SLS case, using a notation analogous to that found in Zellner and Theil (1962) and a similar set of basic assumptions, $\tilde{V}(\hat{\underline{\delta}})$ can be approximated by:

$$\tilde{V}(\hat{\underline{\delta}}) \doteq \frac{1}{N} \begin{bmatrix} s^{11} \widehat{\widehat{\frac{Z_1'X}{N}}} \left(\widehat{\frac{X'X}{N}}\right)^{-1} \widehat{\widehat{\frac{X'Z_1}{N}}} , \ldots\ldots, s^{1M} \widehat{\widehat{\frac{Z_1X}{N}}} \left(\widehat{\frac{X'X}{N}}\right) \widehat{\widehat{\frac{X'Z_M}{N}}} \\ \vdots \\ s^{M1} \widehat{\widehat{\frac{X_M'X}{N}}} \left(\widehat{\frac{X'X}{N}}\right)^{-1} \widehat{\widehat{\frac{X'Z_1}{N}}} , \ldots\ldots, s^{MM} \widehat{\widehat{\frac{Z_M'X}{N}}} \left(\widehat{\frac{X'X}{N}}\right) \widehat{\widehat{\frac{X'Z_M}{N}}} \end{bmatrix}^{-1} \tag{6.2}$$

where $\hat{\underline{\delta}}$ is the complete vector of GIO estimators of the unknown structural parameters, M is the number of stochastic equations, s^{ij} (i,j=1,...,M) designates the elements of the inverse S, S is the two-stage least-squares estimate of the residual errors covariance matrix derived from the subset of complete observations, Z_i (i=1,...,M) is the m atrix of endogenous and exogenous variables appearing on the RHS of the i-th equation, X is the matrix of exogenous variables, a single circumflex over the cross-product expressions indicates that these expressions are approximated by the method described in equation (2.7) and a double circumflex indicates that the cross-products are estimated by the first term only of the RHS of equation (2.7).

Experiments were made for the multiple regression and the 3SLS-GIO estimators described in subsections 5.1 and 5.4. In all cases, the MSE of the variance estimates of the GIO estimators(10) were markedly smaller than the MSE of the variance estimates of the corresponding estimators based only on the subsets of complete observations; they were almost as small as the MSE of the variance estimates of the corresponding estimators based on the total samples, before deleting the "missing" data.

Note that in the experiments with 3SLS estimators, the auxiliary regressions used to approximate the missing data contained extraneous independent variables not included in the structural model. Yet, the variance approximations still appeared to be quite satisfactory.

7. CONCLUSIONS

Given that the GIO estimator is very easy to generalize to a great number of estimation methods used in econometrics or in other applied fields of statistics and that it is quite robust with respect to the hypothesis underlying the statistical models as well as with respect to the nature of the auxiliary regressions used to approximate the missing values, this estimator should prove very useful in a great number of situations.

In many cases, simple approximate formulas can be found to evaluate the asymptotic covariance matrices of the estimators. Exact formulas can also be obtained for these matrices through lengthy but rather straightforward algebraic manipulations.

In his last book: De l'économie qualitative à l'économe quantitative, our lamented friend and colleague Luigi Solari (1977, p. 284) mentioned that it was "natural" to terminate his book by a chapter devoted to the estimation of economic models. The steps which lead from qualitative formalization to quantification must involve the statistical techniques of econometrics. In line with these considerations, we trust that the present paper may contribute to facilitate the passage from qualitative to quantitative economics, when there are missing data among the available observations.

Professor Solari also pointed out elsewhere (Solari, 1966, p.391) that econometrics calls for the combined use of theoretical reasoning and experimentation, in the broad sense of the word. Our approach, which is based on the intuitive conviction that incomplete observations ought to contain some useful information, relies on theoretical statistical considerations but uses also experimental results from Monte Carlo studies; it is therefore in close correspondance with Solari's conception of econometric research.

NOTES

(1) The procedure suggested in this paper may be seen as a generalization of an approach applied earlier under more restrictive assumptions to the multiple regression model by Lynch (1972) and previously, with some variants by Buck (1960) and Dagenais (1971).
Lynch (1972, p. 34, equation (4.6)) gives also the formula for $\tilde{V}(\hat{\beta}_2)$ but it differs from that shown in equation (4.2) above and appears to be erroneous. The difference between Lynch's formula for $\tilde{V}(\beta_2)$ and ours explains that his table showing the ratios of $\tilde{V}(\beta_2)$ to $V(\beta_2^g)$ does not agree with our table 1.

(2) This result becomes intuitively clear if one considers the more simple case where x_{3t} is available for all observations (i.e. $\overline{P}_3 = 0$) and only x_{2t} is missing for a subset of observations; it is then readily seen from equation (4.2) that $\tilde{V}(\beta_2 < \tilde{V}(\beta_2^c)$; it could also be shown that in this case
$\tilde{V}(\beta_3) < \tilde{V}(\beta_3^c)$. This agrees with the intuition that since, in this simple case, the incomlete observations bring in additional information on y and x_3 but none on x_2, these observations may contribute to improve our estimate of β_3 but do not improve our estimate of β_2.

(3) The asymptotic multiple correlation coefficient is defined here as follows: $R^2 = (\beta_2^2 + \beta_3^2 + 2r\beta_2\beta_3)/(\beta_2^2 + \beta_3^2 + 2r\beta_2\beta_3 + \sigma^2)$. .

(4) This estimator has been suggested by Pindyck and Rubinfeld (1976).

(5) The experiments concerning the case of five fixed independent variables with sample size equal to 20 and proportion of complete observations equal to .35 - i.e. with 7 complete observations - had to be run over a second time, because the first results were rather nonsensical. It was then realized that with 5 independent variables and a constant term and with only 7 complete observations, the first estimator considered for each parameter, namely the OLSC estimator, had a Student distribution with only one degree of freedom. This distribution is therefore a Cauchy distribution with infinite variance. Hence, it is not surprising that in such cases, the results might occasionally be erratic.
Excluding from our results all experiments containing 7 complete observations and 5 independent variables would not, however, have altered any of our conclusions on the relative performance of the different estimators.

(6) Note that only the points corresponding to those indicated on the abscissas have been computed. The lines joining these points are freehand approximations.

(7) This contradicts the assertion made be Langaskens (1975), page XIV.41; it agrees, on the contrary, with the conclusions suggested by Aigner (1974), McCallum (1972) and Wiskens (1972), in somewhat different contexts.

(8) As mentioned at the end of section 2, a sufficient condition for any GIO estimator to be consistent is that each relevant average cross-product involving missing data, be replaced by a consistent approximation. It is possible to show that even if the auxiliary regressions used for approximating the missing data yield inconsistent estimates of the theoretical

regression parameters, approximations used for the average cross-products (see equation (2.7)) will still be consistent, provided the data is missing at random. This point is proven in Dagenais and Dagenais (1979), Appendix, p. 34, note 1.

Our assertion that "the dependent variable can be used as an additional proxy for any x, without impairing the concistency of the estimator" is a direct consequence of the above consideration.

(9) This formula is clearly inspired from the classical covariance formula for OLS estimators of linear regression parameters with complete samples. Several variants of the above formula were tried out: this one gave the best results for the cases considered.

(10) Note that the computation of the MSE implies that the true value of the parameter is known. Here, the true value of the variance of each GIO estimator was assumed to be equal to that computed from repeated sampling, in the Monte Carlo experiments.

REFERENCES

(1) Aigner, D.J., MSE Dominance of Least Squares with Errors-of-Observations, Journal of Econometrics 2, 1974, pp. 365-72.

(2) Buck, S.F., A Method of Estimation of Missing Values in Multivariate Data Suitable for Use with an Electronic Computer, Journal of the Royal Statistical Society, Ser. B, 22, 1960, pp. 302-307.

(3) Dagenais, M.G., "Further Suggestions Concerning the Utilization of Incomplete Observations in Regression Analysis, Journal of the American Statistical Association, 66, March 1971, pp. 93-98.

(4) Dagenais, M.G., The Use of Incomplete Observations in Multiple Regression Analysis, A Generalized Least Squares Approach, Journal of Econometrics, 1, December 1973, pp. 317-28.

(5) Dagenais, M.G., Incomplete Observations and Simultaneous-Equations Models, Journal of Econometrics, 4, 1976, pp. 231-41.

(6) Dagenais, M.G. and Dagenais, D.L., A General Approach for Estimating Econometric Models with Incomplete Observations, Cahier 7902, Département de sciences économiques, Université de Montréal, 1979.

(7) Glasser, M., Linear Regression Analysis with Missing Observations Among the Independent Variables, Journal of the American Statistical Association, 59, September 1964, pp. 834-44.

(8) Haavelmo, T., Methods of Measuring the Marginal Propensity to Consume, Journal of the American Statistical Association, 42, 1947, pp.108-22.

(9) Langaskens, Y., Introduction à l'économétrie, Libraire Droz, Genève, 1975.

(10) Lynch, C.J., Computing Regression Coefficients, Utilizing Incomplete Observations, Ph.D. thesis presented at The American University, Washington, D.C., 1972.

(11) McCallum, B.T., Relative Asymptotic Bias From Errors of Omission and Measurement, Econometrica, 40, 1972, 757-58.

(12) Pindyck, R.S. and Rubinfeld, D., Econometric Models and Economic Forecasts, McGraw-Hill, Inc., New York, 1976.

(13) Rubin, D.B., Inference and Missing Data, Biometrika, 63, 1976, pp. 581-92.

(14) Solari, L., La simulation dans la prévision et la programmation en économétrie, Revue suisse d'économie politiques et de statistique, 102e année, fascicule 3/4, 1966, pp. 391-408.

(15) Solari, L., *De l'économie qualitative à l'économie quantitative*, Masson, Paris, 1977.
(16) Theil, Henri, *Principles of Econometrics*, John Wiley & Sons, Inc., New York, 1971.
(17) Wickens, M.R., A Note on the Use of Proxy Variables, *Econometrica*, 40, 1972, pp. 759-61.
(18) Wilks, S.S., *Mathematical Statistics*, John Wiley & Sons, Inc., New York, 1962.
(19) Zellner, A. and Theil, H., Three-stage Least Squares: Simultaneous Estimation of Simultaneous Equations, *Econometrica*, 30, 1962, pp. 54-78.

CHAPTER 6

DYNAMIC MISSPECIFICATION AND SERIAL CORRELATION

Pietro Balestra*, Universities of Geneva (Switzerland) and Dijon (France)

1. INTRODUCTION

In economic applications, the presence of autocorrelation in the residuals is often the result of a mis-specification of the underlying model(1). One important form of mis-specification occurs when the true model is dynamic and the investigator wrongly assumes that it is static. The estimated residuals from a regression equation are then likely to show some degree of autocorrelation. In such cases, the Durbin-Watson d statistic(2) gives ample warning that something is wrong. But, although the signal is right, the reason for it might not have anything to do with autocorrelation. It might simply mean that some dynamic effect has been neglected.

The trade-off between dynamic specification and stochastic structure of the residuals is a subtle one. In this paper we try to explore some aspects of this interrelationship. Our results indicate that on finding a d statistic significantly different from 2, the investigator had better look at the dynamic formulation of his problem rather than automatically reverting to a transformation of the Cochrane-Orcutt type. Actually, it might reasonably be argued that the d statistics can be used to arrive at a proper dynamic specification of the model.

We consider the following regression problem(3):

$$y_t = \beta_1 x_{1t} + \beta_2 x_{2t} + \dots + \beta_k x_{kt} + \alpha_1 y_{t-1} + \alpha_2 y_{t-2} + \dots + \alpha_s y_{t-s} + \varepsilon_t \tag{1.1}$$

where the x_{it} are k non-stochastic exogenous variables. Equation (1.1) is supposed to represent the true structure of the model. The β_i and α_i are unknown regression parameters to be estimated. There are s lagged endogenous variables and the α_i are such that the model is globally stable(4). The error terms are independent with zero mean and common variance σ^2 (The case of autocorrelated errors will be analyzed in section (4).

By dynamic mis-specification we mean that Model (1.1) is estimated only with h lags instead of s lags, $o \leq h \leq s$. When h is zero, the estimated model is purely static; when h is equal to s the dynamic specification is correct.

In section 2 we study a particular transformation of Model (1.1) which enables us to compute asymptotic properties in a relatively easy way. The effects of mis-specification on the estimated coefficients and on the Durbin-Watson d statistics are studied in section 3. As already noted, section 4 deals with the autocorrelated structure of the residuals. Some concluding remarks follow.

2. THE TRANSFORMED MODEL

In order to study the effects of mis-specification, we find it useful to transform Model (1.1) using a recursive formula.

Let us assume, for the sake of simplicity, that only a constant term appears in Model (1.1) in addition to the s lagged endogenous variables. It is the case in which k=1 and $x_{1t}=1$, all t. (The more general case will be discussed later). By recursion, we can express the model in the following way:

$$y_t = \beta_1(1+c_1+c_2+\ldots) + \varepsilon_t + c_1\varepsilon_{t-1} + c_2\varepsilon_{t-2} + \ldots \tag{2.1}$$

$$y_t = \beta_1 \sum_{i=o}^{\infty} c_i + \sum_{i=o}^{\infty} c_i\varepsilon_{t-i}, \quad c_o=1. \tag{2.2}$$

In this transformed model, the error terms μ_t:

$$\mu_t = \sum_{i=o}^{\infty} c_i\varepsilon_{t-i} \tag{2.3}$$

have the following properties:

$$E(\mu_t) = o \tag{2.4}$$

$$\left.\begin{aligned} E(\mu_t^2) &= \sigma^2 \sum_{i=o}^{\infty} c_i^2 \\ E(\mu_t \mu_{t-1}) &= \sigma^2 \sum_{i=o}^{\infty} c_i c_{i+1} \\ E(\mu_t \mu_{t-p}) &= \sigma^2 \sum_{i=o}^{\infty} c_i c_{i+p} \end{aligned}\right\} \tag{2.5}$$

The errors μ_t form a covariance-stationary stochastic process. (The process is also stationary in the mean). We will denote by r_p the following quantity:

$$r_p = \sum_{i=o}^{\infty} c_i c_{i+p} \tag{2.6}$$

The difficulty is that, except in the particular case of only one lag, the coefficients c_i (which depend on the α_j) are complicated expressions and therefore the quantities r_p are not easily computed. In what follows we give some easy computational formulae for the c_i and the r_p and subsequently study some properties of the variance-covariance matrix of the errors μ_t .

2.1 Computation of the coefficients c_i

Let us denote by $\underline{\alpha}$ the vector of coefficients of the lagged endogenous variables in Model (1.1) and by $\underline{\alpha}^{(m)}$ the vector of coefficients of the lagged endogenous variables after operating the m-th substitution. Clearly $\underline{\alpha}^{(o)} = \underline{\alpha}$, $\underline{\alpha}^{(1)}$ is the vector of coefficient upon substitution of y_{t-1} and so on.

The coefficient c_i is thus the leading coefficient of $\underline{\alpha}^{(i-1)}$ (remember that $c_o=1$; c_1 is thus equal to α_1). If we call $\underline{\ell}_j$ the j-the elementary vector of order s (a vector having 1 in position j and zero in all other positions), we may write

$$\underline{c}_i = \underline{\ell}_1' \, \underline{\alpha}^{(i-1)} , \quad i > o . \tag{2.7}$$

Now, it is easy to see that the vectors $\underline{\alpha}^{(m)}$ are given by the following recursive formulae:

$$\underline{\alpha}^{(o)} = \underline{\alpha}$$

$$\underline{\alpha}^{(1)} = H\underline{\alpha}^{(o)} + c_1\underline{\alpha}$$

$$\underline{\alpha}^{(2)} = H\underline{\alpha}^{(1)} + c_2\underline{\alpha}$$

$$\underline{\alpha}^{(m)} = H\underline{\alpha}^{(m-1)} + c_m\underline{\alpha}$$

where H is the following square matrix of order s:

$$H = \begin{bmatrix} 0 & I_{s-1} \\ 0 & 0 \end{bmatrix}$$

Note that:

$$H^s = 0$$

$$\underline{\ell}_i'H = \underline{\ell}_{i+1}' \qquad i = 1, \ldots, s-1$$

$$\underline{\ell}_s'H = 0$$

$$\underline{\ell}_1'H^m = \underline{\ell}_{m+1}' \qquad m = 1, \ldots, s-1$$

We are now in a position to express $\underline{\alpha}^{(m)}$ (by recursion) as:

$$\underline{\alpha}^{(m)} = H^m\underline{\alpha} + c_1H^{m-1}\underline{\alpha} + \ldots + c_{m-1}H\underline{\alpha} + c_m\underline{\alpha} \qquad m = 1, \ldots, s-1 \qquad (2.8a)$$

$$= c_{m-s+1}H^{s-1}\underline{\alpha} + \ldots + c_{m-1}H\underline{\alpha} + c_m\underline{\alpha} \qquad m \geqslant s \qquad (2.8b)$$

Upon taking the leading element in (2.8), using (2.7) and the fact that $\underline{\ell}_1'H^m = \underline{\ell}_{m+1}'$, we get:

$$c_{m+1} = \alpha_{m+1} + c_1\alpha_m + c_2\alpha_{m-1} + \ldots + c_{m-1}\alpha_2 + c_m\alpha_1 \quad m=1,\ldots,s-1 \qquad (2.9a)$$

$$= c_{m-s+1}\alpha_s + c_{m-s+2}\alpha_{s-1} + \ldots + c_{m-1}\alpha_2 + c_m\alpha_1 \qquad m \geqslant s \qquad (2.9b)$$

From (2.9) we can form the following system of s equations:

$$\begin{bmatrix} c_1 \\ c_2 \\ c_3 \\ \cdots \\ c_s \end{bmatrix} = \begin{bmatrix} 0 & 0 & \cdots & 0 & 0 \\ \alpha_1 & 0 & \cdots & 0 & 0 \\ \alpha_2 & \alpha_1 & \cdots & 0 & 0 \\ \cdots \\ \alpha_{s-1} & \alpha_{s-2} & \cdots & \alpha_1 & 0 \end{bmatrix} \begin{bmatrix} c_1 \\ c_2 \\ c_3 \\ \cdots \\ c_s \end{bmatrix} + \begin{bmatrix} \alpha_1 \\ \alpha_2 \\ \alpha_3 \\ \cdots \\ \alpha_s \end{bmatrix} \qquad (2.10)$$

which in matrix notation becomes:

$$\underline{c}^{(1)} = A\underline{c}^{(1)} + \underline{\alpha} \qquad (2.11)$$

where $\underline{c}^{(1)}$ is the vector of the coefficients c_i, $i=1, \ldots, s$, and A is the matrix shown in (2.10). The unique solution for $\underline{c}^{(1)}$ is given by

$$\underline{c}^{(1)} = (I-A)^{-1}\underline{\alpha} \; . \qquad (2.12)$$

For the next vector of s coefficients c_i, $i=s+1,\ldots,2s$, we get the expression:

$$\underline{c}^{(2)} = A\underline{c}^{(2)} + B\underline{c}^{(1)} \qquad (2.13)$$

where B is the following matrix

$$B = \begin{bmatrix} \alpha_s & \alpha_{s-1} & \alpha_{s-2} & \cdots & \alpha_1 \\ 0 & \alpha_s & \alpha_{s-1} & \cdots & \alpha_2 \\ \cdots \\ 0 & 0 & 0 & \cdots & \alpha_s \end{bmatrix}$$

The solution of equation (2.13) is

$$\underline{c}^{(2)} = (I-A)^{-1} B\underline{c}^{(1)} = (I-A)^{-1} B(I-A)^{-1}\underline{\alpha} \; . \qquad (2.14)$$

The same rule applies to higher order vectors, i.e.

$$\underline{c}^{(q)} = A\underline{c}^{(q)} + B\underline{c}^{(q-1)} \tag{2.15}$$

$$\underline{c}^{(q)} = \left[(I-A)^{-1}B\right]^{q-1} (I-A)^{-1}\underline{\alpha} \; . \tag{2.16}$$

Let us now sum all vectors $\underline{c}^{(q)}$ using (2.15) and initial condition (2.11):

$$\sum_{q=1}^{\infty} \underline{c}^{(q)} = (A+B) \sum_{q=1}^{\infty} \underline{c}^{(q)} + \underline{\alpha} \; .$$

The sum of all coefficients c_i for i=1,2,... is simply obtained by multiplying the expression above by the summation vector $\underline{\iota}$ (whose elements are equal to 1). We get[5]:

$$\underline{\iota}' \sum_{q=1}^{\infty} \underline{c}^{(q)} = \underline{\iota}'(A+B) \sum_{q=1}^{\infty} \underline{c}^{(q)} + \underline{\iota}'\alpha = \bar{\alpha}\underline{\iota}' \sum_{q=1}^{\infty} \underline{c}^{(q)} + \bar{\alpha}$$

where $\bar{\alpha} = \sum_{i=1}^{s} \alpha_i$. Hence we get: $\sum_{i=1}^{\infty} c_i = \frac{\bar{\alpha}}{1-\bar{\alpha}}$ and since $c_o=1$,

$$\sum_{i=o}^{\infty} c_i = \frac{1}{1-\bar{\alpha}} \; . \tag{2.17}$$

2.2 Computation of the quantities r_p

We are not interested in the coefficients c_i per se, but rather in their sum of squares and sum of cross products. These quantities can actually be computed without knowing explicitly the c_i.

Let us consider the system corresponding to (2.9) starting with $p = m+1 < s$. Noting that $c_o=1$, we may write:

$$\left.\begin{array}{l}
c_p \;\;\; = \alpha_1 c_{p-1} + \alpha_2 c_{p-2} + \ldots + \alpha_{p-1}c_1 + \alpha_p c_o \\
c_{p+1} = \alpha_1 c_p \;\;\; + \alpha_2 c_{p-1} + \ldots + \alpha_{p-1}c_2 + \alpha_p c_1 + \alpha_{p+1}c_o \\
\cdots\cdots\cdots\cdots\cdots\cdots\cdots\cdots\cdots\cdots \\
c_s \;\;\; = \alpha_1 c_{s-1} + \alpha_2 c_{s-2} + \ldots + \alpha_{p-1}c_{s-p+1} + \alpha_p c_{s-p} + \alpha_{p+1}c_{s-p-1} + \ldots + \alpha_s c_o
\end{array}\right\}$$

If we multiply through the first equation by c_o, the second one by c_1 and so on and if we sum by columns we obtain:

$$r_p = \alpha_1 r_{p-1} + \alpha_2 r_{p-2} + \dots + \alpha_{p-1} r_1 + \alpha_p r_o + \alpha_{p+1} r_1 + \dots + \alpha_s r_{s-p} . \qquad (2.18)$$

Letting p range from 1 to s-1 we get s-1 linear relationships involving the s quantities r_o to r_{s-1}. To complete the system, we start again from (2.9), square each coefficient and sum (by columns) to get:

$$r_o = r_o \sum_{i=1}^{s} \alpha_i^2 + r_1 . 2 \sum_{i=1}^{s-1} \alpha_i \alpha_{i+1} + r_2 . 2 \sum_{i=1}^{s-2} \alpha_i \alpha_{i+2} + \dots + r_{s-1} . 2\alpha_1 \alpha_s + 1. \qquad (2.19)$$

We now introduce the following notation. The symbol $\underline{r}_n^{(m)}$ is used to denote a column vector containing n quantities r_p in ascending order from r_m to r_{m+n-1}, i.e.

$$\underline{r}_n^{(m)} = [r_m r_{m+1} \dots r_{m+n-1}]' . \qquad (2.20)$$

The system of s equations given in (2.18) and (2.19) may now be expressed in the following way:

$$F\underline{r}_s^{(o)} = \underline{\ell}_1 \qquad (2.21)$$

where $\underline{\ell}_1$ is the first elementary vector and F is the matrix of coefficients obtained from (2.18) and (2.19). The matrix F may be formed in the following way:

$$F = I - A - G - D \qquad (2.22)$$

where I is the identity matrix of order s, A is the matrix defined in (2.10) and G and D are given by:

$$G = \begin{bmatrix} o & o & o & \cdots & o & o & o \\ o & \alpha_2 & \alpha_3 & & \alpha_{s-2} & \alpha_{s-1} & \alpha_s \\ o & \alpha_3 & \alpha_4 & & \alpha_{s-1} & \alpha_s & o \\ \cdots & & & & & & \\ o & \alpha_s & o & & o & o & o \end{bmatrix} \tag{2.23}$$

$$D = \begin{bmatrix} \sum_{i=1}^{s} \alpha_i^2 & 2\sum_{i=1}^{s-1} \alpha_i\alpha_{i+1} & 2\sum_{i=1}^{s-2} \alpha_i\alpha_{i+2} & \cdots & 2\alpha_1\alpha_s \\ o & o & o & \cdots & o \\ \cdots\cdot & & & & \\ o & o & o & \cdots & o \end{bmatrix} \tag{2.24}$$

Pre-multiplying (2.21) by F^{-1}, it is seen that the solution for $\underline{r}_s^{(o)}$ is simply the first column of F^{-1}. If we denote by F_{ij} the cofactor of the element in the (i,j) position of F, the solution for each individual r_p may be expressed as:

$$r_p = \frac{F_{1,p+1}}{|F|} \qquad p = o,1, \ldots, s-1. \tag{2.25}$$

The quantity $|F|$ need not be computed explicitly, since in most applications we are interested in ratios of these quantities. Furthermore, $|F|$ can be incorporated in σ^2 . For higher order p, which we rarely use, we propose the recursive formula:

$$r_p = \alpha_1 r_{p-1} + \alpha_2 r_{p-2} + \cdots + \alpha_s r_{p-s} \qquad p \geq s \tag{2.26}$$

It may help the reader at this point if we write down in full the matrix F for the case s=2 and s=3 and give the corresponding solutions.

Two lag case (s=2)

$$F = \begin{bmatrix} 1 & 0 \\ 0 & 1 \end{bmatrix} - \begin{bmatrix} 0 & 0 \\ \alpha_1 & 0 \end{bmatrix} - \begin{bmatrix} 0 & 0 \\ 0 & \alpha_2 \end{bmatrix} - \begin{bmatrix} \alpha_1^2 + \alpha_2^2 & 2\alpha_1\alpha_2 \\ 0 & 0 \end{bmatrix}$$

$$= \begin{bmatrix} 1 - \alpha_1^2 - \alpha_2^2 & - 2\alpha_1\alpha_2 \\ - \alpha_1 & 1 - \alpha_2 \end{bmatrix}$$

$$r_o = \frac{1-a_2}{|F|} \qquad r_1 = \frac{\alpha_1}{|F|} \qquad r_2 = \alpha_1 r_1 + \alpha_2 r_o = \frac{\alpha_1^2 - \alpha_2^2 + \alpha_2}{|F|}$$

Three lag case (s=3)

$$F = \begin{bmatrix} 1 & 0 & 0 \\ 0 & 1 & 0 \\ 0 & 0 & 1 \end{bmatrix} - \begin{bmatrix} 0 & 0 & 0 \\ \alpha_1 & 0 & 0 \\ \alpha_2 & \alpha_1 & 0 \end{bmatrix} - \begin{bmatrix} 0 & 0 & 0 \\ 0 & \alpha_2 & \alpha_3 \\ 0 & \alpha_3 & 0 \end{bmatrix} - \begin{bmatrix} \alpha_1^2+\alpha_2^2+\alpha_3^2 & 2\alpha_1\alpha_2+2\alpha_2\alpha_3 & 2\alpha_1\alpha_3 \\ 0 & 0 & 0 \\ 0 & 0 & 0 \end{bmatrix}$$

$$= \begin{bmatrix} 1-\alpha_1^2-\alpha_2^2-\alpha_3^2 & -2\alpha_1\alpha_2 - 2\alpha_2\alpha_3 & -2\alpha_1\alpha_3 \\ -\alpha_1 & 1-\alpha_2 & -\alpha_3 \\ -\alpha_2 & -\alpha_1-\alpha_3 & 1 \end{bmatrix}$$

$$r_o = \frac{1}{|F|} \begin{vmatrix} 1-\alpha_2 & -\alpha_3 \\ -\alpha_1-\alpha_3 & 1 \end{vmatrix} = \frac{1-\alpha_2 - \alpha_3(\alpha_1+\alpha_3)}{|F|}$$

$$r_1 = \frac{-1}{|F|} \begin{vmatrix} -\alpha_1 & -\alpha_3 \\ -\alpha_2 & 1 \end{vmatrix} = \frac{\alpha_1 + \alpha_2\alpha_3}{|F|}$$

$$r_2 = \frac{1}{|F|} \begin{vmatrix} -\alpha_1 & 1-\alpha_2 \\ -\alpha_2 & -\alpha_1-\alpha_3 \end{vmatrix} = \frac{\alpha_1(\alpha_1+\alpha_3) + \alpha_2(1-\alpha_2)}{|F|}$$

$$r_3 = \alpha_1 r_2 + \alpha_2 r_1 + \alpha_3 r_o = \frac{(\alpha_1^2-\alpha_3^2)(\alpha_1+\alpha_3) + (\alpha_2\alpha_1+\alpha_3)(1-\alpha_2) + \alpha_1\alpha_2 + \alpha_2\alpha_3^2}{|F|}$$

2.3 Properties of the variance-covariance matrix

Let $\underline{u}_k$ be the following vector of errors:

$$\underline{u}_k = [\mu_1 \quad \mu_2 \quad \dots \quad \mu_k]'$$

where the μ_t are as defined in (2.3). The variance-covariance matrix of this vector is given by

$$E(\underline{u}_k \underline{u}_k') = \sigma^2 \, \Omega_k = \sigma^2 \, [r_{|i-j|}] \qquad \begin{array}{l} i=1, \dots, k \\ j=1, \dots, k \end{array} \qquad (2.27)$$

when the r_p are obtained from (2.25) and (2.26). We want to study some properties of Ω_k which are useful in the sequel. Note that k can be any positive integer, while s, wherever used, will always stand for the number of lags in the true regression equation.

Property 1: $\Omega_k^{-1} \, \underline{r}_k^{(o)} = \underline{\ell}_1$ for any $k > o$.

This property can be established easily by noting that $\underline{r}_k^{(o)}$ is the first column of Ω_k.

Property 2: $\underline{\alpha}' \, \Omega_s = (\underline{r}_s^{(1)})'$.

First, let us note that the second equation in (2.21) states

$$-\alpha_1 r_o + (1-\alpha_2) r_1 - \alpha_3 r_2 - \dots - \alpha_s r_{s-1} = 0$$

which implies that $r_1 = \underline{\alpha}' \underline{r}_s^{(o)}$. Since $\underline{r}_s^{(o)}$ is the first column of Ω_s, the first element of Property 2 is proved.

Consider now the third equation in (2.21):

$$-\alpha_2 r_o - (\alpha_1 + \alpha_3) r_1 + (1-\alpha_4) r_2 - \alpha_5 r_3 - \dots - \alpha_s r_{s-1} = 0$$

which may be arranged as:

$$r_2 = \alpha_1 r_1 + \alpha_2 r_o + \alpha_3 r_1 + \alpha_4 r_2 + \dots + \alpha_s r_{s-1} \, .$$

On the right hand side of the above expression, the coefficients of the α_i are the elements of the second column of Ω_s. The argument may now be repeated for the other columns. To prove the last element of Property 2, we simply use (2.26) with p=s.

Property 3: $r_o - \underline{\alpha}' \underline{r}_s^{(1)} = 1$ or, equivalently:

$$r_o - \underline{\alpha}' \Omega_s \underline{\alpha} = 1 .$$

A simple way to prove this property is to expand the system (2.21) by adding one more equation corresponding to (2.26) for p=s. The new system is:

$$\begin{bmatrix} F & 0 \\ \underline{g}' & 1 \end{bmatrix} \begin{bmatrix} \underline{r}_s^{(o)} \\ r_s \end{bmatrix} = \begin{bmatrix} \underline{\ell}_1 \\ o \end{bmatrix}$$

where $\underline{g}' = [-\alpha_s, -\alpha_{s-1}, \ldots, -\alpha_1]$. A careful inspection of the new coeffi-ient matrix reveals that upon pre-multiplication by the row vector $[1, -\alpha_1, -\alpha_2, \ldots, -\alpha_s]$ it gives again the same vector (which therefore is a left hand eigenvector of that matrix). As a result, from the above expanded system we can get:

$$[1, -\alpha_1, -\alpha_2, \ldots, -\alpha_s] \begin{bmatrix} \underline{r}_s^{(o)} \\ r_s \end{bmatrix} = [1, -\alpha_1, -\alpha_2, \ldots, -\alpha_s] \begin{bmatrix} 1 \\ 0 \end{bmatrix}$$

i.e. $$[1, -\underline{\alpha}'] \begin{bmatrix} r_o \\ \underline{r}_s^{(1)} \end{bmatrix} = 1$$

from which Property 3 obtains immediately. The second line of Property 3 is obtained using Property 2.

For any $1 \leqslant k < s$ we may partition Ω_s in the following way:

$$\Omega_s = \begin{bmatrix} \Omega_k & \Omega_{k,\bar{k}} \\ \Omega_{\bar{k},k} & \Omega_{\bar{k}} \end{bmatrix}$$

where $\bar{k}$ is the complement of k in s ($\bar{k}$ = s-k). Using the inverse of a partitioned matrix, we get:

$$\Omega_s^{-1} = \begin{bmatrix} \Omega_k^{-1}(I+\Omega_{k,\bar{k}}\, T^{-1}\Omega_{\bar{k},k}\, \Omega_k^{-1}) & -\Omega_k^{-1}\, \Omega_{k,\bar{k}}\, T^{-1} \\ -T^{-1}\, \Omega_{\bar{k},k}\, \Omega_k^{-1} & T^{-1} \end{bmatrix}$$

where T is defined in the following way:

$$T = \Omega_{\bar{k}} - \Omega_{\bar{k},k}\, \Omega_k^{-1}\, \Omega_{k,\bar{k}}\ . \tag{2.28}$$

Let us now partition the vector $\underline{\alpha}$ in the same way, i.e.

$$\underline{\alpha}' = [\underline{\alpha}_k' \quad \underline{\alpha}_{\bar{k}}']\ . \tag{2.29}$$

From Property 2, using partitoned matrices, we obtain

$$\Omega_s^{-1} \begin{bmatrix} \underline{r}_k^{(1)} \\ \underline{r}_{\bar{k}}^{(k)} \end{bmatrix} = \begin{bmatrix} \underline{\alpha}_k \\ \underline{\alpha}_{\bar{k}} \end{bmatrix}$$

from which we derive:

$$\left.\begin{aligned} \underline{\alpha}_{\bar{k}} &= -T^{-1}\, \Omega_{\bar{k},k}\, \Omega_k^{-1}\, \underline{r}_k^{(1)} + T^{-1}\, \underline{r}_{\bar{k}}^{(1)} \\ \underline{\alpha}_k &= \Omega_k^{-1}\, \underline{r}_k^{(1)} - \Omega_k^{-1}\, \Omega_{k,\bar{k}}\, \underline{\alpha}_{\bar{k}}^{d} \end{aligned}\right\} \tag{2.30}$$

If we compute the quadratic form $(\underline{r}_s^{(1)})'\, \Omega_s^{-1}\, \underline{r}_s^{(1)}$ directly and use (2.30) we find:

$$(\underline{r}_s^{(1)})'\, \Omega_s^{-1}\, (\underline{r}_s^{(1)}) = (\underline{r}_k^{(1)})'\, \Omega_k^{-1}\, \underline{r}_k^{(1)} + \underline{\alpha}_{\bar{k}}'\, T^{-1}\, \underline{\alpha}_{\bar{k}}\ .$$

From Property 2, however, this quadratic form is equal to $\underline{\alpha}'\underline{r}_s^{(1)}$ which, using Property 3, is equal to $r_o - 1$. We therefore proved the following:

<u>Property 4</u>: $\qquad r_o - (\underline{r}_k^{(1)})'\, \Omega_k^{-1}\, \underline{r}_k^{(1)} = 1 + \underline{\alpha}_{\bar{k}}'\, T^{-1}\, \underline{\alpha}_{\bar{k}}$

Let us now consider a vector $\underline{u}_{k,-1}$ of lagged errors:

$$\underline{u}_{k,-1} = [\mu_o \; \mu_1 \; \cdots \; \mu_{k-1}]'$$

Let us denote by $\Omega_{k,-1}$ the following covariance matrix:

$$\Omega_{k,-1} = E(\underline{u}_k \underline{u}'_{k,-1}) = \begin{bmatrix} r_1 & r_o & r_1 & \cdots & r_{k-2} \\ r_2 & r_1 & r_o & & r_{k-3} \\ & \cdots & & & \\ r_{k-1} & r_{k-2} & r_{k-3} & & r_o \\ r_k & r_{k-1} & r_{k-2} & & r_1 \end{bmatrix} \tag{2.31}$$

In the above matrix, the first column is $\underline{r}_k^{(1)}$ and the following columns are the first k-1 columns of Ω_k. Therefore:

$$\Omega_k^{-1} \Omega_{k,-1} = \left[\Omega_k^{-1} \underline{r}_k^{(1)}, \underline{\ell}_1, \underline{\ell}_2, \ldots, \underline{\ell}_{k-1}\right]$$

If we now pre-multiply by $(\underline{r}_k^{(1)})'$, we get

$$(\underline{r}_k^{(1)})' \Omega_k^{-1} \Omega_{k,-1} = [(r_k^{(1)})' \Omega_k^{-1} r_k^{(1)}, r_1, r_2, \ldots, r_{k-1}]$$

$$= (\underline{r}_k^{(o)})' + [(\underline{r}_k^{(1)})' \Omega_k^{-1} \underline{r}_k^{(1)} - r_o, o, o, \ldots, o]$$

Hence, the following property is established:

<u>Property 5</u>: $$(\underline{r}_k^{(1)})' \Omega_k^{-1} \Omega_{k,-1} = (\underline{r}_k^{(o)})' + \{(\underline{r}_k^{(1)})' \Omega_k^{-1} \underline{r}_k^{(1)} - r_o\} \underline{\ell}_1'$$

Consider now the orthogonal and symmetric matrix Q derived from the unit matrix by interchanging the first and last column, the second and second last column, and so on. The matrix Q has unit elements on the non principal diagonal. Clearly, from the definition of the matrix Ω_k we have:

$$Q\Omega_k Q = \Omega_k \quad \text{and} \quad Q\Omega_k^{-1} Q = \Omega_k^{-1} . \tag{2.32}$$

Let us define the column vector $\tilde{\underline{r}}_k^{(1)}$ which is obtained from $\underline{r}_k^{(1)}$ by inverting the order of its elements, i.e.

$$\underline{\tilde{r}}_k^{(1)} = Q\underline{r}_k^{(1)} \; . \tag{2.33}$$

Calling $\underline{\iota}$ the summation vector of order k, the following property holds.

Property 6: $$\underline{\iota}'\Omega_k^{-1}\,\underline{r}_k^{(1)} = \underline{\iota}'\Omega_k^{-1}\,\underline{\tilde{r}}_k^{(1)}$$

The proof is immediate, using (2.32) and the fact that $\underline{\iota}'Q = \underline{\iota}'$. Indeed, we get:

$$\underline{\iota}'\Omega_k^{-1}\,\underline{r}_k^{(1)} = \underline{\iota}'Q\Omega_k^{-1}\,Q\underline{r}_k^{(1)} = \underline{\iota}'\Omega_k^{-1}\,\underline{\tilde{r}}_k^{(1)} \; .$$

Specific analytical results will be derived in the sequel for the case in which k=s-1. Hence consider the following partitioning of the relationship $\underline{r}_s^{(1)} = \Omega_s\underline{\alpha}$:

$$\begin{bmatrix} r_o & (\underline{r}_k^{(1)})' \\ \underline{r}_k^{(1)} & \Omega_k \end{bmatrix} \begin{bmatrix} \underline{\alpha}_1 \\ \underline{\alpha}_{\bar{1}} \end{bmatrix} = \begin{bmatrix} r_1 \\ \underline{r}_k^{(2)} \end{bmatrix} \qquad k = s-1 \tag{2.34}$$

from which one obtains:

$$\left.\begin{aligned} r_o\alpha_1 + (\underline{r}_k^{(1)})'\underline{\alpha}_{\bar{1}} &= r_1 \\ \alpha_1\,\underline{r}_k^{(1)} + \Omega_k\,\underline{\alpha}_{\bar{1}} &= \underline{r}_k^{(2)} \end{aligned}\right\} \tag{2.35}$$

Pre-multiplying through the second expression above by $(\underline{r}_k^{(1)})'\Omega_k^{-1}$ and using the first expression, one gets:

Property 7: $$r_1 - (\underline{r}_k^{(1)})'\Omega_k^{-1}\underline{r}_k^{(2)} = \alpha_1 r_o - \alpha_1(\underline{r}_k^{(1)})'\Omega_k^{-1}\underline{r}_k^{(1)} \; , \quad k = s-1.$$

3. THE EFFECTS OF MISSPECIFICATION

The ordinary least squares estimation of Model (1.1), when the model is correctly specified and under the hypothesis of homoscedasticity and independence of the errors, produces consistent estimators of all regression coefficients including those of the lagged endogenous variables. Furthermore, the least squares estimator of the error variance is consistent and the probability limit of the Durbin-Watson d statistics is equal to 2.

On the other hand, when the model is incorrectly specified, inconsistent results obtain and the probability limit of d is no longer equal to 2. Armed with the results of the preceding section we are in a position to study analytically the effects of such inconsistencies. We will do this first for the case of no exogenous variables (except for the constant term) and subsequently for the general case. When exogenous variables are present in the regression model, the results will depend not only on the stochastic properties of the model but also on the limits of cross-product matrices of these exogenous variables. In order to study how these limits affect the analytical results, a Monte Carlo experiment is provided.

3.1 The case of no exogenous variables

We assume that the true model is

$$y_t = \beta_1 + \sum_{i=1}^{s} \alpha_i y_{t-i} + \varepsilon_t \tag{3.1}$$

with homoscedastic and independent errors.

To illustrate in a very simple way the effects of dynamic mis-specification, let us suppose that we estimate the purely static counterpart of model (3.1), i.e. we neglect all lagged endogenous variables. Given a sample size n, the least-sqaures estimates are:

$$\hat{\beta}_1 = \frac{1}{n} \Sigma y_t = \bar{y}$$

$$\hat{\sigma}^2 = \frac{1}{n-1} \Sigma (y_t - \bar{y})^2$$

$$d = 2(1 - \hat{\rho})$$

$$\hat{\rho} = \frac{\Sigma (y_t - \bar{y})(y_{t-1} - \bar{y}_{-1})}{\Sigma (y_t - \bar{y})^2}$$

Using expression (2.2) and the properties of the transformed errors μ_t, the probability limits of the above expressions are immediately derived. These are:

$$\text{plim}\ \hat{\beta}_1 = \frac{\beta_1}{1-\bar{\alpha}} \qquad\qquad (\bar{\alpha} = \sum_{i=1}^{s} \alpha_i)$$

$$\text{plim}\ \hat{\sigma}^2 = \sigma^2 r_o$$

$$\text{plim}\ \hat{\rho} = \frac{r_1}{r_o}$$

$$\text{plim}\ d = 2(1 - \frac{r_1}{r_o})$$

As expected, inconsistent estimates of β_1 and σ^2 are obtained. Typically, the asymptotic bias of $\hat{\beta}_1$ is positive ($\bar{\alpha} < 1$). The variance is overestimated, since from Property 3 we can infer that $r_o > 1$ (since the quadratic form $\underline{\alpha}'\ \Omega_s\ \underline{\alpha}$ is positive definite). More importantly, though, the Durbin-Watson d statistics will always show some degree of autocorrelation. It is interesting to compute explicitly the probability limit of the estimated first order autocorrelation coefficient, $\hat{\rho}$ for some typical models. These computations are shown in Table 1.

Table 1. Probability limit of first order autocorrelation coefficient (Estimation of static model/No exogenous variables)

Number of lagged endogenous variables in true model	plim $\hat{\rho}$
s = 1	$\frac{r_1}{r_o} = \alpha_1$
s = 2	$\frac{r_1}{r_o} = \frac{\alpha_1}{1-\alpha_2}$
s = 3	$\frac{r_1}{r_o} = \frac{\alpha_1 + \alpha_2\alpha_3}{1-\alpha_2-\alpha_3(\alpha_1+\alpha_3)}$

Looking at Table 1, the trade-off between dynamic mis-specification and autocorrelation in the residuals is most effectively illustrated in the case of just one lagged endogenous variable. If we omit the lagged variable, the plim of the estimated autocorrelation coefficient is just equal to the coefficient of the omitted variable. The higher the value of α_1, the closer to zero the value of d.

We now turn to the more general case in which only a certain number of lagged endogenous variables are omitted. The true model is assumed to be:

$$y_t = \beta_1 + \alpha_1 y_{t-1} + \dots + \alpha_h y_{t-h} + \alpha_{h+1} y_{t-h-1} + \dots + \alpha_s y_{t-s} + \varepsilon_t \qquad (3.2)$$

and estimation is performed only on the basis of the first h lagged endogenous variables. The most obvious reason for this sort of mis-specification is the lack of knowledge of the true model. Other reasons may be the limited number of observations or the high degree of collinearity in the sample.

Given a sample size n, we write the true model as

$$\underline{y} = \underline{\iota}\beta_1 + Y_h \underline{\alpha}_h + Y_{\bar{h}} \underline{\alpha}_{\bar{h}} + \underline{\varepsilon} \qquad (3.3)$$

where $\underline{y}$ is the vector of observations on y_t, $\underline{\iota}$ is the summation vector, Y_h is the matrix of observations of the first h lagged endogenous variables, $Y_{\bar{h}}$ is the matrix of observations on the following s-h lagged endogenous variables, $\underline{\varepsilon}$ is the vector of errors and $\underline{\alpha}_h$ and $\underline{\alpha}_{\bar{h}}$ are the vectors of parameters associated with Y_h and $Y_{\bar{h}}$.

Taking only h lags into account, the least-squares estimator of $\underline{\alpha}_h$ is:

$$\hat{\underline{\alpha}}_h = (\tilde{Y}_h'\tilde{Y}_h)^{-1}\tilde{Y}_h'\tilde{\underline{y}} \qquad (3.4)$$

where "~" over a matrix or a vector indicates that the variables are expressed as deviations from their respective means.

Referring to (2.2) we see that $\tilde{y}_t = \mu_t - \bar{\mu}$. Therefore the probability limit of $\hat{\underline{\alpha}}_h$ is easily established:

$$\text{plim}\ \hat{\underline{\alpha}}_h = \text{plim}\ (\tfrac{1}{n}\tilde{Y}_h'\tilde{Y}_h)^{-1}\ \tfrac{1}{n}\tilde{Y}_h'\tilde{\underline{y}} = \Omega_h^{-1}\underline{r}_h^{(1)} = \underline{\alpha}_h + \Omega_h^{-1}\Omega_{h,\bar{h}}\underline{\alpha}_{\bar{h}}\ . \qquad (3.5)$$

The estimator is inconsistent. Its asymptotic bias is equal to $\Omega_h^{-1}\Omega_{h,\bar{h}}\ \underline{\alpha}_{\bar{h}}$. To get this bias we used (2.30). For future reference, we give the probability limit of the estimated coefficient of the first lagged variable, i.e. $\hat{\alpha}_1$:

$$\text{plim}\ \hat{\alpha}_1 = \underline{\ell}_1'\ \Omega_h^{-1}\ \underline{r}_h^{(1)} \qquad (3.6)$$

where $\underline{\ell}_1$ is the first elementary vector of order h. Using least-squares, the estimated variance is given by:

$$\hat{\sigma}^2 = \frac{1}{n-h-1} \underline{\tilde{y}}' \left[I - \tilde{Y}_h(\tilde{Y}_h'\tilde{Y}_h)^{-1} \tilde{Y}_h'\right] \underline{\tilde{y}} \tag{3.7}$$

and its probability limit is:

$$\text{plim } \hat{\sigma}^2 = \sigma^2 \left[r_o - (\underline{r}_h^{(1)})' \Omega_h^{-1} \underline{r}_h^{(1)}\right] = \sigma^2 [1 + \underline{\alpha}_{\bar{h}} T^{-1} \underline{\alpha}_{\bar{h}}] \quad , \tag{3.8}$$

using Property 4. This estimator is also inconsistent and its asymptotic bias is positive, given the fact that T is a positive definite matrix.

We are chiefly interested in the effect of the dynamic mis-specification on the autocorrelation structure of the estimated residuals. To this end we compute the Durbin-Watson d statistics and its probability limit. (Of course we could also compute d statistics of higher order than one). The Durbin-Watson d statistic is defined as follows:

$$d = \frac{\underline{\hat{\varepsilon}}' D \underline{\hat{\varepsilon}}}{\underline{\hat{\varepsilon}}' \underline{\hat{\varepsilon}}} \tag{3.9}$$

where $\hat{\varepsilon} = \left[I - \tilde{Y}_h(\tilde{Y}_h' \tilde{Y}_h)^{-1} \tilde{Y}_h'\right] \underline{\tilde{y}}$ is the vector of least-squares residuals and D is the matrix:

$$D = \begin{bmatrix} 1 & -1 & 0 & 0 & 0 \\ -1 & 2 & -1 & 0 & 0 \\ 0 & -1 & 2 & 0 & 0 \\ 0 & \cdots\ 0 & 0 & 2 & -1 \\ 0 & 0 & 0 & -1 & 1 \end{bmatrix} \tag{3.10}$$

Dividing by n the numerator and the denominator of (3.9), we see that the probability limit of the denominator is simply equal to the expression in (3.8). As for the numerator, we write down the full expression:

$$\hat{\underline{f}}' D \hat{\underline{\varepsilon}} = \tilde{\underline{y}}' D\tilde{\underline{y}} - 2\tilde{\underline{y}}'\tilde{Y}_h(\tilde{Y}_h'\tilde{Y}_h)^{-1}\tilde{Y}_h' D\tilde{\underline{y}} + \tilde{\underline{y}}'\tilde{Y}_h(\tilde{Y}_h'\tilde{Y}_h)^{-1}\tilde{Y}_h' D\tilde{Y}_h(\tilde{Y}_h'\tilde{Y}_h)^{-1}\tilde{Y}_h'\tilde{\underline{y}}$$

$$\simeq 2\,\tilde{\underline{y}}'\tilde{\underline{y}} - \tilde{\underline{y}}'\tilde{\underline{y}}_{-1} - \tilde{\underline{y}}'\tilde{\underline{y}}_{+1} - 4\tilde{\underline{y}}'\tilde{Y}_h(\tilde{Y}_h'\tilde{Y}_h)^{-1}\tilde{Y}_h'\tilde{\underline{y}} + 2\tilde{\underline{y}}'\tilde{Y}_h(\tilde{Y}_h'\tilde{Y}_h)^{-1}\tilde{Y}_h'\tilde{\underline{y}}_{-1}$$

$$+ 2\tilde{\underline{y}}'\tilde{Y}_h(\tilde{Y}_h'\tilde{Y}_h)^{-1}\tilde{Y}_h'\tilde{\underline{y}} + 2\tilde{\underline{y}}'\tilde{Y}_h(\tilde{Y}_h'\tilde{Y}_h)^{-1}\tilde{Y}_h'\tilde{\underline{y}}$$

$$- \tilde{\underline{y}}'\tilde{Y}_h(\tilde{Y}_h'\tilde{Y}_h)^{-1}\tilde{Y}_h'\tilde{Y}_{h,-1}(\tilde{Y}_h'\tilde{Y}_h)^{-1}Y_h\tilde{\underline{y}} - \tilde{\underline{y}}'\tilde{Y}_h(\tilde{Y}_h'\tilde{Y}_h)^{-1}\tilde{Y}_h'\tilde{Y}_{h,+1}(\tilde{Y}_h'\tilde{Y}_h)^{-1}\tilde{Y}_h'\tilde{\underline{y}} \,.$$

Dividing by n and taking the limit we get:

$$\text{plim}\,\frac{1}{n}\,\hat{\underline{\varepsilon}}' D\,\hat{\underline{\varepsilon}} = 2r_o - 2r_1 - 4(\underline{r}_h^{(1)})'\Omega_h^{-1}\underline{r}_h^{(1)} + 2(\underline{r}_h^{(1)})'\Omega_h^{-1}\underline{r}_h^{(o)}$$

$$+ 2(\underline{r}_h^{(1)})'\Omega_h^{-1}\underline{r}_h^{(2)} + 2(\underline{r}_h^{(1)})'\Omega_h^{-1}\underline{r}_h^{(1)}$$

$$- (\underline{r}_h^{(1)})'\Omega_h^{-1}\Omega_{h,-1}\Omega_h^{-1}\underline{r}_h^{(1)} - (\underline{r}_h^{(1)})'\Omega_h^{-1}\Omega_{h,+1}\Omega_h^{-1}\underline{r}_h^{(1)} \,.$$

Using Property 5 on the last two terms (noting that they are equal since one is the transpose of the other), we can simplify them as follows:

$$(\underline{r}_h^{(1)})'\Omega_h^{-1}\Omega_{h,-1}\Omega_h^{-1}\underline{r}_h^{(1)} = \underline{\ell}_1'\underline{r}_h^{(1)} + [(\underline{r}_h^{(1)})'\Omega_h^{-1}\underline{r}_h^{(1)} - \underline{r}_o]\underline{\ell}_1'\Omega_h^{-1}\underline{r}_h^{(1)}$$

where we used the fact that $(\underline{r}_h^{(o)})'\Omega_h^{-1} = \underline{\ell}_1'$. Now noting that $\underline{\ell}_1'\underline{r}_h^{(1)} = r_1$ and also that $(\underline{r}_h^{(1)})'\Omega_h^{-1}\underline{r}_h^{(o)} = r_1$, we get:

$$\text{plim}\,\frac{1}{n}\,\hat{\underline{\varepsilon}}' D\,\hat{\underline{\varepsilon}} = 2r_o - 2r_1 - 2(\underline{r}_h^{(1)})'\Omega_h^{-1}\underline{r}_h^{(1)} + 2(\underline{r}_h^{(1)})'\Omega_h^{-1}\underline{r}_h^{(2)}$$

$$+ 2[r_o - (\underline{r}_h^{(1)})'\Omega_h^{-1}\underline{r}_h^{(1)}]\underline{\ell}_1'\Omega_h^{-1}\underline{r}_h^{(1)} \,. \tag{3.11}$$

Collecting the results, we are in a position to state:

$$\text{plim } d = 2(1 - \text{plim } \hat{\rho}) \tag{3.12}$$

$$\text{plim } \hat{\rho} = \frac{r_1 - (\underline{r}_h^{(1)})' \Omega_h^{-1} \underline{r}_h^{(2)}}{r_o - (\underline{r}_h^{(1)})' \Omega_h^{-1} \underline{r}_h^{(1)}} - \ell_1' \Omega_h^{-1} \underline{r}_h^{(1)} \ . \tag{3.13}$$

Note that in the above expression for plim $\hat{\rho}$ the second term on the right hand side is equal to plim $\hat{\alpha}_1$, see (3.6).

Formula (3.13) gives us a good indication of how the dynamic mis-specification is reflected in the autocorrelation structure of the least-squares residuals. Obviously, if h=0 we are back to the pure static case and

$$\text{plim } \hat{\rho} = \frac{r_1}{r_o} \qquad h = 0 < s. \tag{3.14}$$

If h=1, the formula simplifies to

$$\text{plim } \hat{\rho} = r_1 \frac{r_o - r_2}{r_o^2 - r_1^2} - \frac{r_1}{r_o} \qquad h = 1 < s. \tag{3.15}$$

At the other extreme, if h=s, the model is correctly specified and

$$\text{plim } \hat{\rho} = 0 \qquad h = s \ . \tag{3.16}$$

An interesting case arises when h = s-1, not only because the result becomes extremely simple but also because it will shed some light on the problem of autocorrelated errors in the true model (see section 4).

From Property 7 we see that the numerator of the first term in (3.13) is α_1 times the denominator. We therefore can state that:

$$\text{plim } \hat{\rho} = \alpha_1 - \text{plim } \hat{\alpha}_1 \qquad h = s-1 \tag{3.17}$$

or equivalently that

$$\text{plim } (\hat{\rho} + \hat{\alpha}_1) = \alpha_1 \qquad h = s-1 \tag{3.18}$$

The asymptotic limit of the first order autocorrelation coefficient of the least-squares residuals is thus equal to the negative of the asymptotic bias of the estimator of α_1 . This result does not depend on the number of lags in the true model, as long as only the last lag is omitted in the process of estimating the model.

The case h = s-1 has another important feature. In many economic applications we are interested in the overall (or long term) dynamic effect which is a function of $\bar{\alpha} = \Sigma\alpha_i$. From (3.5), for the case h = s-1, we obtain

$$\Omega_h^{-1}\underline{r}_h^{(1)} = \underline{\alpha}_h + \Omega_h^{-1}\underline{\tilde{r}}_h^{(1)}\underline{\alpha}_s \qquad (3.19)$$

where $\underline{\tilde{r}}_h^{(1)}$ is equal to $\underline{r}_h^{(1)}$ with the elements in inverse order, i.e. $\tilde{r}^{(1)} = Q\underline{r}_h^{(1)}$ (see (2.33) for the definition of the orthogonal matrix Q). Now, using Property 6 and solving, we get

$$\underline{\iota}'\Omega_h^{-1}\underline{r}_h^{(1)} = \frac{1}{1-\alpha_s}\underline{\iota}'\underline{\alpha}_h \qquad h = s-1 \qquad (3.20)$$

where $\underline{\iota}$ is the summation vector. This leads us to the following result

$$\text{plim } \underline{\iota}'\hat{\underline{\alpha}}_h = \frac{1}{1-\alpha_s}\iota'\underline{\alpha}_h = \frac{\bar{\alpha}-\alpha_s}{1-\alpha_s} = \bar{\alpha} - \alpha_s\frac{1-\bar{\alpha}}{1-\alpha_s} \,. \qquad (3.21)$$

Hence, if we use $\underline{\iota}'\hat{\underline{\alpha}}_h$ to estimate $\bar{\alpha}$ the asymptotic bias is equal to $-\alpha_s\frac{1-\bar{\alpha}}{1-\alpha_s}$. If α_s is positive and small relative to $\bar{\alpha}$, the bias is less than α_s.

To illustrate some of the preceding results, we give in the accompanying table (Table 2) the exact probability limits of the estimated regression coefficients and of the first order autocorrelation coefficient for dynamic models of up to three lags.

Table 2. Effects of dynamic mis-specification

Number of lags in true model	number of lags in estimated equation	plim $\hat{\alpha}_1$	plim $\hat{\alpha}_2$	plim $\sum_{i=1}^{h} \hat{\alpha}_i$	plim $\hat{\rho}$
s = 1	h = 0	/	/	/	α_1
s = 2	h = 0	/	/	/	$\frac{\alpha_1}{1-\alpha_2}$
s = 2	h = 0	$\frac{\alpha_1}{1-\alpha_2}$	/	$\frac{\alpha_1}{1-\alpha_2}$	$-\frac{\alpha_1\alpha_2}{1-\alpha_2}$
s = 3	h = 0	/	/	/	$\frac{\alpha_1+\alpha_2\alpha_3}{1-\alpha_2-\alpha_3(\alpha_1+\alpha_3)}$
s = 3	h = 1	$\frac{\alpha_1+\alpha_2\alpha_3}{1-\alpha_2-\alpha_3(\alpha_1+\alpha_3)}$	/	$\frac{\alpha_1+\alpha_2\alpha_3}{1-\alpha_2-\alpha_3(\alpha_1+\alpha_3)}$	$\frac{(\alpha_1+\alpha_2\alpha_3)(-\alpha_2-\alpha_1\alpha_3)}{(1-\alpha_3^2)(1-\alpha_2-\alpha_3\alpha_1-\alpha_3^2)}$
s = 3	h = 2	$\frac{\alpha_1+\alpha_2\alpha_3}{1-\alpha_3^2}$	$\frac{\alpha_2+\alpha_1\alpha_3}{1-\alpha_3^2}$	$\frac{\alpha_1+\alpha_2}{1-\alpha_3}$	$-\frac{\alpha_3(\alpha_2+\alpha_1\alpha_3)}{1-\alpha_3^2}$

3.2 The dynamic model with exogenous variables

We now consider the general dynamic model:

$$y_t = X_t\underline{\beta} + Y_t\underline{\alpha} + \underline{\varepsilon}_t \tag{3.22}$$

where X_t is the k-row-vector of purely exogenous variables and Y_t is the s-row vector of lagged endogenous variables. As before, the error terms are assumed to be homoscedastic and independent.

Given a sample size n, we write the model in the following matrix form:

$$\underline{y} = X\underline{\beta} + Y\underline{\alpha} + \underline{\varepsilon} \ . \tag{3.23}$$

Conceptually, using a recursive formula, we can express the true model as:

$$y_t = \tilde{X}_t\underline{\beta} + \mu_t \tag{3.24}$$

where $\tilde{X}_t = \sum_{i=o}^{\infty} c_i X_{t-i}$ and the μ_t are as defined in (2.3). The matrix counterpart of (3.24) will be denoted by:

$$\underline{y} = \tilde{X}\underline{\beta} + \underline{\mu} \ . \tag{3.25}$$

Let us assume that we neglect all lagged endogenous variables and we estimate the purely static version of the model. We now study the effect of this type of dynamic mis-specification.

The least-squares estimator of $\underline{\beta}$, i.e. $\hat{\underline{\beta}} = (X'X)^{-1}X'\underline{y}$ is clearly inconsistent. Its asymptotic bias is equal to plim $\frac{1}{n}(X'X)^{-1}X'Y\underline{\alpha}$. More relevant to our discussion is the autocorrelation structure of the least-squares residuals. We therefore compute the Durbin-Watson d statistics and its probability limit.

The denominator of d is given by:

$$\begin{aligned} \underline{y}'M_x\underline{y} &= (\underline{\mu}' + \underline{\beta}'\tilde{X}')M_x(\underline{\mu} + \tilde{X}\underline{\beta}) \\ &= \underline{\mu}'M_x\underline{\mu} + 2\underline{\beta}'\tilde{X}'M_x\underline{\mu} + \underline{\beta}'\tilde{X}'M_x\tilde{X}\underline{\beta} \end{aligned} \tag{3.26}$$

where $M_x = I - X(X'X)^{-1}X'$. Upon division by n and taking the limit, one obtains:

$$\text{plim}\ \frac{1}{n}\ \underline{y}'M_x\underline{y} = \sigma^2 r_o + \underline{\beta}'W_o\underline{\beta} \tag{3.27}$$

where $$W_o = \text{plim}\ \frac{1}{n}\ \tilde{X}'M_x\tilde{X}\ . \tag{3.28}$$

The numerator is given by:

$$\begin{aligned}\underline{y}'M_xDM_x\underline{y} &= (\underline{\mu}' + \underline{\beta}'\tilde{X}')M_xDM_x(\underline{\mu} + X\underline{\beta}) \\ &= \underline{\mu}'M_xDM_x\underline{\mu} + 2\beta'\tilde{X}'M_xDM_x\underline{\mu} + \underline{\beta}'\tilde{X}'M_xDM_x\tilde{X}\underline{\beta}\end{aligned} \tag{3.29}$$

Taking the limit, we find:

$$\text{plim}\ \frac{1}{n}\ \underline{y}'M_xDM_x\underline{y} = 2\sigma^2(r_o - r_1) + 2\underline{\beta}'(W_o - W_1)\underline{\beta} \tag{3.30}$$

where $$2(W_o - W_1) = \text{plim}\ \frac{1}{n}\ \tilde{X}'M_xDM_x\tilde{X}\ . \tag{3.31}$$

Collecting the results, we finally get:

$$\text{plim}\ d = 2(1 - \text{plim}\ \hat{\rho}) \tag{3.32}$$

$$\text{plim}\ \hat{\rho} = \frac{r_1\sigma^2 + \underline{\beta}'W_1\underline{\beta}}{r_o\sigma^2 + \underline{\beta}'W_o\underline{\beta}} \tag{3.33}$$

A more interesting interpretation of the above formula can be given. Notice that r_1/r_o is the probability limit of the autocorrelation coefficient of the model with <u>only</u> lagged endogenous variables. Call this limit

$$\text{plim}\ \hat{\rho}_y\ . \tag{3.34}$$

The quantity $\frac{\underline{\beta}'W_1\underline{\beta}}{\underline{\beta}'W_o\underline{\beta}}$ can be viewed as the autocorrelation coefficient of the vector $M_x\tilde{X}\underline{\beta}$ (in the limit); it thus represents some average autocorrelation coefficient of the data. Call it:

$$\text{plim}\ \hat{\rho}_x\ . \tag{3.35}$$

With this notation, formula (3.33) can be expressed as:

$$\text{plim } \hat{\rho} = \lambda \text{ plim } \hat{\rho}_y + (1-\lambda)\text{plim } \hat{\rho}_x \; . \tag{3.36}$$

The autocorrelation coefficient of the least-squares residuals is just a weighted average of the autocorrelation coefficient of the corresponding purely endogenous model and the (average) autocorrelation coefficient of the exogenous variables. The weight λ is determined by the proportion of the variance, i.e.:

$$\lambda = \frac{r_o \sigma^2}{r_o \sigma^2 + \underline{\beta}' W_o \underline{\beta}} \; . \tag{3.37}$$

When the dynamic mis-specification is severe, we expect plim $\hat{\rho}_y$ to be high (in absolute value). Then, for a moderate or low value of $\hat{\rho}_x$, the weighted average of the two is less than plim $\hat{\rho}_y$. It then follows that $\hat{\rho}_y$ overestimates plim $\hat{\rho}$. Or, to put it in a different way, plim $\hat{\rho}$ does not capture the full extent of the dynamic mis-specification.

When the model is estimated with h lagged endogenous variables, $h < s$, analytical results are harder to derive. We would expect, however, a result similar to (3.36) to hold. To check this proposition, we ran a Monte Carlo experiment using a model with one exogenous variable (taken as the series of U.S. GNP annual data) and a varying number of dynamic specification. The details of these experiments are shown in Table 3)[(6)].

Table 3. Monte Carlo experiments

True specification - parameter values				model estimated with one lag			model estimated with two lags			model estimated with three lags		
exogenous	lagged endogenous variables											
β	α_1	α_2	α_3	d*	d		d*	d		d*	d	
.666	.8	-.16		1.779	1.71 (.20)	1.75 (.35)	2	1.97 (.10)	1.98 (.22)	2	1.97 (.09)	2.03 (.22)
.296	1.2	-.36		1.365	1.35 (.22)	1.47 (.37)	2	1.98 (.12)	1.96 (.24)	2	1.97 (.07)	2.02 (.20)
.074	1.6	-.64		.751	.85 (.25)	1.18 (.39)	2	1.99 (.17)	1.97 (.29)	2	1.97 (.08)	2.03 (.20)
.399	1.2	-.48	.064	1.323	1.30 (.21)	1.40 (.35)	1.948	1.93 (.13)	1.97 (.26)	2	1.96 (.08)	2.02 (.21)
.118	1.8	-1.08	.216	.619	.68 (.18)	.89 (.32)	1.687	1.75 (.19)	1.89 (.29)	2	1.94 (.08)	2.01 (.21)
.015	2.4	-1.92	.512	.142	.22 (.10)	.56 (.30)	1.041	1.32 (.26)	1.70 (.40)	2	1.91 (.11)	2.00 (.22)

d* : Theoretical value of plim $2(1-\hat{\rho}_y)$, assuming no exogenous variable.

d : Average value of Durbin-Watson d statistics over 100 runs. Standard errors in parentheses. First number refers to samples of 50 observations; second number refers to sample of 20 observations.

The conclusions emerging from Table 3 can be summarised as follows:

1) Dynamic mis-specification is indeed reflected in the d statistics. Therefore, the d statistics may be an indicator of dynamic mis-specification rather than an indicator of serial correlation in the true residuals.
2) When dynamic mis-specification is severe, the presence of truly exogenous variables attenuates the degree by which the mis-specification is reflected in d. This is in agreement with the theoretical results shown in (3.36).
3) Most importantly, the Durbin-Watson d statistics may be used to achieve the proper dynamic specification. A simple rule would consist in adding additional lags until the d statistic approaches the value of 2.

4. AUTOCORRELATED ERRORS

In this section, we study a dynamic model in which the true errors are generated by a first order Markov process. For the sake of simplicity, we confine our analysis to the case in which only lagged endogenous variables appear in the regression equation (in addition to the constant term).

The model under consideration is:

$$y_t = \beta_1 + \sum_{i=1}^{s} \alpha_i y_{t-i} + \varepsilon_t \tag{4.1}$$

where $$\varepsilon_t = \rho\varepsilon_{t-1} + v_t \qquad \rho < 1 \tag{4.2}$$

the v_t being homescedastic and independent random variables (with variance equal to σ^2).

Using a Koyck transformation (with parameter ρ), we can express the true model as

$$y_t = \beta_1^* + \sum_{i=1}^{s^*} \alpha_i^* y_{t-i} + v_t \tag{4.3}$$

where

$$\left.\begin{aligned} \beta_1^* &= (1-\rho)\beta_1 \\ \alpha_1^* &= \alpha_1 + \rho \\ \alpha_i^* &= \alpha_i - \rho\alpha_{i-1} \qquad i = 2, \ldots, s^*-1 \\ \alpha_s^* &= -\rho\alpha_s \\ s^* &= s + 1 \end{aligned}\right\} \tag{4.4}$$

Model (4.3) is formally equivalent to Model (3.1) and hence the results obtained in section 3.1 immediately apply. Obviously, if one is interested in the α_i and ρ, equation (4.3) is of no help, since in that equation the parameters α_i and ρ are not identifiable. However, equation (4.3) can be used to study the relationship between the model's dynamics and the autocorrelated structure of the residuals.

To begin with, let us analyze the case in which the purely static counterpart of equation (4.1) is estimated. Referring to the previous results, see section 3.1, and noting that

$$\bar{\alpha}^* = \sum_{i=1}^{s^*} \alpha_i^* = (1-\rho)\bar{\alpha} + \rho \tag{4.5}$$

we obtain:

$$\operatorname{plim} \hat{\beta}_1 = \frac{\beta_1}{1-\bar{\alpha}^*} = \frac{\beta_1}{(1-\rho)\bar{\alpha} + \rho}$$

$$\operatorname{plim} \hat{\sigma}^2 = \sigma^2 r_o^*$$

$$\operatorname{plim} \hat{\rho} = r_1^*/r_o^*$$

$$\operatorname{plim} d = 2(1 - r_1^*/r_o^*)$$

where r_i^* are the parameters related to the true model (4.3).

Note that when s=1, estimating the static model has the same consequences as when the true model (4.3), which has two lagged endogenous variables, is estimated without lags. In this case, the exact value of plim $\hat{\rho}$ is:

$$\operatorname{plim} \hat{\rho} = \frac{\alpha_1^*}{1-\alpha_2^*} = \frac{\alpha_1+\rho}{1+\alpha_1\rho} . \tag{4.6}$$

It can be seen from the above expression that the roles of α_1 and ρ are symmetric. A zero limit can result either from independent errors (ρ=o) and no lagged effect (α_1=o) or when the coefficient of the lagged endogenous variable offsets the serial coefficient of the errors ($\alpha_1=-\rho$). There is really no way to separate the two effects.

For the case s=2, plim $\hat{\rho}$ is also easily computed:

$$\operatorname{plim} \hat{\rho} = \frac{\alpha_1 + \rho - \alpha_2\rho(\alpha_2-\rho\alpha_1)}{1 - \alpha_2 + \rho\alpha_1 + \rho\alpha_2(\alpha_1+\rho-\rho\alpha_2)} . \tag{4.7}$$

An interesting question is to ask what is the effect of estimating equation (4.1) assuming, wrongly, that errors are independent. This mis-specification has the same effect as omitting one lag (the last one) from the true model (4.3). Hence, we can state the following general result.

When model (4.1) is estimated by ordinary least-squares, no matter what the number s of lags is, it is always true that

$$\operatorname{plim} \hat{\rho} = \rho + \alpha_1 - \operatorname{plim} \hat{\alpha}_1 \tag{4.8}$$

or, equivalently,

$$\operatorname{plim} (\hat{\rho}+\hat{\alpha}_1) = \alpha_1 + \rho . \tag{4.9}$$

Special situations other than the ones discussed above can be analyzed by reference to the results of section 3.

5. CONCLUDING REMARKS

In empirical research, the presence of autocorrelation in the residuals is often a serious problem. To the investigator confronted with this problem, different estimating techniques are available. However, in many cases autocorrelation is not a phenomenon per se, but rather the result of some form of mis-specification. In such a situation, nothing is gained in terms of understanding the reality under investigation by simply applying a technique designed to eliminate the effect of autocorrelation.

In this paper we have shown that dynamic mis-specification is an important source of apparent autocorrelation in the residuals. Asymptotic values of the first order autocorrelation coefficient have been computed for a variety of relevant forms of dynamic mis-specification. These results suggest that the familiar d statistics may have a more fundamental role to play than that of detecting autocorrelation. It may actually be used as a signal to arrive at a more dynamic formulation of the model.

NOTES

* This paper was prepared, in part, while the author was visiting professor at Northwestern University.

(1) This point has been made by many authors. Z. Griliches (1961), for instance, states that "... as long as we have serial correlation in the disturbances there is still something systematic in the world which our model has not incorporated." See also D. Cochrane and G.H. Orcutt (1949) and J. Johnston (1972). The effects of mis-specification on serial correlation has been examined in a recent article by M. Chaudhuri (1977), following Theil's approach of specification analysis (1957).

(2) J. Durbin and G.S. Watson (1950).

(3) This is the model analyzed by Durbin; see Durbin (1970).

(4) The roots of the characteristic equation must lie inside the unit circle. In particular we shall assume that the sum of α_i is less than unity.

(5) Note that each column (and each row) of the matrix A + B is some permutation of the vector $\underline{\alpha}$ .sHence the sum of elements of each column (and each row) is equal to $\bar{\alpha} = \sum_{i=1} \alpha_i$.

(6) The data for the experiment is contained in C.A. Cadenas (1975); we thank the author for letting us use his runs to compute the statistics shown in Table 3.

REFERENCES

(1) Cadenas, C.A., Les modèles à retards échelonnés: Un experiment de Monte-Carlo sur le profil de Pascal, Fribourg, 1975.

(2) Chaudhuri, M., Autocorrelated Disturbances in the Light of Specification Analysis, Journal fo Econometrics, vol. 5, 1977, pp. 301-13.

(3) Cochrane, D. and Orcutt, G.H., Applications of Least Squares Regressions to Relationships Containing Autocorrelated Error Terms, Journal of the American Statistical Association, vol. 44, 1949, pp. 32-61.

(4) Durbin, J., Testing for Serial Correlation in Least Squares when Some of the Regressors are Lagged Dependent Variables, Econometrica, vol. 38, 1970, pp. 410-21.

(5) Durbin, J. and Watson, G.S., Testing for Serial Correlation in Least Squares Regression, Biometrika, vol. 37, 1950, pp. 409-28.

(6) Griliches, Z., A Note on Serial Correlation Bias in Estimates of Distributed Lags, Econometrica, vol. 29, 1961, pp. 63-73.

(7) Johnston, J., Econometric Models, McGraw Hill, New York, 1972.

(8) Theil, H., Specification Errors and Estimation of Economic Relations, Review of the International Statistical Institute, vol. 25, 1957, pp.41-51

IV PROGRAMMING

CHAPTER 7

ESTIMATING REVEALED PREFERENCES IN MODELS OF PLANNING BEHAVIOUR

A.J. Hughes Hallett, Erasmus University, Rotterdam and Bristol University
J.-P. Ancot, Netherlands Economic Institute and Erasmus University, Rotterdam

1. THE PROBLEM

This paper is concerned with the problem of modelling the behaviour of the planners in any economic system. We are therefore dealing directly with the operation of a self managed economy. Experience in this area has shown that the main difficulty with models intended for either positive or normative analysis is to obtain an adequate representation of the objective function(s) of the planners, even if only to the extent of their (collective) preference ordering. At this point we are essentially dealing with qualitative, potentially political, judgements. But for these models to be operative we generally need to work with some quantitative representation of preferences.

The evident importance of being able to supply some representation of planners' preferences invites an attack on this problem. There is plenty of evidence that planners' actions can influence economic performance to a very large extent - and not only in centrally planned economies - so that no economic model is complete, and no prediction or description of economic performance is reliable without describing the planning process and thereby endogenising the planners and their activities. Clearly such a model of planning behaviour must have as centre piece an analog of the planners' preference system. Some attempts have been made to estimate the preferences explicitly or implicitly via policy reaction functions. However, the results can hardly be said to have been successful for the reasons noted by Ancot et al (1980) and Johansen (1974). Even then there have been no attempts to model planning behaviour explicitly.

The problem of optimising a nonlinear function $f(\underline{z})$ with respect to the n-vector $\underline{z}$ and subject to a number of constraints is standard practice in economics. Its solution through a variety of algorithms, using no more than successive local approximations to $f(\underline{z})$ rather than full knowledge of all its characteristics and contours, is well known. Suppose, however, $f(\underline{z})$ is unknown and instead the optimising value of $\underline{z}$ is known. We consider here the converse problem to the standard one. Given information or observations on variables known to be, or which may reasonably be assumed to be, the outcome of some optimising process, then is it possible to estimate some local approximation to the associated objective function? This converse problem is evidently one of considerable interest in economics because observations on the outcome of some rational choices or optimising decisions are often available, but very little information is available on the priority ordering which led to those choices. One particularly interesting and important case in point (among many others) is that of measuring the preferences of the planners in the management of the economy.

This paper suggests a model of planning behaviour appropriate to economic planning under uncertainty where the planners may have differenct preference orderings and different perceptions of the constraints (section 2). Our main contribution is to provide a method of estimating a collectve preference system within such a model (section 3). "Estimate" is used throughout as a synonym for "providing a suitable approximation", rather than for optimising some statistical criterion of fit and basing inferences on the distributional characteristics of the results. It is possible that such a route can be taken but we have not done so for reasons of simplicity and generality which will appear. The convergence of the algorithm used, and its uniqueness are discussed (sections 4 and 5). The information displayed in a collective preference function is considered (section 6). Finally, the results of two rather interesting exercises in American macroeconomic planning are provided as illustrations, and to indicate the power of the method for such detective work.

2. A MODEL OF PLANNING BEHAVIOUR

Our model of planning behaviour supposes that rational choices are made by the planners when selecting the values for the variables (instruments) under their control. Rational choices of course imply only that a known preference ordering exists over all variables of interest to the planners, and that this preference ordering should satisfy a minimal set of axioms of choice (reflexivity and completeness to yield a properly defined set of options; and transitivity so that a rational and consistent ordering exists). Secondly it is supposed that the planners know their ideal values for the instruments and targets, and that they know that they face certain constraints. It is not assumed that they necessarily know the constraints correctly, but that they at least have some perception and expectations for them and they choose policies on that basis.

2.1 The variables and constraints

The planning system contains variables of three kinds: an m-vector of policy objectives (targets), $\underline{y}_t$; an n*-vector of policy instruments, $\underline{x}_t$; and a vector of variables exogenous both to the economic system and to the planners, $\underline{s}_t$. We consider a planning horizon T, with discrete intervals t=1 ... T. Let $\underline{y}' = (\underline{y}_1' \ldots \underline{y}_T')$, $\underline{x}' = (\underline{x}_1' \ldots \underline{x}_T')$ and $\underline{s}' = (\underline{s}_1' \ldots \underline{s}_T')$ and write $\underline{z}' = (\underline{y}', \underline{x}')$. Supposed the planners have selected ideal but generally infeasible trajectories for the policy variables $\underline{z}$ as $\underline{z}^d = (\underline{y}_1^{d'} \ldots \underline{y}_T^{d'}, \underline{x}_1^{d'} \ldots \underline{x}_T^{d'})$. . Let $\tilde{\underline{z}} = \underline{z} - \underline{z}^d$ and $n = (n^*+m)T$.

The constraints facing the planners, or at least their perceptions of them, may be represented by an econometric model. We take any such model and write it with its t-period final forms stacked up for t=1 ... T (given the initial conditions $\underline{z}_{t=0}$). Thus

$$\underline{y} = R\underline{x} + \underline{s} \tag{2.1}$$

where $R = \begin{bmatrix} R_{11} & & 0 \\ \vdots & \ddots & \\ R_{TT} & \cdots & R \end{bmatrix}$. So $R_{ij} = \partial \underline{y}_i / \partial \underline{x}_j$ for i,j=1 ... T

evaluated at some $\underline{x}$ and some $\underline{s}$ values. R_{ij} is just the m x n* matrix of (i-1) period delay multipliers of instruments in period j on subsequent targets. They summarise the dynamic responses of the economy which the decision makers face. Past targets cannot be influenced by current instruments.

Evidently (2.1) can be constructed numerically for nonlinear models, but the best known example is that obtained from a linear structural econometric model. There the final forms contain submatrices R_{ij} which are all constant for a multiplier of a given delay, and invariant to $\underline{x}$ and $\underline{s}$; i.e. at each t, $R_{i,j} = R_{i-j+1}$ for all i,j=1 ... T. This format corresponds exactly to that given by Theil (1964). We assume $\underline{s}$ follows an unspecified probability density function with known finite mean and that we may ignore the stochastic nature of the estimated values in R beyond their first-order certainty equivalents. Finally we rewrite (2.1) as

$$H\tilde{\underline{z}} = \underline{b} \tag{2.2}$$

with $H = [I\vdots -R]$ and $\underline{b} = \underline{s} - H\underline{z}^d$. We define the feasible set, F, of $\underline{z}$ values as $F \equiv \{\underline{z}\varepsilon E^n | H\tilde{\underline{z}} - \underline{b} = 0\}$. Naturally, since $mT < n$, F is not empty.

2.2 On the preference system and optimal policies

If policy values $\tilde{\underline{z}}$ can be rationally chosen then the value of an index of economic performance can be associated with each $\tilde{\underline{z}}$ value. The ability to do no more than rank $\tilde{\underline{z}}$ values in terms of this index (which is the sole consequence of presuming rational choices as a behavioural theory for planners) implies that index is no more than an ordinal preference function of $\tilde{\underline{z}}$:

$$w = w(\tilde{\underline{z}}) \tag{2.3}$$

satisfying the axioms of choice mentioned, plus convexity so that the optimal policy value is represented by the minimiser of (2.3). $w(\tilde{\underline{z}})$ represents preferences between rival targets and instruments, and trade-offs between conflicting values over time. These preferences are expressed as relative penalties on failing to reach the desired values in each component of $\underline{z}$.

The axioms of choice governing (2.3) need not be extended further if we adopt a game theoretic approach (as in section 2.3 below) to determine the best $\tilde{\underline{z}}$ value. If we further assume, as we do hereafter, that the planners indeed aim at the global minimum of (2.3) and any observations of a $\tilde{\underline{z}}$ value chosen by them corresponds to that, then we need only local convexity at that minimum in the true preferences. Rational choices moreover imply the planners optimise their own perceived self-interests (including "satisficing") which are in the form of (2.3). The ideal values, $\underline{z}^d$, are then by definition the unconstrained optima of (2.3). We cannot exclude the possibility that $\underline{z}^d$ is finite in some elements but infinite in others. Consumption (more goods being preferable to less) is an example of the latter, whereas unemployment is an example of the former. Economic theory provides further examples where $\underline{z}^d$ would take finite values - for example where output and unemployment are to grow at their full employment "natural" levels. Thus monotonicity in $\tilde{\underline{z}}$ cannot be among the axioms underlying (2.3) with the consequence that minimisation of (2.3), subject to (2.2), is only an appropriate characterisation of a rational choice provided $\underline{z}^d$ does indeed represent its unconstrained optimum.

Finally, and for convenience only, we shall treat (2.3) as if it were continuous and smooth to give differentiability. The convenience is to avoid having to specify the precise game theoretic strategy a planner actually follows to select his optimal policies for $\tilde{z}$; we model that as if he did it by differentiation. Therefore, no specific criterion of success, nor specific form of preference function, is imputed by the maintained hypothesis in this model.

A second order approximation to (2.3) about some feasible $\tilde{\underline{z}}^*$ (ignoring the constant to which minimisation is invariant) is

$$w = \tfrac{1}{2}\tilde{\underline{z}}'Q\tilde{\underline{z}} + \underline{q}'\tilde{\underline{z}} \tag{2.4}$$

where $Q = \left(\frac{\partial^2 w}{\partial \underline{z}\partial \underline{z}'}\right)_{\tilde{\underline{z}}^*}$ and $\underline{q} = -Q\tilde{\underline{z}}^* + \left(\frac{\partial w}{\partial \underline{z}}\right)_{\tilde{\underline{z}}^*}$. Thus Q is symmetric and positive definite if (2.3) is strictly convex and twice differentiable at least over F. The ordinality of (2.3) ensures that of (2.4); hence a normalisation will be imposed on Q throughout(1). Now (2.4) contains implicit ideal values $\underline{z}^d - Q^{-1}\underline{q}$. Notice (2.4) may be transformed with no loss of generality to

$$w = w^+ - \tfrac{1}{2}\underline{q}'Q^{-1}\underline{q} \tag{2.5}$$

where $w^+ = \tfrac{1}{2}\tilde{\underline{z}}^{+\prime}Q\tilde{\underline{z}}^+$ and $\tilde{\underline{z}}^+ = \tilde{\underline{z}} + Q^{-1}\underline{q}$. But by definition ideal values were the unconstrained optimisers of (2.3) and we required that particular definition of $\underline{z}^d$ if minimisation was to be a valid method of making rational choices. Thus (2.4), as a consistent local representation of the true preferences (2.3), may have <u>either</u> $\underline{z}^d$ as the true desired value in the sense of being the unconstrained minimiser of $w(\tilde{\underline{z}})$ and $\underline{q}=0$; <u>or</u> $\underline{q}\neq 0$ and $\underline{z}^d$ replaced by some artificial values $\underline{z}^a = \underline{z}^d + Q^{-1}\underline{q}$; <u>or</u> $\underline{z}^d$ may be retained in (2.4) with $\underline{q}\neq 0$ to give preferences asymmetric about $\underline{z}^d$, with $\partial w/\partial \underline{z} = \underline{q}$ at $\underline{z}^d$ and $\underline{q}$ presumably chosen so that the constrained optimum $\tilde{\underline{z}}^*$ has the more desirable sign in each element. The first two possibilities mentioned are equivalent to one another, whereas the last biases (2.4) in such a way as to give results for the optimal policies unavailable from the true approximation to (2.3) at $\tilde{\underline{z}}^*$. Whether this last specification may be used depends on the extent of the prior information available on $\underline{z}^d$ or $w(\tilde{\underline{z}})$. We think that firm information on the precise $\underline{z}^d$ values will be hard to come by - certainly it was not available for the numerical examples below - so one of the first two representations typically must be used.

The planning problem in essence is, given (2.2), $\underline{z}^d$ and (2.3), to solve for $\tilde{\underline{z}}_p$ as

$$\underset{\sim}{z}_p = \min_{\tilde{\underline{z}}} \{w(\tilde{\underline{z}}) \,|\, H\tilde{\underline{z}} - \underline{b} = 0\} \tag{2.6}$$

Define mT lagrange multipliers, $\underline{\mu}$. We approximate (2.6) using (2.4):

$$\min_{\tilde{\underline{z}}} \{L(\tilde{\underline{z}},\underline{\mu}) \,|\, L = w - \underline{\mu}'(H\tilde{\underline{z}} - \underline{b})\} \tag{2.7}$$

First order conditions for (2.7) are

$$\begin{bmatrix} Q & -H' \\ -H & 0 \end{bmatrix} \begin{bmatrix} \tilde{\underline{z}} \\ \underline{\mu} \end{bmatrix} + \begin{bmatrix} \underline{q} \\ \underline{b} \end{bmatrix} = 0 \tag{2.8}$$

yielding $$\tilde{\underline{z}}^* = Q^{-1}(H'(HQ^{-1}H')^{-1}(HQ^{-1}\underline{q} + \underline{b}) - \underline{q}) \tag{2.9a}$$

and $$\underline{\mu}^* = (HQ^{-1}H')^{-1}(HQ^{-1}\underline{q} + \underline{b}) = (I\vdots 0)(Q\tilde{\underline{z}}^* + \underline{q}) \tag{2.9b}$$

where also $$L(\tilde{\underline{z}},\underline{\mu}) = \tfrac{1}{2}\begin{bmatrix} \tilde{\underline{z}} \\ \underline{\mu} \end{bmatrix}' \begin{bmatrix} Q & -H \\ -H & 0 \end{bmatrix} \begin{bmatrix} \tilde{\underline{z}} \\ \underline{\mu} \end{bmatrix} + \begin{bmatrix} \tilde{\underline{q}} \\ \underline{b} \end{bmatrix}' \begin{bmatrix} \tilde{\underline{z}} \\ \underline{\mu} \end{bmatrix}. \tag{2.10}$$

We write $\Theta = Q^{-1}H'(HQ^{-1}H')^{-1}$ and $P = I - \Theta H$. So that, adopting the case of true $\underline{z}^d$ values and $\underline{q}=0$ for (2.4), (2.9a-b) specialise to

$$\tilde{\underline{z}}^* = \Theta\underline{b} \quad \text{and} \quad \underline{\mu}^* = (HQ^{-1}H')^{-1}\underline{b} \tag{2.11a-b}$$

Finally, given (2.2) and (2.4), we replace $\underline{b}$ by its conditional expectation at the moment of calculation for certainty equivalence, i.e. when E(w) replaces w in (2.7) in recognition of the uncertainties in $\underline{b}$. Similarly we replace H by E(H) to give first order certainty equivalence. Updating those expectations and making adjustments to Q, H, $\underline{q}$ and $\underline{b}$ at each t, gives policies to be implemented as $\tilde{\underline{z}}^*_t$ within (2.9)[(2)]. Thus by choice of conditioning information we can generate $\tilde{\underline{z}}^*$ appropriate to any stage of revision from first period certainty equivalent (t=1) values to the actually implemented multiperiod certainty equivalent sequence of values. These two cases are respectively the open loop controls in a discrete time planning problem.

2.3 The decision making process

More generally, algorithms exist to solve (2.6) when $w(\tilde{\underline{z}})$ is known although the decision rule cannot be written algebraically in terms of $w(\tilde{\underline{z}})$, H and $\underline{b}$. The difficulty in the economic planning context is $w(\tilde{\underline{z}})$ can never generally be known a priori. Any planning process in a self managed system, either in a democracy or any but the most extreme dictatorship, involves a number of participants or interested parties each with their own preference system. Policies then emerge from the deliberations of the planners as some kind of agreed and negotiated solution. Since, therefore, the true collective preferences which lie behind this solution cannot be perfectly known over F, if indeed they even exist, we can at most specify them implicitly as in (2.3). Agreement among the planners means that no individual attempts to implement any value for $\tilde{\underline{z}}*$ (under his control) in defiance of the solution of the other planners. We call this situation of "no active dissent" as government by consent; and we note it implies that $\underline{z}$ can only cover policies which can fairly be said to be under the planners' control.

We finally turn to the details of modelling the process by which planners select a policy to be implemented. We need (2.4) to obtain (2.9) and also (2.9) to obtain (2.4). That is the classic predicament in minimising non-quadratic functions analytically. Several numerical search procedures exist to solve this difficulty.

When $w(\tilde{\underline{z}})$ is known, the Newton-Raphson algorithm computes (2.4) for some trial solution $\tilde{\underline{z}}^{(s)}$ and with that $\tilde{\underline{z}}^{(s+1)}$ from (2.9). Assuming convergence, $\tilde{\underline{z}}_p = \lim_{s\to\infty} \tilde{\underline{z}}^{(s)}$, but global convergence is not guaranteed for an arbitrary $\tilde{\underline{z}}^{(0)}$. MModifications, which are also designed to avoid evaluating and inverting potentially large Hessian matrices, abandon (2.9) and select $\tilde{\underline{z}}^{(s+1)}$ such that $w(\tilde{\underline{z}}^{(s+1)}) < w(\tilde{\underline{z}}^{(s)})$ so that economy of searches in many dimensions is retained. The conjugate gradient, variable metric and parallel tangent algorithms (without line searches) result. Of interest here is that some variable metric algorithms yield, at convergence, a quadratic approximation to $w(\tilde{\underline{z}})$ (Dixon (1975)). And, of course, $\tilde{\underline{z}}^{(s)}$ must be restricted to F for each s. So we would in fact work with $L(\tilde{\underline{z}},\underline{\mu}) = w(\tilde{\underline{z}}) - \underline{\mu}'(H\tilde{\underline{z}} - \underline{b})$ in place of $w(\tilde{\underline{z}})$ in any of these algorithms. But, to obtain preferences revealed in some outcome $\underline{z}_p$ given in (2.2), i.e. in our converse problem, it is (2.4) or (2.3) and not (2.9) which is unknown. Then none of these algorithms are possible. Yet none of the latter group requires more than an evaluation of $\partial L/\partial\tilde{\underline{z}}$ over F and the knowledge that each step reduces the function value. The two situations are similar in minimising $w(\tilde{z})$ without knowledge of its derivatives which are themselves dependent on the variables whose minimising values we seek. They differ in that normally, given $\tilde{z}$, $\partial L/\partial \underline{z}$ is known but $\tilde{z}_p$ is not; whereas our situation is the reverse. But the requirement $L(\tilde{z}^{(s+1)}) < L(\tilde{z}^{(s)})$ is achieved by forcing the equivalent condition under our assumptions:

$$\|\tilde{z}^{(s+1)} - \tilde{z}_p\|_2 < \|\tilde{z}^{(s)} - \tilde{z}_p\|_2 \qquad \text{all } s > 0. \tag{2.12}$$

Consider how the policy maker would now select his optimal policies. We assume that some $\underline{z}_p$ exists preferred to $\underline{z}^{(s)}$ and that the intersection of F and the set of $\underline{z}$ values acceptable to the planner is non-empty to ensure some decision can be made. If each member of the sequence $\{\tilde{z}^{(s)}\}$ is the constrained optimum of (2.4) corresponding to each member of the possibility set $\{Q^{(s)}\}$ for Q, then $\underline{z}_p$ could be any point preferred to every $\underline{z}^{(s)}$ so far, i.e. $w(\tilde{z}_p) < w(\tilde{z}^{(i)})$ $\quad i=0 \ldots s$. Suppose, the policy maker picks a sequence of $\underline{z}_p$ vectors in order to sample the Pareto optimal frontier of F (with respect to $\underline{z}^d$). Each $\underline{z}_p$ is one in a series of experiments to locate which feasible positions are preferable to $\underline{z}^{(s)}$; and therefore ultimately to locate the most preferred feasible position (the policy recommendation) while $\underline{z}^d$ remains the ideal. We define each $\underline{z}_p$ to ensure a systematic search of the frontier, but otherwise the switch from one $\underline{z}_p$ to another, when and by how much, is unrestricted. Our scheme has an inner iteration in $\underline{z}^{(s)}$, and an outer one in $\underline{z}_p$; but that in $\underline{z}^{(s)}$ need not be fully exploited. If the inner iteration is completed we obtain the solution (given $\underline{z}_p$) to

$$\underline{z}^{(p)} = \min_{\underline{z}} \{\|\underline{z} - \underline{z}_p\| \mid H\tilde{z} = \underline{b}\} \tag{2.13}$$

i.e. $$\underline{z}^{(p)} = (I - H'(HH')^{-1}H)\underline{z}_p + H'(HH')^{-1}\underline{s}. \tag{2.14}$$

Evidently (2.14) is a special case of (2.11a) with $Q = I$ and $\underline{z}_p = \underline{z}^d$. Moreover (2.11a) shows that

$$d\underline{z}^* = Pd\underline{z}^d \tag{2.15}$$

Therefore every point on the Pareto optimal frontier of F (with respect to $\underline{z}^d$) can be generated as candidates for $\underline{z}^*$ by choice of $\underline{z}_p$; for example as $\underline{z}^{(p)} + d\underline{z}^*$, where in the special case of (2.14) $d\underline{z}^* = (I-H(HH')^{-1}H)d\underline{z}_p$ for appropriate choices of $d\underline{z}_p$.[(3)] Therefore it is only necessary to experiment with different $\underline{z}_p$ values in order to sample that frontier.

We wish to avoid the necessity of evaluating the gradient vector when (2.3) is unknown and thus avoid associating our model with any particular solution algorithm. We suppose the planner plays a "game" against the model. At each step a new $\underline{z}_p$ is selected such that the $\underline{z}^{(p)}$ resulting from (2.14) implies a lower evaluation in the implicit function (2.3) than at the previous trial. These steps continue until a $\underline{z}_p$, and thus a $\underline{z}^{(p)}$, cannot be beaten; and this situation must eventually be reached.

This model of planning behaviour is designed so that all points on the Pareto optimal frontier of F are implicitly considered and evaluated by the planners where the start is arbitrary. Its final outcome (in terms of $\underline{z}_p$ and $\underline{z}^{(p)}$) may formally be regarded as the outcome of a bargaining game. In section 3 we develop a particular algorithm to make this model operative. Provided that we can also show convergence of this algorithm to the same final outcome (this is done in section 4) the interpretation of this final outcome as the result of a bargaining game remains intact. The essential link between this formal planning model in terms of game theory, and the particular form of it which follows and which is based on methods of differential calculus, is of course the equivalence of (2.13) and (2.6) - (2.11) and the demonstration that (2.13) may also be used to trace the whole Pareto optimal frontier of F.

2.4 The planning model in the context of revealed preferences

A special case of this planning model is where we represent only the final outcome of the planning process, rather than model how the planners arrived at that outcome. We can simply go on to model the decision process of a planner by supposing he used any of these algorithms - say the variable metric one - provided that we ensure the downhill property in terms of (2.3), and that we can approximate the gradient vector. In the case of revealed preferences we anyway only have knowledge of the policies finally recommended and implemented, i.e. the last $\underline{z}_p$. We could therefore imitate the last stage of this selection procedure by making that $\underline{z}^{(p)}$ play the role of $\underline{z}_p$ in the model of the previous paragraph, and force the convergence of $\underline{z}^{(s)}$ onto it. This means that hereafter $\underline{z}_p$ now represents the finally recommended and observed policy choice. Since we wish to find the $Q^{(s)}$ which would yield the given and observed optimal policy choice $\underline{z}_p$ we design the algorithm to choose candidate $Q^{(s)}$ matrices for (2.7) via a variable metric algorithm in such a way that the associated constrained optima, $\underline{\tilde{z}}^{(s)}$, converge to $\underline{\tilde{z}}_p$. The existence of $\underline{z}_p$ ensures it is preferred to any $\underline{z}^{(s)} \neq \underline{z}_p$ and the intersection of F and the acceptable set is nonempty. The final $Q^{(s)}$ reflects revealed preferences because the planners must have used their implicit, if unspecified, preferences in accepting $\underline{z}_p$ as the final and best policy recommendation. And those revealed preferences contain, of course, the compromise position reached as a result of the bargaining among the participants in selecting $\underline{z}_p$.

2.5 On the existence of collective preferences

Modelling planning behaviour by rational choices and then estimating an objective function inevitably raises the question of what precisely (2.3) represents, and how far may we interpret the estimate as showing "preferences". If so, whose preferences?

At its simplest we are here only uncovering an (possibly 'the') objective function which could give rise to the observed policy choice. It seems to be universally accepted in models of this kind that governments can be said to optimise some performance index. It may not represent collective preferences exactly but rather any of the other possible allied interpretations - such as vote or utility maximisation, vote share maximisation, popularity indices, or office maximisation - which could be the relevant objectives for any of the policy makers. It is therefore the government's (collective) preference criteria which we uncover here, not that of the voters or policy consumers. The distinction may very well prove important with the introduction of ideology and self interest by the government and its supporting groups(4).

2.6 On the specification of $\underline{z}_p$

One final remark is required about the values used in $\underline{z}_p$. They may be intended policies of a planning authority which have been published in some form; or they may be historical figures being those policies actually implemented by that authority. In either case we estimate revealed preferences but the two possibilities may not be strictly comparable if mistakes or other changes occur in implementation.

The vital point here is that the target elements must be what the authority would have expected at the moment of implementation of the instruments - not actual realisations. It must be conditioned on the information available to the planners when it was selected. Given values of the instruments, $\underline{x}_p$, the target elements will be

$$E(\underline{y} \mid \underline{x}_p, H, E_t(\underline{s})) = \underline{y}_p \ . \qquad (2.16)$$

$E_t(.)$ is a conditional expectation of the uncertain variables at the start of period t; t=1 ... T. Therefore, we can investigate different $\underline{z}_p$'s varying from initial first period certainty equivalence to multiperiod certainty equivalence (i.e. by inserting from $E_1(.)$ to $E_T(.)$ in (2.16)). Each $\underline{z}_p$ leads to an associated set of estimated preference function parameters. Thus, for example, $E_1(.)$ and $E_T(.)$ themselves lead to preferences over the planning interval viewed ex ante and ex post respectively. If those periods coincide with a particular political administration we obtain the associated preferences as viewed on entering office and on leaving (running for reelection etc.). There is no reason to suppose $\underline{z}_p$ is necessarily feasible (within F) in this special case. It may have been computed by the planners using some model different from (2.2); the expectations conditioning $\underline{z}_p$ in (2.16) may not be those in (2.2); or "tactical" policies may have been recommended (defined as $E(H\underline{z}_p \mid \underline{x}_p, \underline{b}) \neq \underline{b}$) corresponding to "judgmental" forecasts reflecting consideration of factors not included in (2.2) or reflecting prior knowledge of the shortcomings of (2.2).

3. THE ALGORITHM SPECIFICATION

A general variable metric algorithm[5], in minimising some convex function $w(\tilde{\underline{z}})$, generates at step s:

$$\tilde{\underline{z}}^{(s+1)} = \tilde{\underline{z}}^{(s)} + \hat{\alpha}_s G^{(s)} \underline{g}^{(s)} \qquad (3.1)$$

and

$$G^{(s+1)} = G^{(s)} + \frac{\underline{\delta}^{(s)}\underline{\delta}^{(s)\prime}}{\underline{\delta}^{(s)\prime}\underline{\gamma}^{(s)}} - \frac{G^{(s)}\underline{\gamma}^{(s)}\underline{\gamma}^{(s)\prime}G^{(s)}}{\underline{\gamma}^{(s)\prime}G^{(s)}\underline{\gamma}^{(s)}} + \nu_s \underline{v}^{(s)}\underline{v}^{(s)\prime} \qquad (3.2)$$

where

$$v^{(s)} = \frac{\underline{\delta}^{(s)}}{\underline{\delta}^{(s)\prime}\underline{\gamma}^{(s)}} - \frac{G^{(s)}\underline{\gamma}^{(s)}}{\underline{\gamma}^{(s)\prime}G^{(s)}\underline{\gamma}^{(s)}} \ ; \ \underline{\gamma}^{(s)} = \underline{g}^{(s+1)} - \underline{g}^{(s)}; \ \underline{\delta}^{(s)} = \tilde{\underline{z}}^{(s+1)} - \tilde{\underline{z}}^{(s)} \ ;$$

for arbitrary and independent starts $\tilde{\underline{z}}^{(0)}$ and $G^{(0)}$. Also $\underline{g}^{(s)} = [\partial w/\partial \underline{z}]_{\tilde{\underline{z}}^{(s)}}$, the scalar ν_s determines the algorithm family member, and the scalar α_s is defined such that $w(\tilde{\underline{z}}^{(s+1)}) < w(\tilde{\underline{z}}^{(s)})$, the "downhill" property. An accurate line search is to select at each step

$$\hat{\alpha}_s \text{ as } \min_{\alpha} w(\tilde{\underline{z}}^{(s)} + \hat{\alpha} G^{(s)} \underline{g}^{(s)})$$

and thereby generate conjugate search directions. However, we shall not use $\hat{\alpha}_s$ this way, apart from ensuring the "downhill" property.

We select the Symmetric Rank One family member[6], so (3.2) becomes:

$$G^{(s+1)} = G^{(s)} + \frac{(\underline{\delta}_o^{(s)} - G^{(s)}\underline{\gamma}_o^{(s)})(\underline{\delta}_o^{(s)} - G^{(s)}\underline{\gamma}_o^{(s)})'}{\underline{\gamma}_o^{(s)\prime}(\underline{\delta}_o^{(s)} - G^{(s)}\underline{\gamma}_o^{(s)})} \tag{3.3}$$

3.1 Implementing the planning behaviour model for forward planning

Consider the application of a variable metric algorithm as a method for determining $\underline{z}_p$, the policies finally selected. That is the application of (3.2) and (3.3) to our model of planning behaviour at the forward planning stage as described in subsection 2.3. If we are to be put in the planners' shoes we must assume exactly the same knowledge as they would have had over the economic model used, $\underline{z}^d$, and $w(\tilde{\underline{z}})$. This means, for the purpose of constructing an algorithm by which $\underline{z}_p$ notionally could have been selected, we can use their perception of the economic constraints, be it implicit or explicit, in the form of (2.2), the true $\underline{z}^d$ values, and knowledge of the "downhill" property to $\tilde{\underline{z}}_p$, which of course is feasible in this set up. However, when, in the next subsection and thereafter, we attempt to reproduce this algorithm for the case of $w(\tilde{\underline{z}})$ unknown then we must insert our own estimates of (2.2), $\underline{z}^d$, the "downhill" property etc. $\tilde{\underline{z}}_p$ in that context will no longer necessarily be feasible with respect to (2.2) in use for any of the reasons given earlier.

Since it is the constrained optimisation of (2.6) and (2.7) which leads to $\tilde{\underline{z}}_p$, $w(\tilde{\underline{z}})$ must be replaced by $L(\tilde{\underline{z}}, \underline{\mu})$ in (3.1) to (3.3). That implies the following for (3.1) to (3.3): $(\tilde{\underline{z}}, \underline{\mu}')$ replaces $\tilde{\underline{z}}$;

$$G^{(s)} = \begin{bmatrix} Q^{(s)} & -H' \\ -H & 0 \end{bmatrix}^{-1} ; \quad \underline{g}^{(s)} = \begin{bmatrix} \partial L/\partial \underline{z} \\ \hline \partial L/\partial \underline{\mu} \end{bmatrix}_{\tilde{\underline{z}}^{(s)},\, \underline{\mu}^{(s)}} ;$$

$$\underline{\gamma}_o^{(s)} = \underline{g}^{(s+1)} - \underline{g}^{(s)} = \begin{bmatrix} \underline{\gamma}^{(s)} \\ \underline{\gamma}_1^{(s)} \end{bmatrix} ; \quad \underline{\delta}_o^{(s)} = \begin{bmatrix} \tilde{\underline{z}}^{(s+1)} - \tilde{\underline{z}}^{(s)} \\ \underline{\mu}^{(s+1)} - \underline{\mu}^{(s)} \end{bmatrix} = \begin{bmatrix} \underline{\delta}^{(s)} \\ \underline{\delta}_1^{(s)} \end{bmatrix}$$

It is well known that at convergence $G^{(s)}$ is the inverse of the hessian of

(2.6) evaluated at its minimum. One explanation of a variable metric algorithm here is that it takes steps to minimise a sequence of quadratic approximations to $w(\underline{\tilde{z}})$ such as (2.10), culminating at $\underline{\tilde{z}}_p$ for the last. So (3.3) is an advantageous choice not only for simplicity but, significantly, because for a general w(.) it will identify a quadratic approximation to $L(\underline{\tilde{z}}, \underline{\mu})$ at that minimum, (Dixon (1975)). That approximation is (for convergence at s=p)

$$\frac{1}{2}\begin{bmatrix}\underline{\tilde{z}} - \underline{\tilde{z}}^{(p)} \\ \underline{\mu} - \underline{\mu}^{(p)}\end{bmatrix}' G^{(p)^{-1}} \begin{bmatrix}\underline{\tilde{z}} - \underline{\tilde{z}}^{(p)} \\ \underline{\mu} - \underline{\mu}^{(p)}\end{bmatrix} + \underline{g}^{(p)'} \begin{bmatrix}\underline{\tilde{z}} - \underline{\tilde{z}}^{(p)} \\ \underline{\mu} - \underline{\mu}^{(p)}\end{bmatrix} \tag{3.4}$$

(3.4) becomes $\frac{1}{2}\begin{bmatrix}\underline{\tilde{z}} \\ \underline{\mu}\end{bmatrix}' G^{(p)^{-1}} \begin{bmatrix}\underline{\tilde{z}} \\ \underline{\mu}\end{bmatrix} + \begin{bmatrix}\underline{q} \\ \underline{b}\end{bmatrix}' \begin{bmatrix}\underline{\tilde{z}} \\ \underline{\mu}\end{bmatrix}$ (ignoring constants) since

$$\underline{g}^{(p)} = \begin{bmatrix}\underline{q} \\ \underline{b}\end{bmatrix} + G^{(p)^{-1}} \begin{bmatrix}\underline{\tilde{z}}^{(p)} \\ \underline{\mu}^{(p)}\end{bmatrix} \tag{3.5}$$

follows from (2.10) at $\underline{\tilde{z}}^{(p)}$, $\underline{\mu}^{(p)}$. Notice (3.4) is independent of $\underline{z}^d$. After convergence in the hessian matrix, any variable metric algorithm computes the minimum, $\underline{z}_p$, $\underline{\mu}_p$ in a final step;

$$\begin{bmatrix}\underline{z}_p \\ \underline{\mu}_p\end{bmatrix} = \begin{bmatrix}\underline{z}^{(p)} \\ \underline{\mu}^{(p)}\end{bmatrix} - G^{(p)}\underline{g}^{(p)} \tag{3.6}$$

Inserting the value of $\underline{g}^{(p)}$ from the function $L(\underline{\tilde{z}}, \underline{\mu})$ of (2.6) we have

$$G^{(p)}\underline{g}^{(p)} = G^{(p)} \left[G^{(p)^{-1}} \begin{bmatrix}\underline{\tilde{z}}^{(p)} \\ \underline{\mu}^{(p)}\end{bmatrix} + \begin{bmatrix}\underline{q} \\ \underline{b}\end{bmatrix} \right] = \begin{bmatrix} P^{(p)}Q^{(p)^{-1}}\underline{q} \\ Q^{(p)}\underline{q} \end{bmatrix} \tag{3.7}$$

If the true values $\underline{z}^d$ are inserted, then $\underline{q}=0$ and $\underline{z}_p = \underline{z}^{(p)}$. The algorithm may be used as it stands. If, however, assumed values $\underline{z}^a \neq \underline{z}^d$ were inserted, then we have $\underline{q} \neq 0$ and $\underline{\delta}_0^{(p)} = G^{(p)}\underline{g}^{(p)}$ by (2.9a-b). In general, therefore, after convergence we must reset <u>either</u>

$$\underline{z}^a \text{ to } \underline{z}^d = \underline{z}^a + \underline{\delta}^{(p)} \quad \underline{\text{or}} \quad \underline{q} = Q^{(p)}\underline{\delta}^{(p)} \tag{3.8a-b}$$

as implied by the transformed variables of (2.5). Moreover, since[7] by (2.9a-b)

$$d\underline{z}^* = P^{(p)} d\underline{z}^d \quad \text{and} \quad d\underline{z}^* = -P^{(p)} Q^{(p)^{-1}} d\underline{q} \tag{3.9a-b}$$

this ensures that $\underline{z}_p = \underline{z}^*$ is attained as the minimiser in place of $\underline{z}^{(p)}$. In view of (2.12), these adjustments to $\underline{z}^d$ or $\underline{q}$ are minimised. In other words, (3.7) shows that the final step mentioned at (3.6) is none other than the requirement that $\underline{z}^d$ or $\underline{q}$ must be reset at the end because either this algorithm has used the transformed variables of (2.5) or has had both $\underline{z}^a \neq \underline{z}^d$ and $\underline{q} = 0$ inserted. It is nevertheless possible to run this algorithm as it stands, and then adjust $\underline{z}^a$ or $\underline{q}$ via (3.8a-b) after convergence.

The application of (3.1) - (3.6) to $L(\tilde{\underline{z}}, \underline{\mu})$ is a standard representation of a variable metric algorithm for the constrained minimisation of $w(\tilde{\underline{z}})$. Of course we should iterate in both $\tilde{\underline{z}}^{(s)}$ and $\underline{\mu}^{(s)}$ but, in fact, we can suppress the $\underline{\mu}^{(s)}$ part. There is no loss of information in simplifying the problem by designing the algorithm for the case when the true w(.) is quadratic. For our problem it is observationally equivalent to a more general w(.). But this does not imply that we assume w(.) is itself generally quadratic. At step s

$$\underline{g}^{(s)} = \begin{bmatrix} Q^{(p)} & -H' \\ -H & 0 \end{bmatrix} \begin{bmatrix} \underline{z}^{\sim(s)} \\ \underline{\mu}^{(s)} \end{bmatrix} + \begin{bmatrix} \underline{q} \\ \underline{b} \end{bmatrix} \tag{3.10}$$

so that

$$\gamma_o^{(s)} = \begin{bmatrix} Q^{(p)} & -H' \\ -H & 0 \end{bmatrix} \underline{\delta}_o^{(s)} \tag{3.11}$$

Then

$$(G^{(s)^{-1}}\underline{\delta}_o^{(s)} - \underline{\gamma}_o^{(s)}) = \left\{ \begin{bmatrix} Q^{(s)} & -H' \\ -H & 0 \end{bmatrix} - \begin{bmatrix} Q^{(p)} & -H' \\ -H & 0 \end{bmatrix} \right\} \underline{\delta}_o^{(s)} \tag{3.12}$$

$$= \begin{bmatrix} (Q^{(s)} - Q^{(p)}) & \underline{\delta}^{(s)} \\ 0 & \end{bmatrix} \tag{3.13}$$

Hence we can drop the subscripts "o" throughout (3.3) since by writing

$$(\underline{\delta}_o^{(s)} - G^{(s)}\underline{\gamma}_o^{(s)}) = G^{(s)}\,(G^{(s)^{-1}}\underline{\delta}_o^{(s)} - \underline{\gamma}_o^{(s)}) \tag{3.14}$$

(3.3) reduces to an iteration in $Q^{(s)^{-1}}$. Then, we replace that iteration by its inverse:

$$Q^{(s+1)} = Q^{(s)} + \frac{(\underline{\gamma}^{(s)} - Q^{(s)}\underline{\delta}^{(s)})(\underline{\gamma}^{(s)} - Q^{(s)}\underline{\delta}^{(s)})'}{\underline{\delta}^{(s)'}(\underline{\gamma}^{(s)} - Q^{(s)}\underline{\delta}^{(s)})} \tag{3.15}$$

Now
$$G^{(s)}\underline{g}^{(s)} = \left\{\begin{bmatrix} Q^{(s)} & -H' \\ -H & 0 \end{bmatrix}^{-1} \begin{bmatrix} Q^{(p)} & -H' \\ -H & 0 \end{bmatrix} \begin{bmatrix} \underline{\tilde{z}}^{(s)} \\ \underline{\mu}^{(s)} \end{bmatrix} + \begin{bmatrix} \underline{q} \\ \underline{b} \end{bmatrix}\right\} \tag{3.16}$$

Hence, upon manipulation and using the fact that $\underline{\tilde{z}}^{(s)} \varepsilon F$ and $P^{(s)}Q^{(s)^{-1}}H' = 0$, we can write:

$$\underline{\tilde{z}}^{(s+1)} = \underline{\tilde{z}}^{(s)} + \hat{\alpha}_s P^{(s)}\,Q^{(s)^{-1}}(Q^{(p)}\underline{\tilde{z}}^{(s)} + \underline{q}) \tag{3.17}$$

which is independent of $\underline{\mu}$. Therefore we also drop $\underline{\mu}$ from (3.2). Using $-P^{(s)}Q^{(s)-1}Q^{(p)}\underline{\tilde{z}}_p = P^{(s)}Q^{(s)-1}\underline{q}$ obtained from (2.9a) with some manipulation, we can also write (3.17) as

$$\underline{\tilde{z}}^{(s+1)} = \underline{\tilde{z}}^{(s)} - \hat{\alpha}_s P^{(s)}Q^{(s)^{-1}}Q^{(p)}(\underline{\tilde{z}}_p - \underline{\tilde{z}}^{(s)}) \tag{3.18}$$

Therefore an algorithm which makes the model of planning behaviour operative in the sense of forward planning, when $w(\underline{\tilde{z}})$ is known, reduces to using (3.15) and (3.17) from an arbitrary start $Q^{(0)}$ and $\underline{\tilde{z}}^{(0)}$ and choosing $\hat{\alpha}_s$ to ensure the "downhill" property.

3.2 Implementing the planning behaviour model for revealed preferences

If $w(\underline{\tilde{z}})$ is not known a priori, (3.15) and (3.17) cannot be used. There are two cases of interest here. Either $\underline{z}_p$ is known but $w(\underline{\tilde{z}})$ is not, or neither are known completely but the implicit function $w(\underline{\tilde{z}})$ is known at least to the extent that a "downhill" direction can be specified from every $\underline{\tilde{z}}^{(s)} \varepsilon F$.

The former is the converse (to forward planning) problem introduced at the start, and is the classic situation for the estimation of revealed preferences.

The latter, rather than when $w(\tilde{\underline{z}})$ is known accurately a priori, is probably the typical situation for forward planning in an economy and that situation is treated elsewhere (Hughes Hallett (1979c, and 1980)).

The next step then is to set up an iterative scheme to simulate (3.15) and (3.17) and to guide $\underline{z}^{(s+1)}$ to $\underline{z}_p$. Therefore we must set $\tilde{\underline{z}}^{(s+1)}$ to minimise (2.4) with $Q^{(s+1)}$, given $\tilde{\underline{z}}^{(s)}$ and $Q^{(s)}$, if only to ensure (2.6) is eventually achieved[8]. (2.11a), with (3.15) inserted, gives $\tilde{\underline{z}}^{(s+1)}$ in terms of $\tilde{\underline{z}}^{(s)}$ and $Q^{(s)}$ as:

$$\tilde{\underline{z}}^{(s+1)} = \tilde{\underline{z}}^{(s)} - \alpha_s P^{(s)} (Q^{(s)^{-1}} \underline{\gamma}^{(s)} - \underline{\delta}^{(s)}) \tag{3.19}$$

$$\alpha_s = \frac{(Q^{(s)^{-1}} \underline{\gamma}^{(s)} - \underline{\delta}^{(s)})' H (H Q^{(s)^{-1}} H')^{-1} \underline{b}}{(Q^{(s)^{-1}} \underline{\gamma}^{(s)} - \underline{\delta}^{(s)})' [Q^{(s)} (I - P^{(s)}) (Q^{(s)^{-1}} \underline{\gamma}^{(s)} - \underline{\delta}^{(s)}) - \underline{\gamma}^{(s)}]}$$

From (3.11) and $P^{(s)} Q^{(s)^{-1}} = Q^{(s)^{-1}} P^{(s)'}$ with $P^{(s)} \tilde{\underline{z}}^{(s)} = 0$, direct calculation shows (3.19) can be rewritten as:

$$\tilde{\underline{z}}^{(s+1)} = \tilde{\underline{z}}^{(s)} - \left[\frac{\alpha_s}{1-\alpha_s}\right] P^{(s)} Q^{(s)^{-1}} Q^{(p)} \underline{\delta}^{(s)} \tag{3.20}$$

(3.20) (and thus (3.19)) is identical to (3.18) (and thus (3.17)) for suitable values of α_s and $\hat{\alpha}_s$, provided the $\underline{\delta}^{(s)}$ in (3.20) is replaced by

$$\underline{\delta}^{(s)} = \underline{z}_p - \underline{z}^{(s)} \tag{3.21}$$

Then (3.15) and (3.20) would identically reproduce the steps of a variable metric algorithm. But $\underline{\gamma}^{(s)}$ is a function of $\underline{\delta}^{(s)}$ because post-multiplying (3.15) by $\underline{\delta}^{(s)}$ yields[9]

$$\underline{\gamma}^{(s)} = Q^{(s+1)} \underline{\delta}^{(s)} \tag{3.22}$$

Therefore to tie together the forms of the algorithm, (3.15) and (3.17) or (3.15) and (3.19), by making the adjustment to $\delta^{(s)}$ in (3.21) implies the adjustment of the whole term

$$(Q^{(s)^{-1}} \underline{\gamma}^{(s)} - \underline{\delta}^{(s)}) \tag{3.23}$$

throughout (3.15) and (3.19). Equation (3.21), rather than the earlier definition, is taken to define $\underline{\delta}^{(s)}$ hereafter in this paper.

Now (3.15) and (3.19) imitate that particular variable metric algorithm in (3.15) and (3.17) which attempts to reach $\tilde{\underline{z}}_p$ at each step, but is so arranged as to go only that fraction of the distance which leaves $\tilde{\underline{z}}^{(s+1)}$ as the minimiser of (2.10) containing $Q^{(s+1)}$. So $\tilde{\underline{z}}^{(0)}$ is required from (2.11a) given the start $Q^{(0)}$. Naturally (3.15) and (3.19) with (3.21) cannot be identical to (3.15) and (3.17) in the original version, given $Q^{(0)}$, because of the alterations to $\underline{\delta}^{(s)}$ throughout (3.15). Nevertheless these two versions converge in the sense that the differences between iterates vanish as $s\to\infty$, provided, of course, we can show that convergence to $\tilde{\underline{z}}^{(p)}$ follows. And the relationship constructed between $\tilde{\underline{z}}^{(s)}$ and $Q^{(s)}$ in our version of (3.15) and (3.19), ensures that each step is a valid "start" to the following step[10]. Therefore we refer to (3.15) and (3.19), with (3.21) inserted, as the exact algorithm despite the fact that its interpretation as a legitimate variable metric algorithm is only valid for some steps before convergence.

The fact that (3.15) and (3.19) are now only an imitation of a variable metric algorithm in the earlier steps is no disadvantage, because to be made operative (3.15) and (3.19) must also include some approximation for $\underline{\gamma}^{(s)}$. That approximation will anyway destroy the exact correspondence with the case of (3.15) and (3.17) when $\underline{\gamma}^{(s)}$ (equivalently $Q^{(p)}$ or $Q^{(s+1)}$) is known at each s. In fact (3.17) indicates that the required variable metric algorithm moves, from $\tilde{\underline{z}}^{(s)}$, along a direction vector which is the current projection of the true gradient at $\tilde{\underline{z}}^{(s)}$ onto F, orthonormalised using the current metric. That is a move towards $\underline{z}_p$ in the sense of (2.12).

Finally, gradient evaluations are introduced by the approximation suggested by (3.22)

$$\underline{\gamma}^{(s)} = \phi_s Q^{(s)} \underline{\delta}^{(s)} \tag{3.24}$$

for some scalar ϕ_s. Now by inspection (3.19) has a direction vector identical to that in (3.17) only when $Q^{(p)} = Q^{(s)}$. But that is the case when (3.17) has the projection of the current true gradient vector onto F (orthonormalised in the current metric) passing through $\tilde{\underline{z}}_p$ from $\tilde{\underline{z}}^{(s)}$. In the true variable metric algorithm the minimum point can then be reached with the final step (3.6). Again, therefore, (3.15) and (3.19) including (3.24) will at best converge on some true variable metric algorithm in the later steps, if convergence to

$\underline{\tilde{z}}^{(p)}$ indeed follows. In addition we must now also insert our own explicit estimates of the economic constraints and $\underline{z}^d$ in order to make (3.15) and (3.17) operational.

The operational algorithm from (3.19) and (3.15) is now[11]

$$Q^{(s+1)} = Q^{(s)} + \frac{(\phi_s - 1)Q^{(s)}\underline{\delta}^{(s)}\underline{\delta}^{(s)'}Q^{(s)}}{\underline{\delta}^{(s)'}Q^{(s)}\underline{\delta}^{(s)}} \tag{3.25}$$

and $$\underline{z}^{(s+1)} - \underline{z}^{(s)} = \alpha_s P^{(s)}\underline{\delta}^{(s)} \tag{3.26}$$

where $$\alpha_s = \frac{(\phi_s - 1)a^{(s)}}{(\phi_s - 1)b^{(s)} - \phi_s c^{(s)}} \; ; \quad a^{(s)} = \underline{\delta}^{(s)'}Q^{(s)}\underline{\tilde{z}}^{(s)} \; ; \qquad (3.26)$$

$$b^{(s)} = \underline{\delta}^{(s)'}Q^{(s)}(I-P^{(s)})\underline{\delta}^{(s)} \quad \text{and} \quad c^{(s)} = \underline{\delta}^{(s)'}Q^{(s)}\underline{\delta}^{(s)} \; .$$

The step length, α_s, is chosen so that the "downhill" property is guaranteed if (2.12) is forced at every step.

The fact that $\underline{\delta}^{(s)}$ contains $\underline{z}_p$ in place of $\underline{z}^{(s+1)}$ and that $\underline{\gamma}^{(s)}$ has to be approximated are two approximations to the true symmetric rank one algorithm. Convergence in $\underline{\gamma}^{(s)}$ will require $\lim_{s\to\infty} \phi_s = 1$. Then the exact algorithm converges on some variable metric algorithm in the sense that the difference between their direction vectors (and hence iterates) vanishes as $s\to\infty$ (suggesting a rather tight convergence test must be used). As each pair $\underline{z}^{(s)}, Q^{(s)}$ may be regarded as fresh arbitrary starts, the interpretation of their convergent values is unimpaired in terms of standard variable metric theory. But these two approximations prevent any appeal to convergence theorems from that standard theory. It remains to prove convergence, and independence of the starts, to the required variable metric algorithm and thus establish the legitimacy or our adaptation of such an algorithm.

4. PARAMETER RESTRICTIONS AND PROOF OF CONVERGENCE

We prove that $Q^{(s)}$ and $\underline{z}^{(s)}$ obtained from the iterations (3.25) and (3.26) converge simultaneously on their fixed points:

$$Q^{(p)} = \lim_{s\to\infty} Q^{(s)} \quad \text{and} \quad \underline{z}^{(p)} = \lim_{s\to\infty} \underline{z}^{(s)} \tag{4.1}$$

We consider an arbitrary positive definite, symmetric and normalised matrix, $Q^{(0)}$, as a start, and arbitrary fixed values for $\underline{z}_p$ and $\underline{z}^d$. $\underline{z}^{(0)}$ then follows by (2.11a). We derive a necessary and sufficient condition for convergence in this algorithm, and hence a simple convergence test.

4.1 Steplength restrictions

Certain restrictions must be imposed a priori on the steps generated by (3.25) and (3.26) in order that these iterates shall conform exactly to the algorithm derived in the previous section. A variable metric algorithm requires that $\underline{z}^{(s)}$ must satisfy (2.12) and yet at the same time be the constrained minimiser of w for the current $Q^{(s)}$. The latter requirement ensures that each $Q^{(s)}$ remains within the possibility set for Q; i.e. that each $Q^{(s)}$ is positive definite, symmetric and normalised. The imposition of these conditions on (3.25) guarantees both that the second order condition for a minimum is observed, and also that the integrability condition on $\underline{z}^{(s)}$ is satisfied at each s. Without forcing such restrictions we ultimately destroy optimising behaviour as the rationale for the choice of $\underline{z}_p$ in our model of planning behaviour, as well as any assurance that a consistent preference ordering in fact underlies an observed choice, $\underline{z}_p$.

Now one, and only one, of α_s and ϕ_s is subject to choice at step s. That choice determines the step length, and the sequence of those values the convergence path. Therefore the required prior restrictions may be imposed by restricting the values of α_s or ϕ_s available for choice.

From this observation we have a starting point for proving convergence. The argument which follows is largely technical. To preserve its flow we have relegated all but the simplest proofs to appendix B (in an ordering conformable to that of the text).

Since (3.25) and (3.26) presume that $\underline{z}^d$ contains the true unconstrained optimum of (2.3) and that $\underline{q}=0$, we can reset either $\underline{z}^d$ or $\underline{q}$, according to the relevant interpretation, after convergence. This point therefore does not affect questions of convergence or its uniqueness.

Theorem 1:

(2.12) holds, with any arbitrary $\underline{z}^d$ and $\underline{z}_p$, if $0 \leq \alpha_{s-1} \leq 2$ is used in (3.26); and strict inequality is observed if $0 < \alpha_{s-1} < 2$.

In order to show the conditions under which $Q^{(s)}$ remains within the possibility set for Q we need only find those conditions preserving its positive definiteness. (3.25) ensures symmetry, and the normalisation can be imposed at each step.

Theorem 2:

$Q^{(s)}$ is positive definite (positive semi-definite) if and only if $\phi_{s-1} > 0$ ($\phi_{s-1} \geq 0$), given $Q^{(s-1)}$ positive definite.

Theorems 1 and 2 set the bounds on α_s and ϕ_s so that (2.12) is satisfied and $\underline{z}^{(s)}$ remains the optimiser of (2.4).

4.2 The necessary and sufficient conditions for the convergence of (3.25) and (3.26)

We turn to proving convergence. The points of particular interest are (i) to show global convergence in both $\underline{z}^{(s)}$ and $Q^{(s)}$, (ii) to find a convergence test for both, (iii) to demonstrate that $\underline{z}^{(p)}$ and $Q^{(p)}$ are independent of the start (done in the following section), and (iv) to show consistent values of α_s and ϕ_s, always exist within the restrictions imposed by theorems 1 and 2.

Theorem 3:

(i) $c^{(s)} > 0$ (ii) $b^{(s)} \geq 0$ (iii) $b^{(s)} - c^{(s)} \leq 0$;

all $s \geq 0$ if $\phi_{s-1} > 0$

Proof:

(i) by theorem 2; (ii) obvious since $P^{(s)}$ is idempotent;

(iii) from $b^{(s)} - c^{(s)} = -\underline{\delta}^{(s)\prime} Q^{(s)} P^{(s)} \underline{\delta}^{(s)}$.

Corollary 1:

$\phi_{s-1} > 1$ implies $Q^{(s)} - Q^{(s-1)}$ positive definite

$0 < \phi_{s-1} < 1$ implies $Q^{(s-1)} - Q^{(s)}$ positive definite

Proof:

Obvious from theorem 3 and (3.25).

Corollary 2:

$(\phi_s - 1)a^{(s)} \leqslant 0$ all $s \geqslant 0$, $\phi_s \geqslant 0$

Proof:

$\alpha_s > 0$; by theorem 1, in (3.26) with denominator written as $\phi_s(b^{(s)} - c^{(s)}) - b^{(s)} \leqslant 0$ (from theorem 3).

Corollary 3:

Two possible regimes for α_s and ϕ_s now exist at each step s:

either $a^{(s)} < 0$ when $\phi_s \geqslant 1$ and $\alpha_s \varepsilon[0, \min(2, \frac{a^{(s)}}{b^{(s)} - c^{(s)}})]$

or $a^{(s)} \geqslant 0$ when $0 \leqslant \phi_s \leqslant 1$ and $\alpha_s \varepsilon[0, \min(2, a^{(s)}/b^{(s)})]$.

Both intervals on α_s are closed.

Corollary 3 states that the values of α_s and ϕ_s are related through a hyperbola (reproduced in figures 1 and 2) as shown by (3.26). But since $b^{(s)} - c^{(s)} \leqslant 0$ for all s, whatever the start, we need only consider the two regimes $a^{(s)} < 0$ or $a^{(s)} > 0$.

Combining the results so far we require simultaneously the following: α_s in [0,2] to preserve (2.12); $\phi_s > 0$ so that $Q^{(s+1)}$ is positive definite all s; plus α_s and ϕ_s values consistent with those restrictions and (3.26). All these restrictions are satisfied if we honour the inequalities of corollary 3.

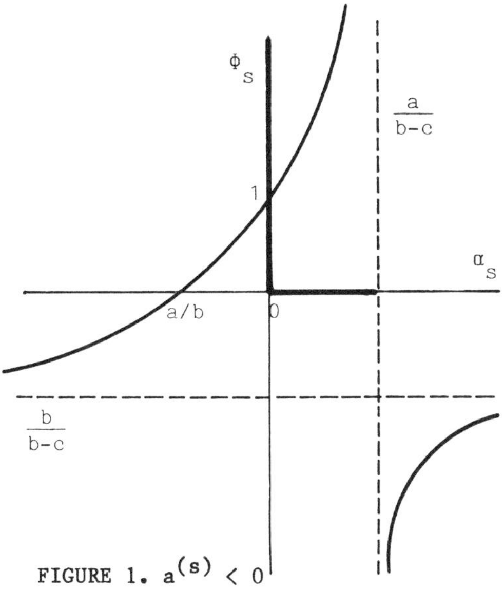

FIGURE 1. $a^{(s)} < 0$

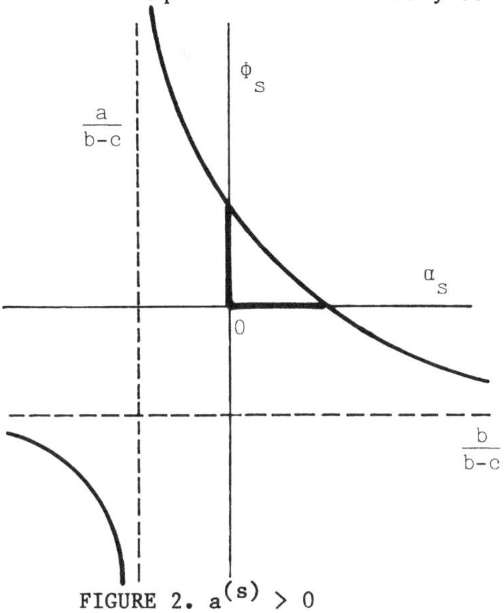

FIGURE 2. $a^{(s)} > 0$

Next we need expressions for all quantities in terms of their previous values. We take (3.25). Next (3.26) implies

$$\underline{\delta}^{(s)} = (I-\alpha_{s-1}P^{(s-1)})\underline{\delta}^{(s-1)} \qquad (4.2)$$

Then we can obtain

$$a^{(s)} = a^{(s-1)} - \alpha_{s-1}b^{(s-1)} \qquad (4.3)$$

$$b^{(s)} = b^{(s-1)} - \frac{\alpha_{s-1}}{a^{(s-1)}}(b^{(s-1)})^2 \qquad (4.4)$$

$$c^{(s)} - b^{(s)} = c^{(s-1)} - b^{(s-1)} \alpha_{s-1}(2-\alpha_{s-1})(b^{(s-1)} - c^{(s-1)}) \qquad (4.5)$$
$$+ \left(\frac{\phi_{s-1}{}^{-1}}{c^{(s-1)}}\right)\left[c^{(s-2)} + \alpha_{s-1}(b^{(s-1)} - c^{(s-1)})\right]^2 + \frac{\alpha_{s-1}}{a^{(s-1)}}\left(b^{(s-1)}\right)^2$$

which are derived in appendix A, theorems 1A, 2A and 3A.

Corollary 4:

(i) if $a^{(0)} > 0$; $a^{(s-1)} \geqslant a^{(s)} \geqslant 0$ ⎫ all $s \geqslant 1$

(ii) if $a^{(0)} < 0$; $a^{(s)} \leqslant a^{(s-1)} < 0$ ⎭

(iii) $\lim_{s\to\infty}(a^{(s)}, b^{(s)}, c^{(s)})$ = nonzero constants iff $\lim_{s\to\infty} \alpha_s = 0$

(iv) $a^{(s)}/b^{(s)}$ = constant all $s \geqslant 0$.

Proof:

(i), (ii) use (4.3), and the limits on α_s from corollary 3 plus theorem 3.
(iii) from (4.3), (4.4) and (4.5); note $\lim_{s\to\infty} \alpha_s = 0$ implies $\lim_{s\to\infty} \phi_s = 1$.
(iv) from (4.3) and (4.4) together.

Corollary 4 shows that $a^{(s)} \neq 0$ for any finite s unless $\alpha_{s-1} = a^{(s-1)}/b^{(s-1)}$ is used following a start of $a^{(0)} > 0$. This possibility will be excluded until the discussion following theorem 6 below.

Theorem 4:

A necessary and sufficient condition for the simultaneous convergence of $\underline{z}^{(s)}$ and $Q^{(s)}$ to their respective fixed points is $\lim_{s\to\infty} \alpha_s = 0$. Hence α_s small enough is the convergence test.

4.3 Convergence for the case of $a^{(0)} < 0$

The start, only in the form of the sign of $a^{(0)}$, dictates entirely which regime is relevant. If convergence is guaranteed in general when $a^{(0)} < 0$, it can only be because the upper bound on $\alpha_s \leqslant a^{(0)}/(b^{(s)} - c^{(s)})$ reduces to zero for large enough s. A similar approach does not hold good if $a^{(0)} > 0$ since then the upper bound on $\alpha_s \leqslant a^{(s)}/b^{(s)}$ is constant and non-zero.

Theorem 5 :

$\lim_{s\to\infty} \alpha_s = 0$ is guaranteed, if $a^{(0)} < 0$, by $\lim_{s\to\infty} a^{(s)}/(b^{(s)} - c^{(s)}) = 0$ provided only that, if $\alpha_s = \lambda_s a^{(s)}/(b^{(s)} - c^{(s)})$ defines λ_s, λ_s is chosen in the nonempty interval $[\lambda_{min}, \lambda_{max}]$.

$$\text{Here } \lambda_{min} = \max\left[0, \frac{(b^{(s)}-c^{(s)})(2a^{(s)}+c^{(s)})}{(a^{(s)})^2 + (2a^{(s)}+c^{(s)})b^{(s)}}\right]$$

$$\text{and } \lambda_{max} = \min\left[\frac{2(b^{(s)}-c^{(s)})}{a^{(s)}}, 1\right]$$

Corollary 5:

If $a^{(0)} < 0$ and λ_{s-1} each satisfies theorem 5, then λ_{min} is a nonincreasing and λ_{max} a nondecreasing function of $s \geqslant 0$.

Provided only that $a^{(0)} < 0$ and λ_s is chosen as in theorem 5, we now have guaranteed simultaneous convergence to $\underline{z}^{(p)}$ and $Q^{(p)}$ for any arbitrary $Q^{(0)}$, $\underline{z}_p$ and $\underline{z}^d$. Moreover, corollary 5 shows that if λ_0 satisfies theorem 5, then any λ_s, $s \geqslant 1$, which is in the interval $[\lambda_{min}, \lambda_{max}]$ computed at the start (s=0) will also satisfy theorem 5. The simplest strategy is to select λ_0 to satisfy theorem 5 and set $\lambda_s = \lambda_0$ all $s \geqslant 1$.

4.4 Extensions to theorem 5

Theorem 5 effectively screens out certain paths to the convergence point. Principally these are the inefficient paths in which $\underline{z}^{(s)}$ is allowed to meander at each step either without progress towards $\underline{z}_p$ or without introducing new information on the objective function; that is without forcing the downhill property or the positive definiteness of $Q^{(s)}$. Omission of either of these characteristics is anyway illegitimate in a variable metric algorithm, which is why they must be excluded here.

Two particular cases of potential convergence difficulties are that mentioned in corollary 6 below and that when $a^{(0)} \geq 0$. It turns out that (3.25) and (3.26) will "jam up" in these cases whereas the exact algorithm does not. The former difficulty is ruled out as an inefficient convergence path. The latter difficulty is treated after the convergence theory for $a^{(0)} < 0$ has been completed.

Corollary 6:

The selection of $\alpha_s = a^{(0)}/(a^{(0)} + b^{(0)})$ is excluded if α_s is chosen according to theorem 5 when $a^{(0)} < 0$.

Corollary 7:

$c^{(s)} \geq c^{(s-1)} > 0$ all s given $a^{(0)} < 0$, with weak inequality only if $\alpha_{s-1}=0$.

Theorem 6:

The average (hence asymptotic) rate of convergence of (3.25) and (3.26) is maximised by

$$\lambda_s^* = \min \left[1, \frac{\alpha_s^*(b^{(s)} - c^{(s)})}{a^{(s)}}\right] \quad \text{where} \quad \alpha_s^* = \frac{\underline{\delta}^{(s)\prime} P^{(s)} \underline{\delta}^{(s)}}{\underline{\delta}^{(s)\prime} P^{(s)\prime} P^{(s)} \underline{\delta}^{(s)}} \geq 1 .$$

Comment:

Since in practice α_s is likely to be restricted by corollary 3 so that α_s^* is an infeasible choice, it is more useful to implement the algorithm only for values $\lambda_s \leq \lambda_s^*$. That corresponds to selecting $\alpha_s \leq \alpha_s^*$ such that $\alpha_s^* - \alpha_s$ is minimised. Moreover λ_s^* never implies $\alpha_s = a^{(0)}/(a^{(0)} + b^{(0)})$.

Corollary 8:

If $\alpha_s > \alpha_s^*$ then $\underline{z}^{(s+1)}$ overshoots $\underline{z}_p$ in that $\underline{\delta}^{(s)}$ and $\underline{\delta}^{(s-1)}$ form an obtuse angle; if $\alpha_s < \alpha_s^*$ then $\underline{z}^{(s+1)}$ undershoots $\underline{z}_p$. Conjugate directions can only be generated when $\alpha_s = \alpha_s^*$.

Comment:

The selection of $\lambda_s \leq \lambda_s^*$ means we approach the convergence point from "one side".

Theorem 6 shows that $\alpha_s \neq \alpha_s^*$ must be chosen whenever $\lambda_s^* = 1$. Indeed, by theorem 5, some s_1 ixists large enough such that $\lambda_s^* = 1$ for all $s \geqslant s_1$. Since $\alpha_s = \alpha_s^*$ is the only case where conjugate directions may be generated, that possibility never arises when $\alpha_s^* > a^{(s)}/(b^{(s)}-c^{(s)})$; and therefore that possibility never arises for any $s \geqslant s_1$. At least, the later steps of our algorithm cannot generate such direction vectors, and they never need be chosen at any earlier stage either.

4.5 Convergence for the case $a^{(0)} \geqslant 0$

Now consider the case of $a^{(0)} \geqslant 0$, to complete a global convergence theory.

Theorem 7:

(i) $\lim_{s\to\infty} (a^{(s)}, b^{(s)}, \phi_s) = 0$ if $a^{(0)} > 0$

(ii) if $\alpha_s = a^{(s)}/b^{(s)}$ then $a^{(s+1)} = 0$ and $\phi_s = 0$ given $a^{(0)} \geqslant 0$.

(iii) an $s=s_0$ exists for which $Q^{(s+1)}$ is singular under (i) or (ii).

Thus if $a^{(0)} \geqslant 0$, the algorithm must be restarted after $a^{(s)} = 0$ has been reached; and $a^{(s)} = 0$ can always be reached in one step. For example, using theorem 7(ii) at s=0 ensures $a^{(1)} = 0$. And then when we restart we will need $a^{(2)} < 0$. The justification for these remarks is, of course, that in an algorithm such as (3.25) and (3.26) any step $Q^{(s)}$ may be regarded as a fresh arbitrary start for $Q^{(s+1)}$, where the associated $\underline{\tilde{z}}^{(s+1)}$ can be obtained by (2.11a) for the $\underline{\tilde{z}}$ iterates. Therefore we need only find some small alterations to the singular $Q^{(s)}$ such that $a^{(s+1)} < 0$ when $a^{(s)} = 0$ has been achieved, and then proceed by theorem 5 as before. It remains to be shown that such a $Q^{(s+1)}$ exists and to provide a method for computing it. This we do next.

Returning to the exact variable metric algorithm which we wish to simulate - that is (3.15) and (3.19) incorporating (3.21) and (3.24) - we find that, when $a^{(s)} = 0$, $\hat{\alpha}_s$ reduces to

$$\beta_s = \frac{\underline{\delta}^{(s)\prime} Q^{(s+1)} \underline{\tilde{z}}^{(s)}}{\underline{\delta}^{(s)\prime} Q^{(s+1)} P^{(s)} (Q^{(s)})^{-1} Q^{(s+1)} \underline{\delta}^{(s)} - \underline{\delta}^{(s)\prime} Q^{(s+1)} \underline{\delta}^{(s)}} \tag{4.6}$$

Since we do not, and eventually cannot, generate conjugate directions the numerator of β_s (i.e. $\underline{\gamma}^{(s)'}\ \tilde{\underline{z}}^{(s)}$) is non-zero. Therefore the exact algorithm would not stop even if (3.25) and (3.26) does so.

Define $dQ^{(s)} = Q^{(s+1)} - Q^{(s)}$ and $d\tilde{\underline{z}}^{(s)} = \tilde{\underline{z}}^{(s+1)} - \tilde{\underline{z}}^{(s)}$. We require these two quantities such that $Q^{(s+1)}$ is positive definite and $a^{(s+1)} < 0$. Consider small values for $dQ^{(s)}$ and $d\tilde{\underline{z}}^{(s)}$ so that linear approximations for linking them are justified. Reformulate the policy optimisation problem in the form presented by Theil (1964): (2.11a) becomes

$$\tilde{\underline{x}}^{(s)} = -(H^{*\prime}Q^{(s)}H^*)^{-1}H^{*\prime}Q^{(s)}\hat{\underline{b}} \qquad (4.7)$$

and $$\tilde{\underline{y}}^{(s)} = R\tilde{\underline{x}}^{(s)} + \underline{b} \quad \text{for} \quad H^{*\prime} = (R' \vdots I) \quad \text{and} \quad \hat{\underline{b}}' = (\underline{b}' \vdots 0) \qquad (4.8)$$

Direct calculation shows (using $H^*\tilde{\underline{x}} + \hat{\underline{b}} = \tilde{\underline{z}}$) (12)

$$d\tilde{\underline{z}}^{(s)} = -(\tilde{\underline{z}}^{(s)'} \otimes H'(H^{*\prime}Q^{(s)}H^*)^{-1}H^{*\prime})\ \mathrm{vec}(dQ^{(s)}) \qquad (4.9)$$

There is therefore a neighbourhood about $\tilde{\underline{z}}^{(s)}$ and $Q^{(s)}$ in which, given a preference system and its optimiser, we can calculate the new optimiser for any small perturbation in that preference system.

Now the required $\tilde{\underline{z}}^{(s+1)}$ and $Q^{(s+1)}$ evidently do exist. We could use (3.25) and (3.26) to $s = s_o$. Then we must pick $dQ^{(s)}$ and $d\tilde{\underline{z}}^{(s)}$ to be small and such that $Q^{(s+1)}$ is symmetric, normalised and positive definite, and such that $a^{(s+1)} < 0$. The latter in terms of $dQ^{(s)}$ and $d\tilde{\underline{z}}^{(s)}$ (to the same linear approximation) is in this case:

$$a^{(s+1)} \simeq \underline{\delta}^{(s)'}Q^{(s)}d\tilde{\underline{z}}^{(s)} + \underline{\delta}^{(s)'}dQ^{(s)}\tilde{\underline{z}}^{(s)} - d\tilde{\underline{z}}^{(s)'}Q^{(s)}\tilde{\underline{z}}^{(s)} \qquad (4.10)$$

Thus $a^{(s+1)} < 0$ is implied if $d\underline{z}^{(s)}$ and $dQ^{(s)}$ are chosen such that the right of (4.10) is negative. So we have to solve for at least $\frac{1}{2}n(n+\frac{3}{2})$ elements subject to n+3 constraints. A solution always exists.

Whereas the preceding argument is useful to establish the legitimacy of stepping to $Q^{(s_o+1)}$ and $\tilde{\underline{z}}^{(s_o+1)}$, we may simplify it for performing the actual calculations. Use (3.25) and (3.26) to $s = s_o$. Then revert to (3.15) and (3.19) and consider one step of arbitrary distance along that direction vector, subject only to (2.12) and the restrictions on $Q^{(s+1)}$. Suppose some distance β_s^* is chosen, and that (3.15) is also used. This much is merely to switch to simulating a different exact variable metric algorithm from the one we started with - but with the same "downhill" property. Now insert the familiar approximations (3.24) and (3.22) for $\underline{\gamma}^{(s)}$ and $\underline{\delta}^{(s)}$ in (3.15) and the remainder of (3.19) to yield:

$$\tilde{\underline{z}}^{(s+1)} = \tilde{\underline{z}}^{(s)} + \alpha_s^* P^{(s)} \underline{\delta}^{(s)} \qquad \text{for} \quad \alpha_s^* = \beta_s^*(\phi_s - 1) \tag{4.11}$$

$$Q^{(s+1)} = Q^{(s)} + \left(\frac{\phi_s - 1}{c^{(s)}}\right) Q^{(s)} \underline{\delta}^{(s)} \underline{\delta}^{(s)\prime} Q^{(s)} \tag{4.12}$$

Restrictions on α_s^* and ϕ_s come from theorems 1 and 2; $\phi_s > 0$ and $0 < \alpha_s^* < 2$. Finally define a constant, d, by choosing

$$0 < \frac{(\phi_s - 1)(a^{(s)} + d)}{(\phi - 1) b^{(s)} - \phi_s c^{(s)}} = \beta_s^*(\phi_s - 1) = \alpha_s^* < 2 \tag{4.13}$$

Since $a^{(s)} = b^{(s)} = 0$, (4.13) reduces to

$$\alpha_s^* = \frac{(\phi_s - 1) d}{-\phi_s c^{(s)}} \tag{4.14}$$

In order to ensure the chosen β_s^* is such that $\alpha_s^* > 0$ we take $d < 0$; and since corollary 1 indicates $\phi_s > 1$ if $Q^{(s+1)}$ is to be positive definite in this modification, $\alpha_s^* < 2$ is ensured by $-2\phi_s c^{(s)}/(\phi_s - 1) < d < 0$. However, within these limits d is a free choice; $-2c^{(s)} < d < 0$ is adequate. We can continue (3.25) and (3.26) from the new start, $Q^{(s+1)}$, thus obtained.

5. ON THE UNIQUENESS AND THE LOCAL VALIDITY OF THE RESULTS

We must now consider the independence of the convergence point $Q^{(p)}$ from the arbitrary start $Q^{(0)}$ given and arbitrary $\underline{z}^d$ and $\underline{z}_p$. $\underline{z}_p$ is by observation or hypothesis (in the form of the axioms of choice in (2.3)) a unique outcome of a rational choice, so it is the uniqueness of $Q^{(p)}$ which is at issue. By (2.13) and the argument following, $\underline{z}^{(p)}$ is the unique point nearest $\underline{z}_p$ which is both feasible and consistent with convexity in (2.4). Given a unique decision to reset either $\underline{q}$ or $\underline{z}^d$ after convergence we may transfer any independence results to $\tilde{\underline{z}}_p$. Indeed $Q^{(p)}$ is unaffected by the resetting.

The algorithm ensures that the second order conditions for a minimum are satisfied at $\tilde{\underline{z}}^{(p)}$. (2.4) is therefore convex in $\tilde{\underline{z}}$ and concave in μ. By hypothesis therefore $w(\tilde{\underline{z}})$ has similar properties with the consequence that $\underline{\mu}_p$ (and equivalently $\underline{\mu}^{(p)}$) was uniquely chosen by the planners. These remarks follow from the saddle point property of constrained optimisation:

$$L(\tilde{\underline{z}},\underline{\mu}^{(p)}) > L(\tilde{\underline{z}}^{(p)},\underline{\mu}^{(p)}) > L(\tilde{\underline{z}}^{(p)},\underline{\mu}) \text{ for } \underline{\mu}\neq\underline{\mu}^{(p)},\ \tilde{\underline{z}}\neq\tilde{\underline{z}}^{(p)} \text{ in F} \quad (5.1)$$

Indeed substituting (2.11) into (2.10) verifies (5.1) locally. The problem remains whether other versions of (2.10) are consistent with the same saddle point, i.e. whether $Q^{(p)}$ depends on $Q^{(0)}$ or the route taken (the λ_s sequence).

5.1 Conditions for independence of the start

Suppose $Q_1 = Q^{(p)}$ and $Q_2 = Q_1 + \Delta Q$, $\Delta Q \neq 0$, are considered for generating $\tilde{\underline{z}}^{(p)}$. It is convenient to return to the notation of (4.7) and (4.8) because ΔQ is singular by virtue of the normalisation. Q_1 and Q_2 both generate $\tilde{\underline{z}}^{(p)}$, $\underline{\mu}^{(p)}$ via

$$\tilde{\underline{x}}^{(p)} = -(H^{*\prime}Q_1H^*)^{-1}H^{*\prime}Q_1\hat{\underline{b}} = -(H^{*\prime}Q_2H^*)^{-1}H^{*\prime}Q_2\hat{\underline{b}} \quad (5.2)$$

iff $\quad H^{*\prime}\Delta QH^*\tilde{\underline{x}}^{(p)} + H^{*\prime}\Delta Q\hat{\underline{b}} = 0. \quad (5.3)$

But $\quad H^*\tilde{\underline{x}}^{(p)} + \hat{\underline{b}} = \tilde{\underline{z}}^{(p)}$ so (5.3) implies $H^{*\prime}\Delta Q\tilde{\underline{z}}^{(p)} = 0.$

Similarly if also $\underline{\mu}^{(p)} = (I\vdots 0)Q_1\tilde{\underline{z}}^{(p)} = (I\vdots 0)Q_2\tilde{\underline{z}}^{(p)}$ then $\Delta Q\tilde{\underline{z}}^{(p)} = 0$.
Overall we now have

$$\begin{bmatrix} I & 0 \\ R' & I \end{bmatrix} \Delta Q\tilde{\underline{z}}^{(p)} = 0 \quad \text{or} \quad \Delta Q\tilde{\underline{z}}^{(p)} = 0 \quad (5.4)$$

Notice that (5.4) shows that the gradient vector of (2.3) has been uniquely estimated at $\underline{z}^{(p)}$. That ensures that all the marginal rates of substitution at $\underline{z}^{(p)}$

$$m_{ij} = \frac{dz_i}{dz_j} = -\frac{\partial w/\partial z_j}{\partial w/\partial z_i} \qquad \begin{matrix} i = 1 \ldots n,\ j = i+1 \ldots n \\ (m_{ii} = -1,\ m_{ij} = m_{ji}^{-1}) \end{matrix} \quad (5.5)$$

are uniquely estimated. The same remarks then apply, after resetting either $\underline{z}^d$ or $\underline{q}$, for (2.3) at $\underline{z}_p$. But the gradient is all that this algorithm has estimated.

To establish independence from the start we must further check if more than one of the candidate matrices, such as Q_1 and Q_2, which conform to (5.4) are also consistent with the a priori known gradient $(\partial w/\partial \underline{z})_{\underline{z}^d} = \underline{g}(\underline{z}^d) = 0$, the normalisation $(Q_1)_{11} = (Q_2)_{11} = 1$; the known (estimated) gradient $\underline{g}(\underline{z}^{(p)})$ and the fact that w is purely quadratic. If so, is there also more than one ordering of Q_{ij} elements (the estimated preference ordering) consistent with all those restrictions? The latter question is, of course, the only point at issue here but it is instructive to go as far as possible in answering the former problem in order to answer the latter. This we do by showing that the curvature of a quadratic surface is fixed when two gradients and a normalisation are known.

5.2 Proof of local uniqueness

Take the case $Q = Q_1$. From (5.5) we can write out $\frac{1}{2}n(n-1)$ equations in $\frac{1}{2}n(n-1)$ unknowns, if we pretend to know Q_{ii}, i=1 ... n, as:

$$m_{ij} \sum_{k \neq i} Q_{ik}\tilde{z}_k^{(p)} + \sum_{k \neq j} Q_{jk}\tilde{z}_k^{(p)} = m_{ij}Q_{ii}\tilde{z}_i^{(p)} - Q_{jj}\tilde{z}_j^{(p)} \qquad (5.6)$$

for i=1 ... n and j=1 ... (i-1) for each i. Now (5.6) can be rewritten as

$$B\underline{q}^* = \underline{h} \qquad (5.7)$$

B is a square matrix of order $\frac{1}{2}n(n-1)$ constructed by the rules given in Appendix C; $q_k^* = Q_{ij}$ and $h_k = \left(m_{ij}Q_{ii}\tilde{z}_i^{(p)} - Q_{jj}\tilde{z}_j^{(p)}\right)$ where k = i+j-2 for i=2 ... n and j=1 ... (i-1) (i.e. vectorising m_{ij} and Q_{ij}). (5.7) has no unique solution for $\underline{q}^*$ if $r(B, \underline{h}) \leqslant r(b) < \frac{1}{2}n(n-1)$ but no solution at all if $r(B,\underline{h}) \geqslant r(B) \neq \frac{1}{2}n(n-1)$; where r(.) denotes rank. There is no reason why, in general when $m_{ij} \neq 0$ and $\tilde{z}^{(p)} \neq 0$, $r(B, \underline{h}) \leqslant r(B)$ whether or not B is singular - indeed there is no reason why B should in general be singular[13]. Weighting the elements of B by Q_{ik} and Q_{jk} in (5.7) does not provide linear dependency except by chance; and, even if it did, replacing each column of B in turn by $\underline{h}$ would destroy that linear dependency since the elements of $\underline{h}$ introduce new information via $Q_{ii}\tilde{z}_i^{(p)}$ and $Q_{jj}\tilde{z}_j^{(p)}$ which are themselves not wholly determined by the elements of B or their components. Thus, except for a set of measure zero, $r(B, h) = r(B) = \frac{1}{2}n(n-1)$; and to have no solution to (5.7) at all for $\underline{q}^*$ would be a contradiction as at least one exists in $Q^{(p)}$. Thus $\underline{q}^*$ is uniquely determined as a function of $\underline{g}(\underline{z}^{(p)})$, $g(\underline{z}^d)$ and Q_{ii}.

Now to deal with Q_{ii} i=1 ... n. Consider the two dimensional example in figure 3.

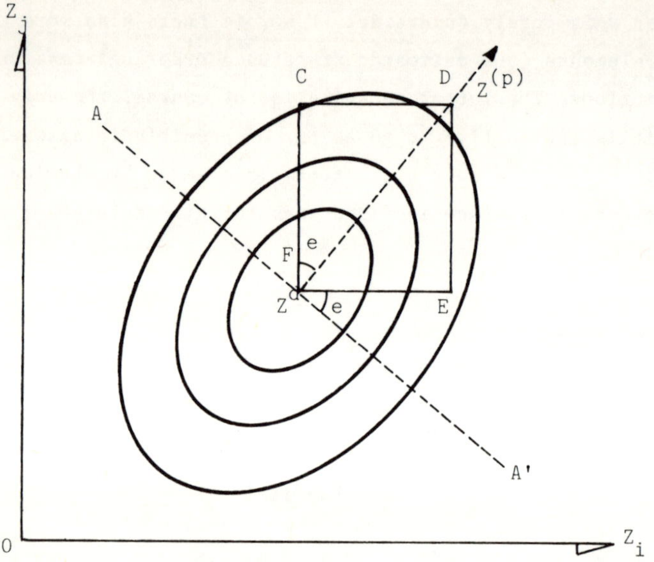

FIGURE 3. A projection of the priorities onto a 2 dimensional subspace of $\underline{z}$ space

If we treat the metric as fixed, the quadratic nature of (2.4) shows a constant curvature in each dimension as:

$$\frac{\partial^2 w}{\partial z_j^2} = \frac{g_j(\underline{z}^{(p)}) - g_j(\underline{z}^d)}{z_j^{(p)} - z_j^d} \qquad \text{(i.e. } z_i \text{ held constant)}$$

(5.8)

and

$$\frac{\partial^2 w}{\partial z_i^2} = \frac{g_i(\underline{z}^{(p)}) - g_i(\underline{z}^d)}{z_i^{(p)} - z_i^d} \qquad \text{(i.e. } z_j \text{ held constant)}$$

where $g(\underline{z}^{(p)})$ and $g(\underline{z}^d)$ are the two known gradients.

The implication of (5.8) is that we cover the whole set of candidate matrices for Q by expansion or contraction of the metric a ›ng AA' using, say, multiplicative factors $0 < \psi < \infty$, but with no changes orthogonally (i.e. through $\underline{z}^d$ and $\underline{z}^{(p)}$). Consider Q_2 as the alternative to Q_1 which gave figure 3. The projection of DE onto AA' has length $(z_j^{(p)} - z_j^d)\sin\Theta$, and that of DC length $(z_i^{(p)} - z_i^d)\cos\Theta$. Now $\psi \neq 1$ is the metric change if $\Delta Q \neq 0$, so these projection lengths become $\psi(z_j^{(p)} - z_j^d)\tan\Theta$ and $\psi(z_i^{(p)} - z_i^d)\cot\Theta$ respectively. In that case

$$\frac{\partial^2 w}{\partial z_j^2} = \frac{g_j(\underline{z}^{(p)}) - g_j(\underline{z}^d)}{\psi(z_j^{(p)} - z_j^d)\cot\Theta} \quad \text{and} \quad \frac{\partial^2 w}{\partial z_i^2} = \frac{g_i(\underline{z}^{(p)}) - g_i(z_i^d)}{\psi(z_i^{(p)} - z_i^d)\tan\Theta} \tag{5.9}$$

since we have g(.) independent of ψ and Θ. Since $\tan\Theta = \dfrac{z_i^{(p)} - z_i^d}{z_j^{(p)} - z_j^d}$ we have finally

$$\left[\frac{\partial^2 w/\partial z_i^2}{\partial^2 w/\partial z_j^2}\right]_{\psi\neq 1} = \frac{(g_j(\underline{z}^{(p)}) - g_j(\underline{z}^d))(z_i^{(p)} - z_i^d)}{(g_i(\underline{z}^{(p)}) - g_i(\underline{z}^d))(z_j^{(p)} - z_j^d)} = \left[\frac{\partial^2 w/\partial z_i^2}{\partial^2 w/\partial z_j^2}\right]_{\psi=1} \tag{5.10}$$

So the ratio of the second derivatives (curvatures) is invariant to ψ and Θ, and hence all candidate Q matrices, whereas the curvatures themselves are not.

To generalise for n dimensions take $z_i = z_1$ and treat the above argument as that for the two dimensional projection of (2.4) onto (z_1, z_j) subspace and repeat for j=2 ... n. (5.4) implies that Q_2, say, can be represented by expanding or contracting the metric along AA', but not along $\underline{z}^d$ to $\underline{z}^{(p)}$, by the set of factors $\psi_j \varepsilon (0,\infty)$, one for each z_j. Then each other candidate gives rise to a new set of ψ_j values. So the argument generalises directly. Then the ratio Q_{jj}/Q_{11} for j=2 ... n are uniquely determined. But we anyway forced the normalisation $Q_{11} = 1$. So we have a Q matrix unique only up to a factor of proportionality and up to additions orthogonal to the given $\tilde{\underline{z}}^{(p)}$. After resetting $\underline{z}^d$ or $\underline{q}$, the latter orthogonality is to $\tilde{\underline{z}}_p$ itself.

5.3 Comments on the restriction of locally unique results

The result just obtained is stronger than necessary when a preference ordering only is required, but it is important to emphasise the local nature of the estimated objective function. The significance of this point lies in the interpretation that may be given to the results obtained from (3.25) and

(3.26).

If we take a set of vectors which form a basis spanning $\underline{z}$ space, we can regard each member of that set as a notional basic policy component mutually uncorrelated with the others. The observed $\tilde{\underline{z}}_p$ is spanned by a subset of that basis. Then (5.4) shows we have no uniquely estimated preferences over those components which do not enter a basis for $\tilde{\underline{z}}_p$ itself. The latter policy components are, of course, those not chosen by the planners. Thus we have no estimate of preferences over subspaces orthogonal to that containing $\tilde{\underline{z}}_p$ but a unique estimate for that in which $\tilde{\underline{z}}_p$ lies. This is as it should be. Working from one $\tilde{\underline{z}}_p$, it is unreasonable to expect to be able to deduce relative priorities over policies or components that have been rejected. In other circumstances these rejected components may contribute. So if we had more than n linearly independent observations on $\underline{z}_p$ (5.4) could not generally hold. Otherwise, we claim an approximation to $w(\tilde{\underline{z}})$ defined on the subspace of policy space spanned by a basis for $\tilde{\underline{z}}_p$. Moreover, being normalised, Q represents only relative priorities. Thus we can, in any case, extract at most a preference ordering from it, rather than cardinal values. Yet we can extend $Q^{(p)}$ to apply to all policies within a neighbourhood of $\tilde{\underline{z}}_p$ for which that ranking (signs included) is invariant but where (5.4) no longer holds precisely. This is the extent to which we may generalise the local nature of the estimated preferences.

The estimate of $w(\tilde{\underline{z}})$ obtained is therefore local in the following senses: (a) we have only the quadratic approximation at $\tilde{\underline{z}}_p$; (b) knowledge that $\tilde{\underline{z}}_p$ was optimal permits only the assumption of local convexity in $w(\tilde{\underline{z}})$ and we have estimated only that local approximation - multiple turning points may exist in $w(\tilde{z})$ itself; (c) there is a neighbourhood of values over which priority orderings are uniquely determined for each observation on $\tilde{\underline{z}}_p$. Thus, in recognising (c) we have lost nothing in generality because in any event (a) and (b) applied. There is no disadvantage in practical terms to have the estimated preferences only locally valid: it is a special feature of particular significance in problems of social choice that the relative penalties on the policy failures $\tilde{\underline{z}}$ are themselves heavily dependent on the values of those variables (Hughes Hallett (1979b)). For example, the trade-off between unemployment and inflation accepted by a government facing 1% of both will be quite different from that accepted when it faces 20% of both. In recognition of this we have specified $w(\tilde{\underline{z}})$ as potentially nonquadratic. Other studies in this field have attempted to obtain globally valid preference orderings by imposing prior zero restrictions and time invariance on Q. Not only in both exercises below do we find strong evidence which contradicts both these assumptions, but the wildly varying estimates, which result from different forms of these assumptions on the same trial problem, make it impossible to determine which reflect unjustified assumptions and which reflect the preferences (Ancot, Hughes Hallett and Paelinck (1980)). We have relaxed the maintained hypothesis on Q and trade global results for local ones in recognition that in any event no more generality is justified.

6 THE ANALYSIS OF THE REVEALED PREFERENCES IN (2.4)

At convergence the algorithm (3.25) and (3.26) yields an estimate of the true preference function (2.3); being the quadratic approximation (2.4) evaluated at an observed optimal choice $\underline{z}_p$. Now (2.4), when $\underline{q}=0$ and $\underline{z}^d$ are the true desired values, can be separated with respect to time:

$$w = \sum_{i=1}^{T} \sum_{j=1}^{T} \tilde{\underline{z}}_i' Q_{ij} \tilde{\underline{z}}_j \tag{6.1}$$

and again with respect to all variables:

$$w = \sum_{i=1}^{T} \sum_{j=1}^{T} \left(\sum_{k=1}^{n^*+m} \sum_{\ell=1}^{n^*+m} (Q_{ij})_{k\ell} \tilde{z}_{ik} \tilde{z}_{j\ell} \right) \tag{6.2}$$

We may therefore examine the preferences in Q by variables within one time period; or by time periods for one variable; or both. Indeed

$$Q = \begin{bmatrix} Q_{11} & \cdots\cdots & Q_{1T} \\ \vdots & & \vdots \\ Q_{1T} & \cdots\cdots & Q_{TT} \end{bmatrix} \tag{6.3}$$

shows the submatrices of (6.1) for different time periods; each of which has typical element $(Q_{ij})_{k\ell}$ for the two policy variables in (6.2).

The diagonal elements of Q, $(Q_{ii})_{kk}$, i=1 ... T, k=1 ... n*+m, show penalties assigned to squared deviations of variables from their desired values in each period. In particular we will look cross-sectionally to see how the implied preference ranking alters over time and how the relative gaps in that ordering increase or decrease. We will also look at the time series behaviour of those weights in order to rank preferences on any one variable over the planning exercise.

The remainder of the submatrices of order m+n* on the diagonal of Q, Q_{ii} i=1 ... T, show penalties on joint failures, over and above the penalties on the individual failures, to reach desired values of two variables simultaneously at a given moment. Thus, with the example of taxation and government expenditure, pressure to maintain a balanced budget follows from a negative weight on their joint failures in each period. If taxation overshoots its desired value then the penalties are reduced below the weighted sum of their individual penalties whenever government expenditure also does so; but they are increased if it does not. In contrast, if consumption overshoots penalties would presumably be reduced if investment did not, so as not to increase the pressure of aggregate demand unacceptably. Negative off-diagonal elements encourage "extreme" positions, positive elements "intermediate" ones. The variables concerned are revealed to have been considered complements and substitutes, respectively, by the planners.

Finally, the remaining submatrices contain penalties which perform a similar function but for the joint failures at different points of time. Intertemporal penalties may be assigned so that accelerating penalties accrue to persistent failures, to penalise the timing with which a unit failure occurs, or to encourage substitutability or complementarity over time; in addition to the basic pattern of preferences in each time period as set up in the block diagonal components of Q. Examples are, respectively, penalising units of a balance of payments deficit proportionally more the longer it persists; penalising undershooting the employment target proportionally more the closer to an election it occurs; penalising consecutive consumption failures of the same sign, or rewarding a taxation failure and a consecutive public expenditure failure of the same sign, when a balanced budget is desirable in the long run, but a deficit or surplus are permissable in the short term.

Finally there is the choice of resetting $\underline{q}$ or $\underline{z}^d$ after convergence. We have pointed out that if, for any reason, $\underline{z}^a \neq \underline{z}^d$ had been used the true desired values can be obtained by resetting $\underline{z}^d$ so that $\underline{q}=0$; or by resetting $\underline{q}$ whereupon $\underline{z}^d$ is represented in (2.4) by $\underline{z}^a - Q^{-1}\underline{q}$. Thus $\underline{q}$ appears to play no role in the interpretation of the revealed preferences as computed by (3.25) and (3.26).

7. NUMERICAL EXAMPLES

We now use this algorithm for estimating the preferences revealed in American macroeconomic policy in the periods 1933-36 and 1957-62 respectively. The reasons for this choice were as follows.

Firstly, the re-election dates facing American politicians are not determined by them but are known by all in advance; this avoids the problem of interpreting the targets a policy maker has set himself when the date by which we presume that he will wish to reach them is also set by him.

Secondly, these two periods cover well defined political situations whose events provide us with strong prior expectations of what the preferences would be. Both periods start with the economy in a recession following a sustained boom. In as much as there can be a break with previous policies it will be at such moments. The preferences of the administration - and their policies - will have been reassessed in the light of the current situation because those situations, at least, are points of closed loop control in a discrete time planning problem. Both recessions are followed by a presidential election in which the incumbent president and vice-president respectively are candidates.

Thirdly, both periods contain a complete presidency. But the second shows the aftermath to an election in which the administration changes. We see the differences between the preferences of a first term president up for re-election and those of a second term president not up for re-election and uncertain at the time of planning that his vice-president will obtain his party's nomination, and yet most of whose cabinet are quite sure that they will not serve the subsequent administration. Simple comparisons are possible for the Eisenhower and Kennedy administrations; we can observe how preferences alter after an election and in transferring from one administration to another.

Exercise 1 used the model Klein 1 and the details are obtained from a well-known study by Theil (1964). Consumption (C), investment (I) and distribution of income (D) ($D = W_1 - 2\pi$; W_1 = private sector wage bill, π = profits) are selected as targets and W_2 (public sector wage bill), T (tax yield) and G (government expenditure) are available as instruments; allvariables being in constant dollars. Noncontrollables are the constant and a time trend, so uncertainty and closed loop control considerations are confined to the stochastic errors. We took $Q^{(0)} = I$, the identity matrix, $\underline{z}^{(0)}$ and $\underline{z}^{d}$ from Theil.

Exercise 2 used a quarterly model presented by Pindyck (1973). We used the first optimal control example given there. The targets are consumption (C), nonresidential investment (IN), residential investment (IR), prices (P), unemployment (U) and the instruments available are changes in money supply (DM), government expenditure (G) and supertax (TO). C,IN, IR, DM, and G are in constant dollars; P is in an index (1958.4 = 100); U is a fraction of the labour force. TO is defined by Pindyck as a surcharge or threshold (TO 0) but is probably best thought of as discretionary adjustments the authorities may (with increasing penalties) make outside some fixed tax regime. $Q^{(0)}$ is taken to penalise all percentage deviations from $\underline{z}^d$ in each variable equally (but TO twice as much) for each t=1 ... T. Desired values were constant rates of growth 4% for C, G; 6% for IN, IR; 2% for P; whereas TO = 0, U = 2% and DM = 1.4$b were constant from the initial positions since the objective of the exercise was stabilisation. Noncontrollables were the constant and full capacity disposable income, so again uncertainty and closed loop problems are confined to stochastic errors; but, like Pindyck, we have not pursued this aspect.

7.1 The first Roosevelt administration (1933 - 1936)

We start by considering the results of the multiperiod certainty equivalent plans: tables 1 and 2. These are the preferences associated with the closed loop policies. Each period's policies are conditioned on the information available to the planner at the start of that period. Hence the preferences are genuinely revealed (ex post) preferences. After discussing these, we will discuss preferences associated with some open loop policies; in this case those conditioned on the information available to the planners at the start of the administration. A comparison can then be made between our estimate of what they intended to do on assuming office and what they in fact did, particularly as the 1936 election approached.

The revealed preferences in this exercise are analysed in three steps, corresponding to the partitioning of the matrix Q employed in section 6. First we look at the diagonal elements (relative penalties on individual variables at individual time intervals); then the block diagonal submatrices (relative joint penalties at individual time intervals); and finally the off-diagonal submatrices (relative single or joint penalties at two time intervals together).

Three principal results are apparent from table 1, the diagonal elements of Q. First, there is a major difference between 1933-34 and 1936 in the penalties the administration assigned to individual failures. During 1933-34 the descending order of importance was C - G - T - I - D - W_2 (for 1934 the penalties were 1.7, 1.1, .25, .15, .019, .015, respectively). By the re-election year the preference ordering had clearly altered to D - C - I - G - T - W_2

(for 1936, 7.4, 4.8, 1.6, .96, .2, .13, respectively). Both the movement of D from fifth to first position and that of G and T from second and third to fourth and fifth respectively commences in 1935, but neither are complete until 1936.

Table 1. The diagonal elements of Q in exercise 1 (multiperiod certainty equivalent results)

	C	I	D	W_2	T	G
1933	1.000	0.0114	0.0466	0.0310	1.1000	2.6080
1934	1.731	0.1533	0.0198	0.0149	0.2525	1.0860
1935	3.057	0.4744	1.2050	0.0149	0.0043	1.1760
1936	4.801	1.6400	7.4010	0.1342	0.2060	0.9613

Table 2. The block diagonal submatrices of Q in exercise 1 (multiperiod certainty equivalent results)

		C	I	D	W_2	T	G
Q_{11}					1933		
	C	1.00	0.10	0.21	0.17	1.05	1.61
	I	0.10	0.01	0.02	0.02	0.11	0.16
	D	0.21	0.02	0.05	0.04	0.22	0.34
1933	W_2	0.17	0.02	0.04	0.03	0.18	0.28
	T	1.05	0.11	0.22	0.18	1.10	1.69
	G	1.61	0.16	0.34	0.28	1.69	2.60
Q_{22}					1934		
	C	1.73	0.51	0.18	-0.15	0.66	1.37
	I	0.51	0.15	0.05	-0.05	0.20	0.41
	D	0.18	0.05	0.02	-0.02	0.07	0.14
1934	W_2	-0.15	-0.05	-0.02	0.01	-0.06	-0.12
	T	0.66	0.20	0.07	-0.06	0.25	0.52
	G	1.37	0.41	0.14	-0.12	0.52	1.09
Q_{33}					1935		
	C	3.06	1.20	-1.92	-0.03	0.10	1.90
	I	1.20	0.47	-0.75	-0.01	0.04	0.75
	D	-1.92	-0.75	1.21	0.02	-0.06	-1.19
1935	W_2	-0.03	-0.01	0.02	0.00	-0.00	-0.02
	T	0.10	0.04	-0.06	-0.00	0.00	0.06
	G	1.90	0.75	-1.19	-0.02	0.06	1.18
Q_{44}					1936		
	C	4.80	2.81	-5.96	-0.80	-0.99	2.15
	I	2.81	1.64	-3.48	-0.47	-0.58	2.16
	D	-5.96	-3.48	7.40	0.99	1.23	-2.67
1936	W_2	-0.80	-0.47	0.99	0.13	0.17	-0.36
	T	-0.99	-0.58	1.23	0.17	0.21	-0.44
	G	2.15	1.26	-2.67	-0.36	-0.44	0.96

Table 3. Intertemporal penalties for exercise 1
(multiperiod certainty equivalent results)

		C	I	D	W_2	T	G
Q_{12}				1934			
	C	1.31	0.39	0.14	-0.12	0.50	1.04
	I	0.13	0.04	0.01	-0.01	0.05	0.11
	D	0.28	0.08	0.03	-0.02	0.11	0.22
1933	W_2	0.23	0.07	0.02	-0.02	0.09	0.18
	T	1.38	0.41	0.14	-0.12	0.53	1.09
	G	2.12	0.63	0.22	-0.19	0.81	1.68
Q_{13}				1935			
	C	1.75	0.69	-1.10	-0.02	0.06	1.08
	I	0.18	0.07	-0.11	-0.00	0.01	0.11
	D	0.37	0.15	-0.23	-0.00	0.01	0.23
1933	W_2	0.30	0.12	-0.19	-0.00	0.01	0.19
	T	1.83	0.72	-1.15	-0.02	0.06	1.14
	G	2.82	1.11	-1.77	-0.03	0.09	1.75
Q_{14}				1936			
	C	2.19	1.28	-2.72	-0.36	-0.45	0.98
	I	0.22	0.13	-0.27	-0.04	-0.05	0.10
	D	0.47	0.27	-0.58	-0.08	-0.10	0.21
1933	W_2	0.38	0.22	-0.47	-0.06	-0.08	0.17
	T	2.30	1.34	-2.85	-0.38	-0.47	1.03
	G	3.54	2.07	-4.39	-0.59	-0.73	1.58
Q_{23}				1934			
	C	2.30	0.90	-1.44	-0.02	0.07	1.43
	I	0.68	0.27	-0.43	-0.01	0.02	0.42
	D	0.24	0.09	-0.15	-0.00	0.01	0.15
1934	W_2	-0.20	-0.08	0.13	0.00	-0.01	-0.13
	T	0.88	0.34	-0.55	-0.08	0.03	0.54
	G	1.82	0.73	-1.14	-0.02	0.06	1.13
Q_{24}				1936			
	C	2.88	1.68	-3.58	-0.48	-0.60	1.29
	I	0.85	0.50	-1.06	-0.14	-0.18	0.38
	D	0.30	0.17	-0.37	-0.05	-0.06	0.13
1934	W_2	-0.26	-0.15	0.32	0.04	0.05	-0.11
	T	1.10	0.64	-1.36	-0.18	-0.23	0.49
	G	2.28	1.33	-2.83	-0.38	-0.47	1.02
Q_{34}				1936			
	C	3.83	2.24	-4.76	-0.64	-0.79	1.71
	I	1.51	0.88	-1.87	-0.25	-0.31	0.67
	D	-2.40	-1.41	0.99	0.40	0.50	-1.08
1935	W_2	-0.04	-0.02	0.04	0.01	0.01	-0.02
	T	0.12	0.07	-0.15	-0.02	-0.03	0.05
	G	2.38	1.39	-2.95	-0.40	-0.49	1.06

Secondly, the penalties the administration attach to instrument failures fall throughout the period, e.g. G from 2.6 to .96, T from 1.1 to .2. In contrast, the penalties attached to C and I rise continually, by 380% and 1440% respectively, and those for D fall at first from .036 to 0.019 and then increase dramatically to 7.4. For each instrument almost all the decrease in penalty values occurs before the end of 1934. For W_2 and T they fall further in 1935 whereas the penalty values on G remain stable; this latter possibility reflects inertia and the long term committments involved in government expenditure. In 1936 these weights return close to the 1934 levels. In contrast 1935, and more particularly 1936, contain virtually the entire increase in penalty values on targets for the period.

Thirdly, the instrument penalties are relatively higher than those on the targets in 1933, but the generally falling weights of 1934 leave targets marginally more penalised by the administration than instruments. The generally rising target weights of 1935 further reinforce this. Finally in 1936 there is simultaneously a very sharp increase in all target penalties and a decrease in instrument penalties.

Taking these three observations together, there appears to have been an obvious attempt to "get the economy moving" in 1933 and to reach the desired goals in 1936. This was particularly the case with those variables having an immediate impact on the voters (C, D, T and G) and these are, of course, precisely the variables with which the New Deal is associated. If necessary the intervening periods were to be sacrificed; as can be seen in the movement in the penalties on D, in the fall in instrument weights by 1934, and in targets weights failing to rise before 1935. An interpretation consistent with these facts is that pre-set values of the fiscal policies, T and G, were considered most important to start the economic recovery. These instruments were to be freed when the recovery was underway to do whatever was necessary to keep the targets on track. This was particularly emphasised in 1936 in an extra effort to ensure that the targets were achieved in the election year. Of the targets I, and more especially D, could be sacrificed in the earlier periods but all failures were penalised much more heavily in 1936 than at any other point (C, I, and D by 4.8, 23.8 and 157.4 times as much as in 1933 respectively). The reverse is true for the instruments. The revealed preferences of the Roosevelt administration show how economic targets and instruments were geared to the four year cycle of a presidency. To obtain freedom of manoeuvre later, the administration's early concern was with success in its use of the instruments of policy. The later emphasis was markedly that of achieving the targets. Irrespective of what the documents from the era tell us about Roosevelt's publicly proclaimed intentions, here is a case of an elected politician responding to the constraint of re-election by the strategic use of economic planning.

We must now consider a possible objection to our interpretation of these results: they could stem from a transversality problem(14). $\underline{\tilde{z}}$ might be small in the first period because of some well planned movements in $\underline{x}$ of earlier periods, not because of high priorities in the first period. The algorithm, not covering earlier periods, can only assign high weights to the relatively small $\underline{\tilde{z}}$. One may doubt that given the record of the Hoover administration; and, moreover, it does not account for weights relatively higher on instruments than targets compared to later periods.

Similarly, it might be argued that the very high weights of 1936 reflect a concern to achieve targets beyond that year. One may doubt this for a politician in only his first term of office, who himself could only have been too well aware that incumbency did not guarantee electoral success, given his own success against an incumbent. Moreover, this point cannot account for the simultaneous increase in target weights but decrease in instrument weights. If transversality effects were present then we should expect a loosening of restrictions on the targets in order to allow enough flexibility to achieve the more important subsequent targets.

We now turn to examine joint contemporaneous failures. Here we look at the off-diagonal elements of the diagonal submatrices Q_{ii}, i=1 ... 4, in table 2. At the start, the administration considered joint failures in C and G, T and G, then C and T to be the most serious. However, by 1936 C and D, C and I, and D and I were considered the most serious joint failures; these were followed in order by C and G, D and T, D and W_2, C and T, I and G, and D and G as the next most serious (of the same order as the 1933 joint failures), leaving joint failures in instruments as the most insignificant. That grouping provides further support for the interpretation we have offered above. Once again, we see the place of income distribution in the Roosevelt strategy. Immediately after his first election it could be accorded a low priority; but with the approach of the 1936 election there was a need to bind together again the New Deal coalition, and income distribution as a target was of major concern to one component of that coalition: organised labour. Yet, when we examine the sign patterns, we find evidence of an electoral strategy that is more complex than this. The positive sign on C and I indicates that they were perceived as substitutes throughout the period; both are with D for 1933-34. But in 1935-36 the signs for D with C and I reverse. D is thus the first to be sacrificed at the start, but later it emerges as strongly complementary to C and I which are themselves increasingly aimed not to overheat aggregate demand. C and I are substitutes with G and T, as are T and G themselves in 1933-35. In contrast the sign pattern for T in 1936 reverses; implying independent roles for fiscal instruments with disincentives to increasing T in 1936 or decreasing either T or G elsewhere. The positive signs on T and G for 1933-35 indicate there was a conscious attempt to err on the side of expansion and not balance the budget until 1936 (when that sign is reversed). Again joint penalties on targets increase markedly in the last period whereas those on instruments decrease; those on targets and instruments together are higher in 1933 and 1936 than elsewhere.

The significance of the sign pattern should be apparent. Roosevelt believed that he could not put together a winning coalition in 1936 based solely on the electoral support of those who would want an expanded economy at any cost. His concern becomes not to overheat the economy too close to the election, not to increase taxes in that same period, and yet to balance the budget in 1936. We can go further with evidence of a strong "electoral cycle" in the administration's preferences. Intertemporal penalties on the targets increase as we move towards the submatrix Q_{14} of table 3. Submatrices in Q with later dates have that characteristic amplified, so that joint and single failures collect accelerating penalties both the longer they persist and also the closer to the 1936 election they occur. C and D are the most important; although D is only so in conjunction with C, T and G. These results are interesting for an understanding of the relation between political strategy and economic planning. They show considerable concern that the policies of the New Deal should be put into action, but rather more concern that they should be effective in the election year.

We now turn to preferences from the open loop controls; that is as seen ex ante at the start of the administration. The weights mostly remained remarkably similar under a common normalisation; and, in so far as they do not, we can argue for positive evidence of a closed loop control by the government, otherwise we remain agnostic. We reproduce the matrix Q for the first open loop solution in table 4 (that is, plans made at the start of 1933) to show the extent of these revisions. At the beginning the penalties are virtually iden-

Table 4. Q for exercise 1 (first period certainty equivalence)

		C	I	D	W_2	T	G
Q_{11}				1933			
	C	1.00	0.10	0.21	0.17	1.05	1.62
	I	0.10	0.01	0.02	0.02	0.11	0.16
	D	0.21	0.02	0.05	0.04	0.22	0.34
1933	W_2	0.17	0.02	0.04	0.03	0.18	0.28
	T	1.05	0.11	0.22	0.18	1.10	1.69
	G	1.62	0.16	0.34	0.28	1.69	2.61
Q_{12}				1934			
	C	1.61	0.58	-0.69	0.09	0.54	1.27
	I	0.16	0.06	-0.07	0.01	0.05	0.13
	D	0.34	0.12	-0.15	0.02	0.11	0.27
1933	W_2	0.28	0.10	-0.12	0.01	0.09	0.22
	T	1.68	0.61	-0.73	0.09	0.57	1.34
	G	2.59	0.94	-1.12	0.14	0.87	2.06
Q_{13}				1935			
	C	2.28	1.10	-1.44	0.03	0.14	1.05
	I	0.23	0.11	-0.14	0.00	0.01	0.11
	D	0.49	0.23	-0.31	0.01	0.03	0.22
1933	W_2	0.39	0.19	-0.25	0.01	0.02	0.18
	T	2.39	1.16	-1.51	0.04	0.15	1.09
	G	3.69	1.78	-2.32	0.05	0.23	1.69
Q_{14}				1936			
	C	1.97	0.77	-0.39	-0.34	-0.43	0.98
	I	0.19	0.08	-0.04	-0.03	-0.04	0.10
	D	0.42	0.16	-0.08	-0.07	-0.09	0.21
1933	W_2	0.34	0.13	-0.07	-0.06	-0.07	0.17
	T	2.06	0.80	-0.41	-0.36	-0.45	1.03
	G	3.18	1.24	-0.63	-0.55	-0.70	1.59
Q_{22}				1934			
	C	2.58	0.93	-1.12	0.14	0.87	2.05
	I	0.93	0.34	-0.40	0.05	0.31	0.74
	D	-1.12	-0.40	0.48	-0.06	-0.38	-0.89
1934	W_2	0.14	0.05	-0.06	0.01	0.05	0.11
	T	0.87	0.31	-0.38	0.05	0.29	0.69
	G	2.05	0.74	-0.89	0.11	0.69	1.63
Q_{23}				1935			
	C	3.66	1.77	-2.31	0.05	0.23	1.68
	I	1.33	0.64	-0.84	0.02	0.08	0.61
	D	-1.59	-0.77	1.00	-0.02	-0.10	-0.73
	W_2	0.19	-0.09	-0.12	0.00	0.01	0.09
	T	1.23	0.59	-0.78	0.02	0.08	0.56
	G	2.91	1.41	-1.83	0.04	0.18	1.33
Q_{24}				1936			
	C	3.16	1.23	-0.63	-0.54	-0.69	1.58
	I	1.14	0.45	-0.23	-0.20	-0.25	0.57
	D	-1.37	-0.53	0.27	0.24	0.30	-0.68
1934	W_2	0.17	0.06	-0.03	-0.03	-0.04	0.08
	T	1.06	0.41	-0.21	-0.18	-0.23	0.53
	G	2.51	098	-0.50	-0.43	-0.55	1.25
Q_{33}				1935			
	C	5.21	2.52	-3.28	0.07	0.33	2.39
	I	2.52	1.21	-1.58	0.04	0.16	1.15
	D	-3.28	-1.58	2.06	-0.05	-0.21	-1.50
1935	W_2	0.07	0.04	-0.05	0.00	0.00	0.03
	T	0.33	0.16	-0.21	0.00	0.02	0.15
	G	2.39	1.15	-1.50	0.03	0.15	1.09
Q_{34}				1936			
	C	4.49	1.75	-0.89	-0.77	-0.99	2.24
	I	2.17	0.84	-0.43	-0.37	-0.48	1.08
	D	-2.83	-1.10	0.56	0.49	0.62	-1.41
1935	W_2	0.06	0.02	-0.01	-0.01	-0.01	0.03
	T	0.28	0.11	-0.06	-0.05	-0.06	0.14
	G	2.06	0.80	-0.41	-0.35	-0.45	1.03
Q_{44}				1936			
	C	3.87	1.51	-0.77	-0.67	-0.85	1.93
	I	1.51	0.59	-0.29	-0.26	-0.33	0.75
	D	-0.77	-0.29	0.15	0.13	0.17	-0.38
1936	W_2	-0.67	-0.26	0.13	0.12	0.15	-0.33
	T	-0.85	-0.33	0.17	0.15	0.19	-0.42
	G	1.93	0.75	-0.38	-0.33	-0.42	0.96

tical. The intertemporal weights are slightly larger, with thoses involving D changing signs; those larger weights are mostly for failures involving C and G. Diagonal target weights start increasing in 1934, peak in 1935 (above their multiperiod certainty equivalent values) and fall back considerably in 1936, most notably for D which is then only twice its 1933 value. C remains the most important even in 1936. Diagonal instrument weights show very much their multiperiod certainty equivalent pattern. The significance of this open loop analysis is that we see the long term strategy adopted by the Roosevelt administration in 1933. The objective, quite clearly, was to aim for success in its economic policies in 1935; and that C, which affected all voters and was a matter for immediate concern following the depression, rather than D, was considered most important. Not unnaturally, it would be seen as desirable that this success should be achieved in sufficient time for the election; there was less risk involved in aiming for success in 1935 rather than in 1936. But, of course, the "best of all possible worlds" was not realised, and in 1935 it became increasingly important that the objectives were realised in 1936. D then became most important.

Finally, it is of interest to look at the adjustments to the desired values for $\underline{z}$; i.e. $\underline{z}^d$ rather than $\underline{z}^a$ (tables 5 and 6). We have taken the view that the assumed values of $\underline{z}^d$, being arbitrarily chosen, very probably do not accurately reflect the aspirations of the Roosevelt regime. They are constructed to return the economic activity per head, in the targets, back to the previous peak (1929) level by 1936; and with linear trends for the instruments. While this may be a plausible guess we think in those disturbed times other possibilities were also likely, so it is of interest to try resetting $\underline{z}^a$. For the multiperiod certainty equivalent results (table 5), we notice C^d and I^d were set above C^a and I^a (by more for C^d); as was G^d above the trend G^a. Thus Roosevelt was more ambitious than we assumed for those variables, becoming more so towards the election with C, I and less so with G. That agrees with our remarks about holding a New Deal coalition together without emphasising the fiscal "irresponsibility". And for the same reasons T^d is above the trend T^a for 1933-35 but below it for 1936. D^d, however, is slightly above D^a for 1933 to 1934, and below for 1935-36 by a large margin. This suggests that Roosevelt is considerably more sanguine about the feasible economic performance (perhaps as he observed what was achieved in early periods) at least for this variable.

Comparing table 6 with table 5 we see the first period certainty equivalent $\underline{z}^d$ values suggest Roosevelt was initially less ambitious for C and I but very much more so for D. The instrument desired values have scarcely been altered. The 1935 peak in the targets is also clear, but this transfers to 1936 as he raises his sights with the approaching election. There is some balance in his ambitions in that he weights most heavily those failures where desired values had to be revised down and less heavily where they were held up. Thus a somewhat more charitable view may be offered of his ambitions. To some extent, then, we see a falling away of idealism as plans progress and with the realisation that C is more manipulable in the short term than D. But the significant point, here, is the extent and flexibility of the various revisions.

We conclude that preferences and plans for the instruments seem to have been carefully set out at the start and persistently followed. There is a clear pattern of the penalties being evenly placed at the beginning of the administration, yet with particular pressure for their achievement in good time for the election. As time progresses, the middle years do indeed have to be sacrificed as Roosevelt's concern is increasingly to achieve success in his economic goals in 1936.

Table 5. $\underline{\delta}^{(p)}$ for exercise 1 (multiperiod certainty equivalence case)

	C	I	D	W_2	T	G
1933	-3.032	-0.3062	-0.6459	-0.5235	-3.1800	-4.899
1934	-3.990	-1.1830	-0.4138	0.3556	-1.5210	-3.160
1935	-5.304	-2.0870	3.3290	0.0493	- .1679	-3.289
1936	-6.647	-3.8850	8.2530	1.1060	1.3730	-2.973

Table 6. $\underline{\delta}^{(p)}$ for exercise 1
(first period certainty equivalent (open loop case)

	C	I	D	W_2	T	G
1933	-2.969	-0.2994	-0.6362	-0.5126	-3.1170	-4.798
1934	-4.763	-1.7310	2.068	-0.2570	-1.6160	-3.785
1935	-6.783	-3.2770	4.286	- .0935	-0.4290	-3.107
1936	-5.832	-2.2550	1.143	1.0070	1.3250	-2.944

7.2 The administrations of 1957-62 (Eisenhower and Kennedy)

We now turn to examine a period of years in which a president, having been re-elected, cannot himself serve a further period in the White House. He still has some electoral objectives in these years so that economic planning does not become divorced from political considerations. The dominant events of the period are the recession between 1957 third quarter (1957-3) and 1959-1, the mid-term congressional elections of 1958-4, and the presidential election of 1960-4. Table 7 shows the weights from the diagonal of Q. The former is graphed in figure 4. Target weights show an upward trend throughout with a distinctive pattern superimposed. Instrument weights have no overall trend but again a clear pattern. This suggests that there was a steady increase in concentration on achieving economic goals at the expense of the noneconomic goals throughout the period. Interestingly this period follows the ending of the Korean war, and stabilization in the cold war.

Table 7. Diagonal elements of Q in exercise 2; unit penalties

	C	IN	IR	P	$Ux10^8$	$DMx10^4$	G	TO
1957-1	1.00	24.59	17.50	5.827	0.603	1.031	17.42	28.98
2	6.299	56.53	15.24	7.723	2.298	1.182	3.587	10.46
3	5.69	69.45	15.24	14.490	2.403	1.948	10.36	25.37
4	15.17	129.00	15.40	9.437	4.418	3.444	17.20	26.24
1958-1	31.29	271.6	14.91	17.83	10.22	2.87800	36.38	30.99
2	43.54	410.6	15.40	29.38	16.41	0.03259	73.18	34.30
3	55.65	562.2	14.68	46.98	19.65	0.03896	137.20	39.12
4	47.34	562.2	21.26	49.24	15.49	0.03269	160.40	41.20
1959-1	39.72	529.9	54.02	129.0	12.39	0.1072	170.5	43.01
2	34.49	446.2	72.02	157.5	10.97	0.2601	150.0	44.40
3	31.20	403.7	82.36	238.8	8.662	1.129	139.7	44.60
4	35.19	343.8	68.82	283.0	7.483	5.774	114.6	43.50
1960-1	43.86	350.3	52.93	356.7	8.393	5.795	114.50	41.80
2	57.85	369.9	35.22	410.6	8.662	4.974	114.50	40.10
3	58.69	376.5	32.55	483.4	9.639	0.963	108.10	38.70
4	53.44	383.2	29.05	554.0	8.393	1.419	80.59	37.10
1961-1	62.30	417.7	26.52	655.8	8.595	0.5221	73.26	36.10
2	79.40	424.8	28.07	710.0	8.595	0.2819	98.82	35.30
3	92.46	446.3	31.46	785.5	12.280	0.2952	77.63	44.30
4	113.10	484.3	48.75	958.9	11.200	0.0323	42.31	17.40
Compare	1	6	15	6	4	.3	3	6

which penalise all percentage failures equally in each year.

For C, IN, U weights peak coincidentally at 1958-3 having grown rapidly from 1957-3; then they fall rather slower until 1959-4. As these figures reflect multiperiod certainty equivalent plans this behaviour is, in part, the administration's response to the recession. That response is somewhat delayed and initially too cautious. The weights continue to rise from the start of the recession almost until the end. Presumably they revised their plans and had to increase the penalties on failing to end the recession as it continued. This interpretation is confirmed by the generally large intertemporal weights found (of a similar order to the corresponding diagonal elements) indicating that persistent failures collected sharply accelerating penalties. Even a risk averse administration would not still be increasing individual penalties at the end of the recession. But the spread between the tails of these peaks would suggest some risk aversion since the recession could have been predicted, leading to open loop weights having a peak over those dates. These comments are of interest for the issue as to whether government intervention has the effect of further destabilizing an economy. Our study provides some indication, though the evidence is rather weak, that these administrations have had such an effect since reactions are typically initially too cautious and there is some delay in revising weights up or down.

More important for our purposes is the suddenness with which the weights on C, IN, and U rise and peak coincidentally, the dominance of those peaks in their respective series, and the slower falling back of the weights. That pattern suggests that this behaviour is also due to the mid-term elections. That would account for the exact coincidence of the peaks; their timing at exactly the quarter preceding the elections when over the same period penalties are almost totally removed from DM (which we shall argue is the main policy instrument of the Eisenhower administration); and the dramatic rise in target weights and fall of those on DM in the election run up. All these are just the characteristics which we have learnt, from the previous exercise, to expect in the multiperiod certainty equivalent preferences of a government extremely concerned about a particular election. The fact is that these elections produced a landslide victory for the Democratic party in Congress. This possibility, during a 'lame duck' presidency, would have been foreseen by the administration which, in order to carry out its own policies successfully, would actually want to minimise the possibility (or degree) of a hostile Congress for the two years remaining. Indeed to take this line of least resistence would be the most important objective of all for a relatively unambitious administration which was not a candidate for reappointment. Any pressure to upgrade the weights for 1960 by Nixon himself would be offset by the uncertainty of his nomination and the ineffectual position of the vice-president. The 1958 election itself would ensure high weights at that point; and thereafter they would not have fallen much because of the presence of the large Democratic congressional majority.

The movements in target weights in 1958 may therefore have obscured any rises in them during the run up to the presidential election. Certainly they remain at a higher level than before 1958. There are, in fact, coincident local peaks for C, IN, and U in mid 1960 which would be quite significant but for the previous peaks. The exception is IR, and electorally significant policy variable in the long term, which has nearly constant penalties except in the year before the presidential election - a rapid rise from 1958-4 to 1959-3 and falling back thereafter. Because of the long lags involved it is likely that there was little effort in the short term to revise the penalties from an open loop strategy. So the behaviour of penalties on IR may confirm the open loop strategy for the presidential election, as we observed in the case of Roosevelt, in peaking a year early. To a lesser extent IN and U conform to that pattern - the lags here permitting only small revisions and thus minor peaks in 1960. But C, being more flexible, exhibits a peak comparable to 1958. In any event, the clear inference from these figures is that 1958 was the year of major concern for Eisenhower and that only limited support was thereby made available to the Republican candidate in 1960. Naturally, Eisenhower's principal concern would be with maintaining sufficient flexibility during his last two years of office for policy making and for what he considered important for the nation (low inflation, high investment and a balanced budget according to the records of the period), party politics and successors apart. Hence the priority given to economic success immediately before mid-term elections.

This model of planning behaviour therefore provides a full explanation of the second Eisenhower admininstration's economic strategy. Rather than exhibiting perverse behaviour in that an electoral cycle is not immediately apparent, the administration's strategy is a reasonable one and one which was refreshingly different from that of other administrations. If Eisenhower ignored advice and conventional wisdom, it was based on his entirely rational choice to be more concerned with getting his own policies into effect than with re-election problems.

This example has been presented, at least in part, in order to demonstrate the power of our model of planning behaviour. It is not necessary to postulate exactly what the planners' objectives are. The maintained hypothesis which would result would be too rigid and restrictive, since it would be of the vote or utility maximisation, popularity index or office holding maximisation variety. In this model we allow the data to determine the objectives and relax the maintained hypotheses as far as possible by presuming only the optimisation of some implicit objective function satisfying the mentioned axioms of choice.

Turning now to the instruments, the weights on TO and C are both low at the start of the recession but peak at its end. This is consistent with the view that the authorities release the instruments to take values as necessary to start the recovery; but thereafter that recovery is a planned one with desired trajectories for instruments so that the economy emerges from the recession without distortions. The administration is evidently more persistent with TO than G. DM shows clear signs of use in the opposite way to TO and G. In 1957 and the election period DM is obviously intended to follow a prescribed course of policy but as the recession sets in and as both elections approach penalties are nearly completely removed. Overall this suggests that, initially, DM was used more as the "powerhouse" of expansion or contraction (contraction on these occasions since DM $<$ 0, presumably to counteract the demand pressure from the increasingly negative TO, but expansion in 1958 where DM $>$ 0 and G falls) while the fiscal variables were used more for fine tuning the basic movements. The peaks in penalties on G at elections (very clear for 1958) are further evidence for fine tuning, against the normal Republican economic strategies, to arrest the swing to the Democrats. But significantly, from 1960-4 there is a noticeable decrease in weights on G and TO relative to the average on DM representing a shift towards fiscal and away from monetary policies under Kennedy.

We also reset $\underline{z}^d$ by (3.8a). Generally the planners were more ambitious than mere stabilisation for (in order) D, IN, P, DM and G; but less ambitious for IR, U, and TO. Again this shows a realistic view of what manipulation of the economy is possible. The timing of changes showed a clear intention to boost the economy at the 1958 election for C^d, IN^d and G^d (DM^d was muddled, perhaps being used for several other purposes) whereas U^d and TO^d had troughs. All this is remarkably similar to the Roosevelt strategies. Again DM^d (being changes in money supply) peaked at the 1960 election and the 1957 recession which suggests it was intended as the main instrument. G^d has slow changes which indicates some inertia in government expenditure programmes.

Combining these results suggests that Kennedy had a clear and probably longer term plan, and used policy differently to his predecessor (switching from DM to G and TO, less fine tuning, but consistent plans). Eisenhower had a short horizon, was uncertain of his objectives and was inconsistent in his plans to reach them. The consequence is weak trends in policy with many alterations, probably adaptations or changes of mind, in the light of events. Eisenhower's overriding concern with P and a balanced budget irrespective of events is clear. Kennedy uses all the instruments but Eisenhower concentrates on DM. As such it is empirical evidence for the conventional wisdom that Eisenhower clearly chose to run a loose, flexible and decentralised administration, but Kennedy had both more clearly defined objectives and more centralised control.

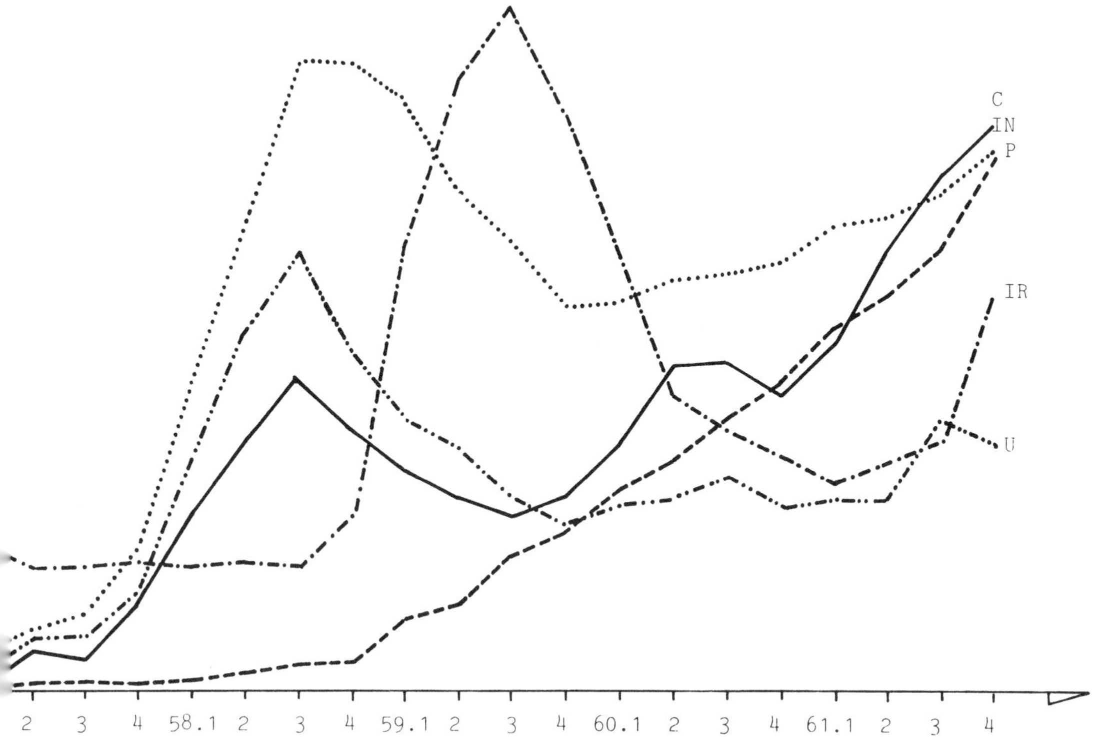

FIGURE 4. Target weights, exercise 2

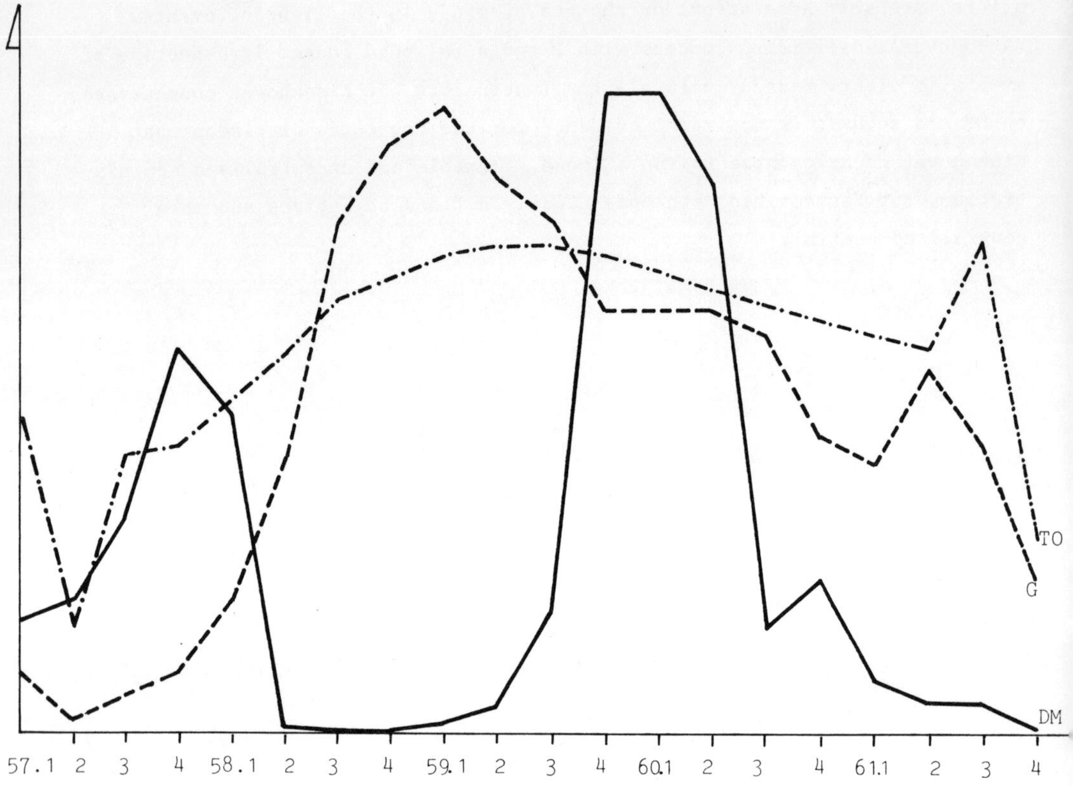

FIGURE 5. Instrument weights, exercise 2

8. CONCLUSIONS

The conclusion to be drawn from the empirical work in this study is inevitably to point out the strength of the connection between the setting of economic instruments, the economic performance and the electoral mechanism in the American economy. We have provided rather a novel analysis of the political cycle phenomenon which has attracted so much comment in the literature. But by concentrating on the objective functions themselves, rather than estimates of the "reaction functions" (2.9a) which show the connection between policy output and the conditioning information while the preferences remain implicit, we have been able to point to something of a "mens rea" for the planners and politicians. There does appear to have been a conscious attempt to control the economy for political ends in these examples - and it would not be hard to extend the examples more widely. Furthermore the preference structure is detailed and shows that fairly complex and sophisticated strategies incorporating various checks, balances and revisions are involved.

We can draw out a few general conclusions from the study as a whole. In the first place, we believe it is important to show how estimates of the preferences of a planner in any given situation can be made, albeit preferences as revealed in his intentions and/or actions. Yet this represents only the first stage in developing the subject in the direction of modelling planners' behaviour. Without such a development, the testing of hypotheses in the framework of any model of behaviour, and the subsequent amendment of hypotheses after confrontation with the data, will remain beyond our reach. The technique demonstrated in this paper seems to offer an opportunity to solve this problem.

Secondly, it is both interesting and important to obtain estimates of the preference system because, as this study makes clear, government activity as regards policy variables is far from exogenous to the economy and its performance. The complexity of the strategies we have seen and the extent of policy revisions vouch for this. Our results show just how dangerous it is to ignore the interaction between the political or planning sphere and the economic sphere. A model which does so will be seriously incomplete in its description and hence in its prescriptions for that economy.

The third point to emphasise us that the results obtained are only strictly applicable to circumstances rather similar to those when the observed decisions were taken. If one tries to apply them to circumstances that are radically different, then it is likely that they will be inappropriate since the policy makers' preferences will also have changed radically. Preferences are inevitably conditioned on the circumstances that obtain at the time. In any case, (2.4) is an approximation that is evaluated at the observed policy values just as any model approximates the behaviour of the real system about the observed levels of its variables. Further, it expresses preferences over policies within a neighbourhood about the chosen $\underline{z}_p$. However, if, as is often the case, the set of policies both feasible and acceptable to the government is highly restricted, this point scarcely detracts from the utility of the results. Moreover, the reliability of the results is dependent on the model employed. Nevertheless, in principle this need not be a valid criticism provided the model is the same as, or a close approximation of, that used by the planners in order to select $\underline{z}_p$.

APPENDIX A. Recursive relations in the quantities used by the iterates (3.25) and (3.26)

(i) the identities:

1. $Q^{(s)-1}P^{(s)'} = P^{(s)}Q^{(s)-1}$ (A1)

2. $P^{(i)}P^{(j)} = P^{(j)}$ (A2)

3. $P^{(s)}(I-\alpha_{s-1}P^{(s-1)}) = P^{(s)} - \alpha_{s-1}P^{(s-1)}$ (A3)

4. $P^{(s-1)}(I-\alpha_{s-1}P^{(s-1)}) = (1-\alpha_{s-1})P^{(s-1)}$ (A4)

5. $P^{(s)'}Q^{(s)}P^{(s)} = Q^{(s)}P^{(s)} = P^{(s)'}Q^{(s)}$ (A5)

6. $(I-\alpha_{s-1}P^{(s-1)})'Q^{(s-1)}P^{(s-1)} = (1-\alpha_{s-1})Q^{(s-1)}P^{(s-1)}$ (A6)

7. $(A+BDB')^{-1} = A^{-1} - A^{-1}B(B'A^{-1}B+D^{-1})^{-1}B'A^{-1}$ (A7)
   where A, D are nonsingular of order p and q respectively

8. $P^{(s)}\underline{\tilde{z}}^{(s)} = 0$ by (2.11) (A8)

(ii) the recursive relations for use with (3.25) and (3.26) in the original variables (the results are necessary for section 4):

Lemma 1A: $$Q^{(s)}P^{(s)} = Q^{(s-1)}P^{(s-1)} + (\phi_{s-1}-1)\frac{Q^{(s-1)}\underline{\delta}^{(s-1)}\underline{\delta}^{(s-1)'}Q^{(s-1)}}{c^{(s-1)}}$$

$$+ \frac{\alpha_{s-1}}{a^{(s-1)}}(I-P^{(s-1)})'Q^{(s-1)}\underline{\delta}^{(s-1)}\underline{\delta}^{(s-1)'}Q^{(s-1)}(I-P^{s-1}).$$

Proof: $$Q^{(s)}P^{(s)} = Q^{(s)} - H'(HQ^{(s)-1}H')^{-1}H \qquad \text{(A9)}$$

Set $A = Q^{(s-1)}$, $B = Q^{(s-1)}\underline{\delta}^{(s-1)}$ in formula (A7) applied to (3.25) and we find ($c^{(s-1)} \neq \infty$, $\phi_{s-1} \neq 1$)

$$H'(HQ^{(s)-1}H')^{-1}H = H'(HQ^{(s-1)-1}H'-\varepsilon_{s-1}H\underline{\delta}^{(s-1)}\underline{\delta}^{(s-1)'}H')^{-1}H \qquad \text{(A10)}$$

where $\varepsilon_{s-1} = (\phi_{s-1}-1)/(c^{(s-1)}\phi_{s-1})$. Applying (A7) again with $A = HQ^{(s-1)-1}H'$ and $B = H\underline{\delta}^{(s-1)}$, we can write (A10) as

$$H'(HQ^{(s-1)-1}H')^{-1}H - H'(HQ^{(s-1)-1}H')^{-1}H\underline{\delta}^{(s-1)}\underline{\delta}^{(s-1)'}H'(HQ^{(s-1)-1}H')^{-1}H\eta_{s-1}.$$

Now
$$\eta_{s-1}^{-1} = b^{(s-1)} - \varepsilon_{s-1}^{-1} = \frac{(\phi_{s-1}-1)b^{(s-1)} - \phi_{s-1}c^{(s-1)}}{\psi_{s-1}-1} = \frac{a^{(s-1)}}{\alpha_{s-1}} \tag{A11}$$

Both insert (A11) and substitute for $Q^{(s)}$ in (A9) and upon sorting out terms we have the result.

We now turn to recursive relations in $a^{(s)}$, $b^{(s)}$ and $c^{(s)}$. The results are displayed in equations (4.3) - (4.5). Hereafter in this appendix we drop sub- or superscripts "s-1".

<u>Theorem 1A</u>: $b^{(s)} = b^{(s-1)} - \alpha_{s-1}(b^{(s-1)})^2/a^{(s-1)}$

<u>Proof</u>: From (3.26) and (4.2),

$$b^{(s)} = \underline{\delta}'(I-\alpha P)'Q^{(s)}(I-P^{(s)})(I-\alpha P)\underline{\delta}$$

$$= \underline{\delta}'(I-P)'Q^{(s)}(I-P^{(s)})\underline{\delta} \quad \text{by (A3)} \tag{A12}$$

$$= \underline{\delta}'(I-P^{(s)})'Q^{(s)}\underline{\delta} \quad \text{by (A5), (A4)} \tag{A13}$$

$$= \underline{\delta}'Q(I-P)\underline{\delta} - \frac{\alpha}{a}\,\underline{\delta}'(I-P)'Q\underline{\delta}\underline{\delta}'Q(I-P)\underline{\delta} \quad \text{by lemma 1A and (3.25)} \tag{A14}$$

which in view of (3.26) gives the result.

<u>Theorem 2A</u>: $a^{(s)} = a^{(s-1)} - \alpha_{s-1}b^{(s-1)}$

<u>Proof</u>: From (3.26), (3.25) and (4.2)

$$a^{(s)} = \underline{\delta}'(I-\alpha P)'(Q + \frac{(\phi-1)}{c}Q\underline{\delta}\underline{\delta}'Q)(\underline{\tilde{z}} + \alpha P\underline{\delta}) \tag{A15}$$

Multiplying out and using (3.26) with (A5) we get

$$a^{(s)} = a^{(s-1)} - \alpha\underline{\delta}'P'Q\underline{\tilde{z}} + \alpha(1-\alpha)\underline{\delta}'QP\underline{\delta} + (\phi-1)(ca+\alpha(b-c)a)/c$$

$$- (\phi-1)(c+\alpha(b-c))(b-c)/c \qquad (A16)$$

Use (A8) and (A5) on the second term so that

$$a^{(s)} = a^{(s-1)} - \alpha(1-\alpha)(b-c) + (\phi-1)(c+\alpha(b-c))(a-\alpha(b-c))/c \qquad (A17)$$

Now substitute for $(\phi-1)$ and sort out the remaining terms using (B16) below.

Theorem 3A: $c^{(s)} - b^{(s)} = c^{(s-1)} - b^{(s-1)} + (2-\alpha_{s-1})\alpha_{s-1}(b^{(s-1)} - c^{(s-1)})$

$$+ \alpha_{s-1}\frac{(b^{(s-1)})^2}{a^{(s-1)}} + (\phi_{s-1}-1)\frac{[c^{(s-1)} + \alpha_{s-1}(b^{(s-1)} - c^{(s-1)})]^2}{c^{(s-1)}}$$

Proof: From (3.26) and (4.2)

$$c^{(s)} - b^{(s)} = \underline{\delta}'(I-\alpha P)'Q^{(s)}P^{(s)}(I-\alpha P)\underline{\delta} \qquad (A18)$$

$$= \underline{\delta}'(I-\alpha P)'QP(I-\alpha P)\underline{\delta} + \frac{\alpha}{a}\underline{\delta}'(I-\alpha P)(I-P)'Q\underline{\delta}\underline{\delta}'Q(I-P)(I-\alpha P)\underline{\delta}$$

$$+ \underline{\delta}'(I-\alpha P)'Q\underline{\delta}\underline{\delta}'Q(I-\alpha P)\underline{\delta}(\phi-1)/c \quad \text{by lemma 1A} \qquad (A19)$$

$$= (1-\alpha)^2(c-b) + (\phi-1)(c+\alpha(b-c))^2/c + \alpha b^2/a \qquad (A20)$$

where (A4), (A5), (A6) and (A1) have been used after multiplying out terms in (A19).

Theorem 4A: $(I-P^{(s)})\underline{\delta}^{(s-1)} = (I-(1-\alpha_{s-1}b^{(s-1)}/a^{(s-1)})P^{(s-1)})\underline{\delta}^{(s-1)}$

Proof: Use (A10)

$$Q^{(s)-1} = Q^{-1} - \underline{\delta}\underline{\delta}'\varepsilon \qquad \text{with} \quad \varepsilon = \frac{\phi-1}{c} = -\alpha/(a-b) \qquad (A21)$$

Thus $\quad (HQ^{(s)-1}H')^{-1} = (HQ^{-1}H')^{-1}(I-H\underline{\delta}\underline{\delta}'H'(HQ^{-1}H')^{-1}\alpha/a) \quad$ by (A11) $\quad$ (A22)

Inserting (A21) and (A22) into the expression for $I-P^{(s)}$ and multiplying out we have

$$I-P^{(s)} = Q^{-1}H'(HQ^{-1}H')^{-1}H - Q^{-1}H'(HQ^{-1}H')^{-1}H\underline{\delta}\underline{\delta}'H'(HQ^{-1}H')^{-1}H\alpha/a \quad (A23)$$

$$- \varepsilon\underline{\delta}\underline{\delta}'H'(HQ^{-1}H')^{-1}H + \varepsilon\underline{\delta}\underline{\delta}'H'(HQ^{-1}H')^{-1}H\underline{\delta}\underline{\delta}'H'(HQ^{-1}H')^{-1}H\alpha/a$$

$$= I-P-(I-P)\underline{\delta}\underline{\delta}'(I-P)'Q\alpha/a - \varepsilon\underline{\delta}\underline{\delta}'(I-P)'Q$$

$$+ \varepsilon\underline{\delta}\underline{\delta}'(I-P)'Q\underline{\delta}\underline{\delta}'(I-P)'Q\alpha/a \quad (A24)$$

Now postmultiply by $\underline{\delta}^{(s-1)}$

$$(I-P^{(s)})\underline{\delta}^{(s-1)} = (I-P)\underline{\delta} - b\varepsilon\underline{\delta} - (I-P)\underline{\delta}b\alpha/a + \varepsilon\underline{\delta}b^2\alpha/a = (I-(1-\alpha b/a)P)\underline{\delta} \quad (A25)$$

as required.

Corollary 1A:

(i) $$\underline{\delta}^{(s)} = \underline{\delta}^{(s-1)} - \alpha_{s-1}\underline{\xi}^{(s-1)} \quad \text{where} \quad \underline{\xi}^{(s)} = P^{(s)}\underline{\delta}^{(s)} \quad (A26)$$

(ii) $$\underline{\xi}^{(s)} = d^{(s-1)}\underline{\xi}^{(s-1)} \quad \text{where} \quad d^{(s-1)} = (1-\alpha_{s-1}(1+b^{(0)}/a^{(0)})) \quad (A27)$$

Proof: (i) by 4.2

(ii) Now $\underline{\xi}^{(s)} = P^{(s)}\underline{\delta}^{(s)} = P^{(s)}(I-\alpha P)\underline{\delta} = P^{(s)}\underline{\delta} - \alpha\underline{\xi}$

and $$P^{(s)}\underline{\delta} = -(I-P^{(s)})\underline{\delta} + \underline{\delta} = [(a-\alpha b)/a]P\underline{\delta} \quad \text{by theorem 4A} \quad (A28)$$

Hence $$\underline{\xi}^{(s)} = (1-\alpha-\alpha b/a)\underline{\xi} \quad (A29)$$

But, in view of theorems 1A and 2A, $b^{(s-1)}/a^{(s-1)} = b^{(0)}/a^{(0)}$. Thus $d^{(s-1)}$ defined by (A29) reduces to that given in (A27).

Theorem 5A: Define $\underline{g}^{(s)} = Q^{(s)}\underline{\delta}^{(s)}$ and $\underline{f}^{(s)} = Q^{(s)}\underline{\xi}^{(s)}$, then

(i) $$\underline{f}^{(s)} = d^{(s-1)}\left[\underline{f}^{(s-1)} - (\phi_{s-1}-1)\frac{(b^{(s-1)}-c^{(s-1)})}{c^{(s-1)}}\underline{g}^{(s-1)}\right]$$

(ii) $$\underline{g}^{(s)} = [\phi_{s-1} + \alpha_{s-1}(\phi_{s-1}-1)\frac{(b^{(s-1)}-c^{(s-1)})}{c^{(s-1)}}]\underline{g}^{(s-1)} - \alpha_{s-1}\underline{f}^{(s-1)}$$

<u>Proof</u>: $$\underline{g}^{(s)} = Q(I-\alpha P)\underline{\delta} + \frac{(\phi-1)}{c} Q\underline{\delta}\,\underline{\delta}'Q(I-\alpha P)\underline{\delta} \quad \text{(A30)}$$

$$= \underline{g} - \alpha Q\underline{\xi} + (\phi-1)\frac{(b-c)}{c}\underline{g} \quad \text{(A31)}$$

which gives (ii). Similarly we have

$$\underline{f}^{(s)} = d^{(s-1)}(Q\underline{\xi} + \frac{(\phi-1)}{c} Q\underline{\delta}\,\underline{\delta}'Q\underline{\xi}) \quad \text{(A32)}$$

Substitute $\underline{\xi} = P\underline{\delta}$ in second term of (A32) to get (i).

<u>APPENDIX B</u>. The proofs required for section 4

<u>Theorem 1, proof</u>:
The projection of $\underline{z}_p$ onto F in the metric of $Q^{(s-1)}$ is

$$\underline{k}^{(s-1)} = \underline{z}_p - Q^{(s-1)-1}H'(HQ^{(s-1)-1}H')^{-1}(H\underline{z}_p - (\underline{b}+H\underline{z}^d)) \quad \text{(B1)}$$

Hence $$\underline{k}^{(s-1)} = \underline{z}_p - (I - P^{(s-1)})\underline{\delta}^{(s-1)} = \underline{z}^{(s-1)} + P^{(s-1)}\underline{\delta}^{(s-1)} \quad \text{(B2)}$$

Since $H\underline{\delta}^{(s-1)} = H\underline{z}_p - (\underline{b} + H\underline{z}^d)$ for any $\underline{\tilde{z}}^{(s-1)} \varepsilon F$.

Immediately we have

$$\underline{z}^{(s)} = \alpha_{s-1}\underline{k}^{(s-1)} + (1 - \alpha_{s-1})\underline{z}^{(s-1)} \quad \text{(B3)}$$

$\therefore$ $\|\underline{z}^{(s)} - \underline{z}^{(s-1)}\|^2 = \alpha^2_{s-1}\|\underline{k}^{(s-1)} - \underline{z}^{(s-1)}\|^2$ follows. (B4)

Next $$(\underline{z}_p - \underline{z}^{(s)})'(\underline{z}^{(s)} - \underline{z}^{(s-1)}) = \alpha_{s-1}(\underline{z}_p - \underline{k}^{(s-1)})'(\underline{k}^{(s-1)} - \underline{z}^{(s-1)})$$

$$+ \alpha_{s-1}(1 - \alpha_{s-1})\|\underline{k}^{(s-1)} - \underline{z}^{(s-1)}\|^2 \quad \text{(B5)}$$

on substitution for $\underline{z}^{(s)}$. Thus by (B4) and (B5) we have

$$2(\underline{z}_p - \underline{z}^{(s)})'(\underline{z}^{(s)} - \underline{z}^{(s-1)}) + \|\underline{z}^{(s)} - \underline{z}^{(s-1)}\|^2$$

$$= 2\alpha_{s-1}\left[(\underline{z}_p - \underline{k}^{(s-1)})'(\underline{k}^{(s-1)} - \underline{z}^{(s-1)}) + \|\underline{k}^{(s-1)} - \underline{z}^{(s-1)}\|^2\right]$$

$$- \alpha_{s-1}^2 \|\underline{k}^{(s-1)} - \underline{z}^{(s-1)}\|^2 \qquad \text{(B6)}$$

However $\|\underline{z}^{(s-1)} - \underline{z}_p\|^2$

$$= \|\underline{z}_p - \underline{z}^{(s)}\|^2 + 2(\underline{z}_p - \underline{z}^{(s)})'(\underline{z}^{(s)} - \underline{z}^{(s-1)}) + \|\underline{z}^{(s)} - \underline{z}^{(s-1)}\|^2 \qquad \text{(B7)}$$

of which the last two terms are given by (B6)[15]. But (B2) gives, for all α,

$$(\underline{z}_p - \underline{k}^{(s-1)})'(\underline{k}^{(s-1)} - \underline{z}^{(s-1)}) = \underline{\delta}^{(s-1)\prime}P^{(s-1)\prime}(I-P^{(s-1)})\underline{\delta}^{(s-1)} \geq 0 \qquad \text{(B8)}$$

whose sign follows from the idempotency of $P^{(s-1)}$, which indicates $P^{(s-1)}$ and $I-P^{(s-1)}$ share eigenvectors.

In fact therefore (B6) is stricly positive for all $0 < \alpha_{s-1} < 2$ and at least nonnegative for $0 \leq \alpha_{s-1} \leq 2$. In the former case

$$\|\underline{z}^{(s-1)} - \underline{z}_p\| > \|\underline{z}^{(s)} - \underline{z}_p\|. \qquad \text{(B9)}$$

<u>Theorem 2, proof</u>: Suppress all sub- and superscripts "s-1". Let $\beta = \frac{-c}{(\phi-1)}$. Take the similarity transform $Q = W \Lambda W'$. By (3.25)

$$Q^{(s)} = W\Lambda^{\frac{1}{2}} \left[I - \frac{\Lambda^{\frac{1}{2}}W'\underline{\delta\delta}'W\Lambda^{\frac{1}{2}}}{\beta}\right] \Lambda^{\frac{1}{2}}W' \qquad \text{(B10)}$$

which is positive definite (semi-definite) iff for $i = 1 \ldots n$

$$\left| I - \frac{\Lambda^{\frac{1}{2}}W'\underline{\delta\delta}'W\Lambda^{\frac{1}{2}}}{\beta} - \psi I \right| = 0 \qquad \text{(B11)}$$

implies $\psi_i > 0$ $(\psi_i \geq 0)$. Now $\beta \neq 0, \neq \infty$ (if it were either, the result follows directly). Hence

$$\left|\beta(1-\psi)I - \Lambda^{\frac{1}{2}}W'\underline{\delta\delta}'W\Lambda^{\frac{1}{2}}\right| = 0 \qquad \text{(B12)}$$

implying $\beta(1-\psi) \geq 0.$ (B13)

However $\Lambda^{\frac{1}{2}}W'\underline{\delta}\underline{\delta}'W\Lambda^{\frac{1}{2}}$ (B14)

is of rank one having its only nonzero eigenvalue[16]

$$\underline{\delta}'W\Lambda W'\underline{\delta} = c > 0. \tag{B15}$$

$\therefore \quad \psi_1 = \phi \qquad$ (or unity)

and the result follows from (B11).

Corollary 3, proof:

Consider $a^{(s)} < 0$. Recall $b^{(s)} - c^{(s)} < 0$ all s and note theorem 1.

Now
$$(\phi_s - 1) = \frac{-\alpha_s c^{(s)}}{a^{(s)} - \alpha_s(b^{(s)} - c^{(s)})} \tag{B16}$$

follows from (3.26). We find in this case

$$a^{(s)} - \alpha_s(b^{(s)} - c^{(s)}) < 0. \tag{B17}$$

This implies
$$\alpha_s < \frac{a^{(s)}}{b^{(s)} - c^{(s)}}$$

is forced if $\phi_s > 0$ is to be maintained. Corollary 2 shows $\phi_s > 1$ is the only possibility in this case. Now consider $a^{(s)} > 0$ and use theorem 1 again. Corollary 2 and (B16) show

$$a^{(s)} - \alpha_s(b^{(s)} - c^{(s)}) > 0.$$

From (B16)
$$\phi_s = \frac{a^{(s)} - \alpha_s b^{(s)}}{a^{(s)} - \alpha_s(b^{(s)} - c^{(s)})} \tag{B18}$$

so that to require $\phi_s > 0$ gives the α_s range. Corollary 2 completes the result.

Theorem 4, proof:

sufficiency: $\underline{z}^{(s)} = \underline{z}^{(s-1)} + \alpha_{s-1}P^{(s-1)}\underline{\delta}^{(s-1)}$, and from (3.25) and (B16)

$$Q^{(s)} = Q^{(s-1)} - \frac{\alpha_{s-1}Q^{(s-1)}\underline{\delta}^{(s-1)}\underline{\delta}^{(s-1)'}Q^{(s-1)}}{a^{(s-1)} - \alpha_{s-1}(b^{(s-1)} - c^{(s-1)})} \qquad \text{(B19)}$$

Sufficiency is now obvious.

necessity: by corollary 1A above

$$\underline{z}^{(s)} - \underline{z}^{(s-1)} = \alpha_{s-1}\underline{\xi}^{(s-1)} = \alpha_{s-1}d^{(s-2)}\underline{\xi}^{(s-2)} \qquad \text{(B20)}$$

$$= \alpha_{s-1}\prod_{j=0}^{s-2}(1 - \alpha_j(1+b^{(0)}/a^{(0)}))\underline{\xi}^{(0)} \qquad \text{(B21)}$$

$$\therefore\ \underline{z}^{(s)} + \underline{z}^{(0)} = [\sum_{i=1}^{s-1}\alpha_i \prod_{j=0}^{i-1}(1 - \alpha_j(1+b^{(0)}/a^{(0)}))]\underline{\xi}^{(0)} \qquad \text{(B22)}$$

At the same time by (B19) with theorem 5A:

$$Q^{(s)} = Q^{(s-1)} - \frac{\alpha_{s-1}\underline{g}^{(s-1)}\underline{g}^{(s-1)'}}{a^{(s-1)} - \alpha_{s-1}(b^{(s-1)} - c^{(s-1)})} \qquad \text{(B23)}$$

Now necessity is obvious, given $\underline{g}^{(0)}$ and $\underline{\xi}^{(0)}$ are nonzero, if simultaneous convergence with $\underline{z}^{(s)}$, as minimiser of (3.25) with $Q^{(s)}$, is to be observed. And that condition is required so that (3.25) and (3.26) may simulate a variable metric algorithm. A potential difficulty for necessity is if

$$\alpha_s = (1 + b^{(s)}/a^{(s)})^{-1} = a^{(0)}/(a^{(0)} + b^{(0)}) \qquad \text{(B24)}$$

The sequence in $\underline{z}^{(s)}$ halts; but as then $\underline{g}^{(s+1)} = \alpha_s\underline{g}^{(s)} \neq 0$ that in $Q^{(s)}$ does not, which would violate the requirements for our algorithm. In essence, $Q^{(s)}$ is an arbitrary start for $Q^{(s+1)}$ and the sequence in $\underline{z}^{(s)}$ is merely a necessary companion iteration to simplify calculations at each step. So the convergence of $Q^{(s)}$ is of first interest. Moreover, reverting to the exact algorithm being simulated, (3.15) and (3.19), we see that does not stop in either part if (B24) were used; neither therefore should (3.26). Of course (B24) is not always feasible. By corollary 3 it cannot be selected when $a^{(0)}<0$ and $c^{(0)} + a^{(0)} > 0$ – which is a common situation. Finally if we obtain convergence we will of course also require the convergence point to be independent of the route taken. Thus (B24) must be ruled out as convergence with a free choice for α_s can only be observed in general if $\lim_{s\to\infty} \alpha_s = 0$. The convergence test, therefore, is $|\alpha_s - \alpha_{s-1}|/\alpha_{s-1} < 10^{-\tau}$ for a suitable $\tau > 0$.

<u>Theorem 5, proof:</u>

By theorem 4 and corollary 3 it is sufficient to show

$$\frac{a^{(s)}}{b^{(s)} - c^{(s)}} - \frac{a^{(s-1)}}{b^{(s-1)} - c^{(s-1)}} \leqslant 0 \tag{B25}$$

Also by corollary 3 $\lambda\varepsilon[0, 1]$, a closed interval. The lower bound rises when $\lambda_{min} > 0$; and the upper bound falls if $\frac{a^{(s)}}{b^{(s)} - c^{(s)}} > 2$. The latter remark establishes λ_{max}. We therefore need to prove

$$\frac{b^{(s)} - c^{(s)}}{b^{(s-1)} - c^{(s-1)}} \geqslant \frac{a^{(s)}}{a^{(s-1)}} \tag{B26}$$

Substitute (4.3) and (4.5) into (B26) and then for α_{s-1} in the result. We obtain, since $\lambda_{s-1} \neq 0$ (so that $\underline{z}^{(s)} \neq \underline{z}^{(s-1)}$ is forced whenever possible),

$$\Big[\lambda_{s-1}^2 (a^{(s-1)})^2 - 2\lambda_{s-1} a^{(s-1)}(b^{(s-1)} - c^{(s-1)}) + \Big(\frac{\lambda_{s-1}}{1-\lambda_{s-1}}\Big). \tag{B27}$$

$$+ \Big(\frac{\lambda_{s-1}}{1-\lambda_{s-1}}\Big)(c^{(s-1)} + \lambda_{s-1} a^{(s-1)})^2 - \lambda_{s-1} a^{(s-1)}(b^{(s-1)} c^{(s-1)})\Big](b^{(s-1)} - c^{(s-1)})^{-2} \geqslant 0$$

Since (B27) is clearly true if $\lambda_{s-1} = 1$, we consider $\lambda_{s-1} < 1$ only. Write the numerator (required to be nonnegative) as

$$k(\lambda_{s-1}) = \lambda_{s-1}[(a^{(s-1)})^2 + 2a^{(s-1)}(b^{(s-1)} - c^{(s-1)}) + c^{(s-1)}(2a^{(s-1)} + b^{(s-1)})]$$

$$+ [c^{(s-1)2} - 2a^{(s-1)}(b^{(s-1)} - c^{(s-1)}) - b^{(s-1)} c^{(s-1)}] \tag{B28}$$

Moreover the solution to $k(\lambda) = 0$ is

$$\hat{\lambda} = \frac{(b^{(s-1)} - c^{(s-1)})(2a^{(s-1)} + c^{(s-1)})}{(a^{(s-1)})^2 + 2a^{(s-1)}b^{(s-1)} + b^{(s-1)}c^{(s-1)}} > 0 \qquad \text{(B29)}$$

which establishes λ_{min}.

Now $$k(1) = (c^{(s-1)} + a^{(s-1)})^2 \geq 0 \qquad \text{(B30)}$$

and $$k(0) = -(b^{(s-1)} - c^{(s-1)})(2a^{(s-1)} + c^{(s-1)}) \geq 0 \qquad \text{(B31)}$$

provided $c^{(s-1)} \geq -2a^{(s-1)}$. Now the theorem follows unless both $c^{(s-1)} < -2a^{(s-1)}$ and $\hat{\lambda} \geq \lambda_{max}$. We can verify

$$\hat{\lambda} - \frac{2(b^{(s-1)} - c^{(s-1)})}{a^{(s-1)}} = \frac{2(c^{(s-1)} - b^{(s-1)})(2a^{(s-1)} + c^{(s-1)}) + a^{(s-1)}c^{(s-1)}}{(a^{(s-1)} + b^{(s-1)})^2 + b^{(s-1)} - b^{(s-1)})} < 0 \qquad \text{(B32)}$$

in this case. Similarly we find

$$\hat{\lambda} - 2 = \frac{-(a^{(s-1)} + c^{(s-1)})^2 - (a^{(s-1)})^2 - b^{(s-1)}c^{(s-1)}}{(a^{(s-1)} + b^{(s-1)})^2 + b^{(s-1)}(c^{(s-1)} - b^{(s-1)})} < 0 \qquad \text{(B33)}$$

in every case. Thus $[\lambda_{min}, \lambda_{max}]$ is nonempty in all circumstances.

<u>Corollary 5, proof</u>:
By corollary 4 (iv)

$$\frac{b^{(s-1)} - c^{(s-1)}}{a^{(s-1)}} = \frac{b^{(s)}}{a^{(s)}} - \frac{c^{(s-1)}}{a^{(s-1)}} \qquad \text{(B34)}$$

so that by theorem 5

$$c^{(s)}/a^{(s)} \leq c^{(s-1)}/a^{(s-1)} \leq 0 \qquad \text{(B35)}$$

which establishes that $\lambda_{min} = 0$ at s whenever $\lambda_{min} = 0$ at s-1. If $\lambda_{min} \neq 0$ at s-1, then corollary 4 (i) implies

$$0 \geq c^{(s)} + 2a^{(s)} \geq c^{(s-1)} + 2a^{(s-1)} \qquad \text{(B36)}$$

Writing the nonzero λ_{min} in the form

$$\left[\frac{b^{(s-1)}}{a^{(s-1)}} - \frac{c^{(s-1)}}{a^{(s-1)}}\right] \left[\frac{2a^{(s-1)} + c^{(s-1)}}{a^{(s-1)} + b^{(s-1)}/a^{(s-1)}(2a^{(s-1)} + c^{(s-1)})}\right] \geq 0 \qquad \text{(B37)}$$

we see, from (B35) and (B36) with corollary 4(iv) and 4(i), that (B37) decreases at each step. Thus (B35) and (B37) establish that λ_{min} is a non-increasing function of $s \geq 0$ under the conditions of theorem 5. Additionally λ_{max} is a nondecreasing function of $s \geq 0$ under those conditions by (B25).

Corollary 6, proof:

The selection of $\alpha_s = \frac{\alpha^{(s)}}{a^{(s)} + b^{(s)}} = \frac{a^{(0)}}{a^{(0)} + b^{(0)}}$ is excluded (given $a^{(0)} < 0$)

if (i) $a^{(0)} + b^{(0)} > 0$ (implying $\alpha_s < 0$); or

(ii) $\frac{a^{(0)}}{a^{(0)} + b^{(0)}} > 2$ i.e. $a^{(0)} + 2b^{(0)} > 0$ (implying $\alpha_s > 2$); or

(iii) $\frac{a^{(0)}}{a^{(0)} + b^{(0)}} > \frac{a^{(0)}}{b^{(0)} - c^{(0)}}$ i.e. $a^{(0)} + c^{(0)} > 0$ which violates corollary 3.

If $a^{(0)} < 0$, we consider only $a^{(0)} + b^{(0)} < 0$ and $b^{(0)} - c^{(0)} < 0$ for finite values of α_s and its limits. Note that (ii) and (iii) here guarantee (i); and theorem 5 ensures that if (iii) holds at s=0 it does subsequently. Now

$\alpha_s = \frac{a^{(0)}}{a^{(0)} + b^{(0)}}$ implies $\lambda_0 = \frac{b^{(0)} - c^{(0)}}{a^{(0)} + b^{(0)}}$. If $\lambda_{min} = 0$ then $2a^{(0)} + c^{(0)} \geqslant 0$ contradicting (iii). Thus this selection of α_s is only possible when $\lambda_{min} = \hat{\lambda}$. But then $\lambda_0 < \lambda_{min}$ since (suppressing superscripts "0")

$$1 < \frac{(a+b)\ (2a+c)}{(a+b)^2 + b(c-b)} \qquad \text{because } a(b-(c+a)) < 0 \tag{B38}$$

when $c + a > 0$.

Corollary 7, proof:

Use (4.4) and (4.5) and $\alpha_s = \frac{\lambda_s a^{(s)}}{b^{(s)} - c^{(s)}}$. Next

$$c^{(s)} - c = \lambda a\left(2 - \frac{\lambda a}{b-c}\right) - \left(\frac{\lambda}{1-\lambda}\right) \frac{(c+\lambda a)^2}{(b-c)} \tag{B39}$$

(B39) is clearly zero if $\lambda=0$, and strictly positive when $\lambda=1$ by theorem 3. For other λ values $c^{(s)} - c > 0$ if

$$(b-c)^{-1}[\lambda(-2a(b-c) - a^2 - 2ca) - c^2 + 2a(b-c)] > 0 \tag{B40}$$

Now (B40) is evidently true for $\lambda=0$, $\lambda=1$ and thus any $0 \leqslant \lambda \leqslant 1$.

Theorem 6, proof:

The average rate of convergence is maximised by maximising, at each s, the average step length by choice of α_s. Since α_s does not affect $\underline{z}^{(s)}$ this procedure minimises $\|\underline{z}^{(s+1)} - \underline{z}_p\|$. The asymptotic rate of convergence is the limit of the average rate as $s\to\infty$. The step length is

$$\|\underline{z}^{(s)} - \underline{z}_p\| - \|\underline{z}^{(s+1)} - \underline{z}_p\| \tag{B41}$$

Consider (B7) and insert (B6). The unique maximum of (B41) at s is given by (the coefficient of α_s^2 being negative)

$$\alpha_s^* = 1 + \frac{(\underline{z}_p - \underline{k}^{(s)})'(\underline{k}^{(s)} - \underline{z}^{(s)})}{\|\underline{k}^{(s)} - \underline{z}^{(s)}\|^2} \tag{B42}$$

Now substitute (B3) and (3.26) in the denominator, and (B8) in the numerator to give α_s^* as quoted in the theorem. Notice (B8) and corollary 3 ensure that $1 \leq \alpha_s^* \leq 2$ all s. However, returning to (B28), $k(\lambda_s)$ has slope

$$(a^{(s)})^2 + b^{(s)}(c^{(s)} + 2a^{(s)}) \geq (a^{(s)} + b^{(s)})^2 > 0 \tag{B43}$$

Thus λ_{max} maximises the steplength whenever $a^{(s)}/(b^{(s)} - c^{(s)}) < 2$. Finally λ_s^* combines λ_{max} and α_s^* so that α_s^* is chosen whenever feasible.

Corollary 8, proof:

$\underline{\delta}^{(s)}$ and $\underline{\delta}^{(s+1)}$ form an obtuse angle iff

$$\|\underline{z}^{(s+1)} - \underline{z}^{(s)}\|^2 + \|\underline{z}^{(s+1)} - \underline{z}_p\|^2 > \|\underline{z}^{(s)} - \underline{z}_p\|^2 \tag{B44}$$

substituting by (B7) for the second term in (B44) and sorting out gives

$$-2(\underline{z}_p - \underline{z}^{(s+1)})'(\underline{z}^{(s+1)} - \underline{z}^{(s)}) > 0 \tag{B45}$$

Substituting now from (B5) gives ($\alpha_s \neq 0$)

$$-(\underline{z}_p - \underline{k}^{(s)})'(\underline{k}^{(s)} - \underline{z}^{(s)}) - (1-\alpha_s)\|\underline{k}^{(s)} - \underline{z}^{(s)}\|^2 > 0 \tag{B46}$$

The quantities $\underline{z}^{(s)}$ and $\underline{k}^{(s)}$ are independent of α_s. So (B46) is true iff $\alpha_s > \alpha_s^*$. The inequality is reversed for $\alpha_s < \alpha_s^*$; and zero is obtained if $\alpha_s = \alpha_s^*$.

Theorem 7, proof:

(i) the result for ϕ_s follows from corollary 6 and (4.4), since $a^{(s)} = 0$ and $b^{(s)} = 0$, in view of (B18). If $\lambda_s \neq 1$ all $s \geq 1$ the results for $a^{(s)}$, $b^{(s)}$ follow at $s_o = \infty$ by corollary 4(i) and (4.4) since $\alpha_s \leq a^{(s)}/b^{(s)}$.

(ii) if $\lambda_s = 1$ is feasible and chosen where $\alpha_s = \lambda_s a^{(s)}/b^{(s)}$ defines λ_s, then it happens at $s_o = s$ in view of (4.3) and (B18).

(iii) this result holds when $\phi_s = 0$ but $\phi_{s-1} \neq 0$ by theorem 2; i.e.

$$Q^{(s+1)} = Q^{(s)}[I - \frac{\underline{\delta}^{(s)}\underline{\delta}^{(s)'}Q^{(s)}}{c^{(s)}}] \quad \text{(B47)}$$

where $\underline{\delta}^{(s)}\underline{\delta}^{(s)'}Q^{(s)}$ is of rank one, with nonzero eigenvalue $c^{(s)}$. Therefore $Q^{(s+1)}$ has rank at most n-1. s_o is given above.

APPENDIX C. On the rank of matrix B of equation (5.7), section 5.

Rules for constructing B:

1. The number of equations in the system (5.6) is the number of ways two indices can be picked from n without replacement such that j > i. Further $Q_{k\ell}$ is missing from the equation for m_{ij} where $\left.\begin{matrix} i\neq k,\ell \\ j\neq k,\ell \end{matrix}\right\}$ so B has coeffcients forn≥4

2. From (5.6), there are ${}^nC_2$ rows and columns in B. In any row there are ${}^{n-2}C_2$ zero elements and ${}^nC_2$ - ${}^{n-2}C_2$ = 2n - 3 nonzero elements. No row or column has more or less zero than that, so it will be possible to permute rows and columns to form a matrix with null matrices of order ${}^{n-2}C_2$ on the block diagonal.

3. The left hand side terms of (5.6) have one element (Q_{ij}) in common with coefficients $m_{ij}\tilde{z}_j$ and $\tilde{z}_i$ which appear on the diagonal of B under the equation ordering given (i≠j).

4. From (5.6) and $Q_{ij} = Q_{ji}$, it follows that m_{ij} is involved in the coefficient of $Q_{k\ell}$, ℓ>k, if <u>either</u> i=k <u>or</u> i=ℓ but not otherwise (but when i=k and j=ℓ then as 3 above).

5. From (5.6), the coefficient of $Q_{k\ell}$, ℓ>k, in the equation of m_{ij} involves either z_k or z_ℓ (unless i=k and j=ℓ as in 3 above) and it is the one whose index appears once only in the set {i,j,ℓ].

From these rules we construct B. As an illustration when n=4

$$B = \begin{bmatrix} m_{12}z_2+z_1 & m_{12}z_3 & m_{12}z_4 & z_3 & z_4 & 0 \\ m_{13}z_2 & m_{13}z_3+z_1 & m_{13}z_4 & z_2 & 0 & z_4 \\ m_{14}z_2 & m_{14}z_3 & m_{14}z_4+z_1 & 0 & z_2 & z_3 \\ m_{23}z_1 & z_1 & 0 & m_{23}z_3+z_2 & m_{23}z_4 & z_4 \\ m_{24}z_1 & 0 & z_1 & m_{24}z_3 & m_{24}z_4+z_3 & z_3 \\ 0 & m_{34}z_1 & z_1 & m_{34}z_2 & z_2 & m_{34}z_4+z_3 \end{bmatrix}$$

It is the fact that there are null submatrices of order ${}^{n-2}C_2$ which can be permuted to the block diagonal which makes it easy to check B is generally nonsingular.

NOTES

(1) We used $Q_{11} = 1$.

(2) The details of these well known operations are shown by Theil (1964).

(3) For any Q, r(P) = n*T < n where r(.) denotes rank. Further $H(p, d\underline{z}^*) = 0$ for $H \neq 0$, since r(H) = mT. So at least one $d\underline{z}^d$ can always be found to give any required $d\underline{z}^*$ since $r(P, d\underline{z}^*) \leq r(P)$.

(4) There is no doubt that collective preferences cannot exist in certain cases, for example, where Arrow's Possibility Theorem applies. But a collective preference function can only be said not to exist if certain strict conditions are met. These conditions have been spelled out in detail by Johansen (1969) and Bailey (1979); the decision process cannot be the outcome of a cooperative game, nor may the domain of the choice set be restricted, and the choice set must be reducible to two options if the non-existence of collective preferences is to be established. By the very nature of economic planning, these conditions cannot be met in preference functions appropriate to a government. We presume therefore that collective preferences may exist where our planning model is appropriate.

(5) Variable metric algorithms form one family of techniques for minimising a convex function; (3.1) and (3.2) encompass that family - see Dixon (1975) and the references therein.

(6) See again Dixon (1975).

(7) See Hughes Hallett (1979a).

(8) It is also implicit in our model of planning behaviour as the representation of the final inner iteration in the choice of $\underline{z}_p$ by (2.13) and again in the discusion of section 2.4.

(9) This also follows from (3.11) with (2.9b) inserted for $\underline{\delta}_1^{(s)}$.

(10) Strictly only "at least as good as other $\underline{z}^{(s)}$ values", but since $\underline{z}_p$ only was chosen there is no information loss in taking $\underline{z}_p$ preferred to $\underline{z}^{(s)}$. Hence, locally, strict convexity was assumed for $w(\tilde{\underline{z}})$.

(11) In fact most variable metric algorithm family members will lead to (3.25) and (3.26) (Rustem et al. (1978)) but for reasons of interpreting the quadratic approximation at (3.4) the symmetric rank one is a convenient choice.

(12) (4.9) is a reformulation of the link between $d\tilde{\underline{z}}^{(s)}$ and $dQ^{(s)}$ given in Hughes Hallett (1979a).

(13) Both statements can be checked by means of the example with n=4 given in appendix C.

(14) As $t \to T$, current $\underline{y}_t$ values may stray from $\underline{y}_t^d$ with less penalty than at earlier periods in a dynamic context since their lagged effects now occur beyond T; whereas earlier their current and lagged effects directly contribute to $w(\tilde{\underline{z}})$. A fuller discussion is in Pindyck (1973).

(15) The idea of using (B6) and (B7) is suggested in Rustem et al. (1978).

(16) Dhrymes (1970), p. 573-4.

REFERENCES

(1) Ancot, J.-P., Hughes Hallett, A.J. and Paelinck, J.H.P., The Determination of Implicit Preferences: To Approaches Compared, European Economic Review, (1980, forthcoming).

(2) Bailey, M.J., The possibility of rational social choice in an economy, Journal of Political Economy, 87, 1979, pp. 37-56.

(3) Dhrymes, P.J., Econometrics Statistical Foundations and Applications, Harper and Row, New York, 1970.

(4) Dixon, L.C.W, Quadratic Termination and Second Order Convergence, in Dixon, L.C.W. and Szegö, G.P. (eds), Towards Global Convergence, North Holland, Amsterdam, 1975.

(5) H.M.S.O., Report of the Committee on Policy Optimisation (Cmnd 7148), 1978.

(6) Hughes Hallett, A.J., The Sensitivity of Optimal Policies to Stochastic and Parametric Changes, in Holly, S., Rustem, B., Zarrop, M. (eds.), Optimal Control for Econometric Models: an Approach to Economic Policy Formulation, McMillan & Co., London, 1979(a).

(7) Hughes Hallett, A.J., Computing Revealed Preferences and Limits to the Validity of Quadratic Objective Functions for Policy Optimisation, Economics Letters, 2, 1979(b), pp. 27-32.

(8) Hughes Hallett, A.J., On Methods for Avoiding the a priori Numerical Specification of Preferences for Policy Selection, Economics Letters, 3, 1979(c), pp. 221-28.

(9) Hughes Hallett, A.J., The Qualitative Design of Economic Policies and Planner-Model Interaction, Proceedings of 3rd IFAC.IFORS World Congress on Dynamic Economics (Warsaw), Jansen, J.M., Pau, L.F. and Strazak, A. (eds.), Pergamom Press Ltd., Oxford, 1980.

(10) Johansen, L., An Examination of the Relevance of Kenneth Arrow's Possibility Theorem for Economic Planning, Economics of Planning, 9, 1969, pp. 5-41.

(11) Johansen, L., Establishing Preference Functions for Macro-economic Decision Models, European Economic Review, 5, 1974, pp. 41-66.

(12) Pindyck, P.S., Optimal Policies for Economic Stabilisation, Econometrica, 41, 1973, pp. 529-60.

(13) Rustem, B., Vellupillai, K., and Westcott, J.H., A Method for Respecifying the Weighting Matrix of a Quadratic Function, Automatica, 14, 1978, pp. 567-82.

(14) Theil, H., Optimal Decision Rules for Government and Industry, North Holland, Amsterdam, 1964.

CHAPTER 8

RECENT EXPERIENCES WITH THE QUALIFLEX MULTICRITERIA METHOD

J.-P. Ancot and J.H.P. Paelinck, Netherlands Economic Institute

1. INTRODUCTION

Since QUALIFLEX was brought before a meeting of the Regional Science Association(1) in 1975, a number of applications have been made and the method has been refined.

This method of multicriteria analysis was originally designed to deal with the most general kind of situation in which the available information for evaluating the alternatives with respect to the criteria can take the simplest ordinal form: the only prerequisite is the existence of an order relation between the alternatives and for each of the criteria selected. It is indeed typical of applications of multicriteria analysis that, at least for some criteria, only minimum information is available or permitted; that may be due not only to the sheer lack of (exact quantitative) information, but also to the fact that a 'vaguer' evaluation reflects the experts' view more exactly than a precise one (although noise nuisance can be measured in decibels, an evaluation based on such a measurement may be misleading), or to an expert's unwillingness to get 'too much involved' (a frequently encountered attitude of ecologists in the absence of general nature conservation programmes). QUALIFLEX finally combines different levels of information accuracy into one integrated treatment.

The technique, which has been exposed elsewhere(2), rests on the permutation idea; such combinatorial algorithms quickly become very time consuming as the number of dimensions of the decision space (the number of items and/or criteria) increases. Although this number is likely to remain fairly small in actual applications, computational methods have been derived to deal with cases involving a large number of alternatives(3).

Applications of QUALIFLEX have been made to water-management project selection (AQUAFLEX)(4), to the selection of optimum location-cum-phasing of airports (AEROFLEX)(5), and to waste disposal and recycling systems (ARA)(6); in these applications the point of view was taken that the decision maker is in general unable to specify exact numerical values for the weighting system of the criteria. That starting point leads to a useful organisation of the decision space, this decision space being defined here as the set of points the coordinates of which correspond to all possible (normalised) combinations of the weights applying to the criteria. Decision space can then be partitioned into a number of subspaces, within each of which a particular priority ranking holds; this organisation of decision space naturally leads to three different orientations for multicriteria analysis: a general description of the whole space (or of a large part of that space), detailed analysis of possible profiles of the decision maker (a hierarchical ranking of the criteria corresponding to a particular subspace), and punctual analysis of specific weight combinations. In this effort to produce a comprehensive picture of the solutions to the choice problem in the presence of a continuum of weight combinations rather than for individual numerical values, attention is also paid to the sensitivity of rankings of the alternatives with respect to movements within the decision (sub)space (variations in the weight combinations of the criteria).

The object of this chapter is to synthesise the actual state of the method, and discuss some of the problems that have been raised on the occasion of its various applications.

Let it be recalled that the original version of the method was based on a purely qualitative object-criteria-weights table, an example of which is reproduced below.

Table 1.

$\underline{w}$	$\underline{c}$ \ $\underline{o}'$	o_1	o_2	o_3
+++	c_1	+	++	+++
++	c_2	+++	++	+
+	c_3	++	+++	+

$\underline{o}'$ is the J-element row vector of objects to be ranked, $\underline{c}$ the I-element column vector of criteria by which the ranking should be done, $\underline{w}$ the column vector of qualitative weights governing the selection.

A ranking of $\underline{o}'$ on the basis of c_1, for example, can be illustrated by the next table, in which o_3 Đ o_2 Đ o_1[7] is reproduced.

Table 2.

	o_3	o_2	o_1
o_3	0	+1	+1
o_2	-1	0	+1
o_1	-1	-1	0

The convention here is that concordances with the dominances in the chosen ranking to be tested are valued +1, discordances -1; that boils down, in fact, to using a Kendall-τ approach[(8)].

A case often encountered is that of mixed information, in which some criteria might for instance be valued numerically; in such a case, an indicative ranking of c_2 (+++ = 47, ++ = 38, + = 35) would make use of the observed differences between these figures.

Table 3.

	o_3	o_2	o_1
o_3	0	-9	-12
o_2	+9	0	-3
o_1	+12	+3	0

This suggests that a possibility to be investigated is the transformation of the ordinal information (e.g. on c_1) into so-called pseudonumerical information[(9)]; the idea is to choose a representative point satisfying the constraints (in this case $o_3 \mathcal{D} o_2 \mathcal{D} o_1$ for c_1). In choosing one such point Abelson and Tukey[(10)] for example propose a maxmin-r^2 criterion, i.e. the minimum correlation of the vector to be chosen inside the admissible domain with any other vector i should be maximised. In the case of c_1, for instance, the Abelson-Tukey algorithm would give the <u>at</u>-solution in figure 1 hereafter; its coordinates are (.58,.24, .18). Another acceptable criterion could be the centre of gravity[(11)], which could be interpreted as the most probable point (expected value) in case of a rectangular distribution of the coordinates; its coordinates are given by

$$x_s = n^{-1} \sum_{i=s}^{n} i^{-1} \qquad (1.1)$$

where s is the sth rank in a series of n. In figure 1, for example, this would give the interior point (.61, .28, .11) shown as <u>g</u>, quite close to <u>at</u>; this is

not necessarily true of larger n; e.g. for n = 6 one has
$\underline{g}$ = (.41, .24, .16, .10, .06, .03) and $\underline{at}$ = (.41, .17, .13, .11, .10, .09).

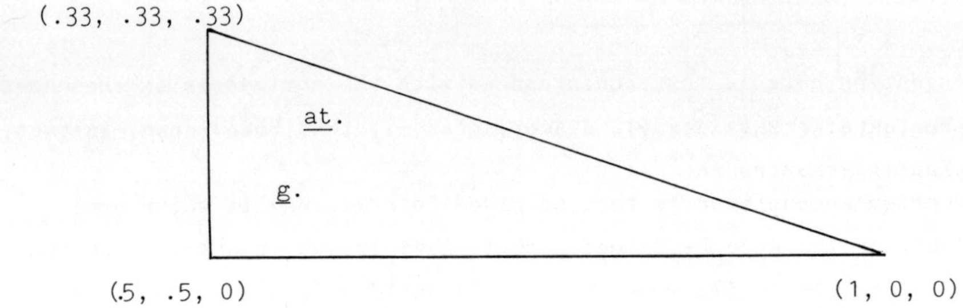

FIGURE 1.

Whatever the option taken, the results of tables like 2 or 3 have to be normalised by dividing them by their sum of positive values (3 in case of table 2, 24 in case of table 3); QUALIFLEX then combines the phase-one results up to the final criterion, by adding the weighted results.

From such tables the optimal ranking may be selected with the help of a maximum a-cyclical subgraph algorithm(12); three algorithms should be mentioned here.

The first is the Korte-Oberhofer relative-optima enumeration algorithm(13), the second the Lenstra branch-and-bound algorithm(14). A third one, first presented in J.-P. Ancot and J.H.P. Paelinck (1979), has been developed at the Netherlands Economic Institute and rests on a 0-1 programming approach(15); a simplification can be introduced, however, when (pseudo-) numerical information is used.

Consider the matrix of evaluations of the J objects with respect to the I criteria(16)

$$X = [x_{ij}], \quad i = 1, ..., I; \; j = 1, ..., J; \qquad (1.2)$$

the typical elements s_{ijk} of the matrix S_i of scores with respect to the ith criterion being defined as

$$s_{ijk} \triangleq x^*_{ij} - x^*_{ik}, \quad i = 1, ..., I; \; j,k = 1, ..., J \qquad (1.3)$$

where $\quad x^*_{ij} = \alpha_i^{-1} x_{ij}$ (1.4)

normalisation being introduced via

$$\alpha_i = \tfrac{1}{2} \sum_{jk} \left| x_{ij} - x_{ik} \right| \tag{1.5}$$

If the weights of the criteria are w_i, $i = 1, \ldots, I$, the total matrix of scores $\bar{S}$ is defined by its typical element:

$$\bar{s}_{jk} = \sum_i w_i s_{ijk} = \sum_i w_i x^*_{ij} - \sum_i w_i x^*_{ik} = \bar{x}^*_j - \bar{x}^*_k \tag{1.6}$$

where $\quad \bar{x}^*_j \triangleq \sum_i w_i x^*_{ij}$ (1.7)

The algorithm alluded to above then consists in rearranging the rows and columns in such a way as to maximise the sum of the elements above the main diagonal; the optimal permutation of the objects is the corresponding sequence of indices.

Consider now the vector $\underline{t}$ with typical element

$$t_j = \bar{x}^*_j, \qquad j = 1, \ldots, J \tag{1.8}$$

In Paelinck (1982, ch. 6) the following theorem is proved:
the optimal permutation of the objects is given by the sequence of indices corresponding to the arrangement by increasing order of magnitude of the elements t_j in $\underline{t}$.

2. SOME EXAMPLES OF THE USE OF QUALIFLEX

On the basis of the preceding developments, a complete computer programme with numerical and graphical output was developed(17); the purpose of this programme is not only to provide the user with the optimal ranking of the competing alternatives for a given set of weights, but also enable him to conduct a general study of the complete decision space and detailed analyses of selected sub-spaces corresponding to particular profiles of the hierarchy of criteria, including the sensitivity of the optimal rankings with respect to variations in the weight combinations. Examples will be developed next.

2.1 An application to an airport location problem

The first important application of the QUALIFLEX method was made in an airport location study set up to prepare decisions about extensions of the civil airport facilities in the Netherlands[18].

The decision problem in this study was the following: given predictions about future (medium-term) needs, what are the possibilities for realising the desired capacity expansions of the airport facilities? If more alternatives exist, the 'best' alternative should be chosen, on the basis not only of aviation-specific points of view, but also of more general criteria.

From the first part of the study it appeared that a number of important alternatives should be considered; these alternatives could be described as follows:

I: optimal use of Schiphol airport

II: stimulation of the regional airports

III: development of a supraregional airport

IV: development of a second national airport, with a fifty-fifty allocation of international commercial traffic between the two national airports

V: development of a new national airport for the major part of the international commercial traffic; Schiphol would be reduced to a regional airport.

The following criteria have been selected in function of four major aspects:

Table 4. The criteria for the airport location problem

Major aspect	Criteria
Aviation	Problems of transport system Capacity surplus traffic system Efficiency of traffic system National air space problems International air space problems
Economy	Decentralisation of airport capacity Rentability of airport Employment Access infrastructure
Space	Urbanisation Direct spatial congestion Compatibility with existing plans Rural areas
Environment	Noise nuisance Rural areas

Another aspect is the socio-cultural aspect of aviation; however, this criteria has not been explicitly included in the list because it is difficult to operationalise and also because it is implicitly present in several of the above criteria. A further aspect is that of civil defense: given that a large civil airport can be seen as a danger prone object, it should preferably be localised at large distance from dense population areas. This aspect thus favours alternatives which degrade the role of Schiphol airport. However, it is difficult to combine this aspect with the others, because it deals with risks for the civil population in exceptional circumstances; a consistent evaluation of this aspect is therefore impossible.

Prior to the detailed evaluation of each aspect, table 5 provides a first round ordinal evaluation process; the purpose of the second round is then to refine these evaluations to end up with cardinal scores, after possible elimination of those alternatives which, on the basis of the first round information, would appear to be completely dominated by the other alternatives.

Table 5. The matrix of first round evaluations

Criterion \ Alternative	I	II	III	IV	V
Aviation					
Transport system	+++++	+++	++	+	++++
Capacity surplus	+++	++	+	++++	+++++
Efficiency	+++++	++++	+++	+	++
Air space (national)	+++++	++++	++	+	+++
Air space (internat.)	+++++	++++	+	++	+++
Economy					
Decentralisation	+++	+++++	++++	++	+
Rentability	+++++	++++	+++	++	+
Employment	+	++	++++	+++	+++
Infrastructure	++++	++++	+++	++	+
Space					
Urbanisation	++	++	++	+++	+
Congestion	+++++	++++	+++	++	+
Compatibility	++	+	++++	+++	++++
Rural areas	++	++	+	+	+
Environment					
Noise	++	+	+++	++++	+++++
Rural areas	+++	++	++++	+	+++++

Each of the four groups was then analysed in detail. Within each group the ordinal evaluations of table 5 were translated into cardinal or numerical scores as the result of a thorough comparative study of the five alternatives with respect to each of the 'sub-criteria'. The working principle was the initial allocation of a score 100 to the 'best' alternative and the subsequent calibration of the other scores with respect to that fixed point; these scores were then normalised per 'sub-criteria' so as to add up to 100. Furthermore, within each of the four main groups a set of numerical weights was selected to express the relative importance of the various sub-criteria within the groups; also a set of weights was decided upon in order to represent the hierarchy existing between the main groups. Table 6 summarises this information.

Table 6. The input data

Criteria	I	II	III	IV	V	sub-weights	main weights
K1: Aviation							
1. Transport system	40	15	13	12	20	30	
2. Capacity system	18	16	14	22	30	11	40
3. Efficiency	34	29	19	4	14	35	
4. Air space (national)	40	35	6	4	15	12	
5. Air space (internat.)	40	30	4	6	20	12	
K2: Economy							
1. Decentralisation	22	30	24	15	9	28	
2. Rentability	31	30	25	9	5	24	20
3. Employment	16	17	27	20	20	33	
4. Infrastructure	30	30	25	10	5	15	
K3: Space							
1. Urbanisation	20	20	20	25	15	35	
2. Congestion	30	28	24	11	7	10	20
3. Compatibility	12	10	28	22	28	30	
4. Rural areas	23	23	18	18	25	25	
K4: Environment							
1. Noise	12	10	13	25	40	75	20
2. Rural areas	17	16	19	14	34	25	

The multicriteria method QUALIFLEX was then used to obtain the optimal ranking of the alternatives given the data of table 6. This optimal solution was as follows, ranking the alternatives from 'best' to 'worst':

Best: 1. alternative I: optimal use of Schiphol
2. alternative V: new national airport
3. alternative II: stimulate regional airports
4. alternative III: supranational airport
Worst: 5. alternative IV: second national airport

The relative distances between the alternatives within this ordering can also be computed; for the above optimal solution they were as follows:

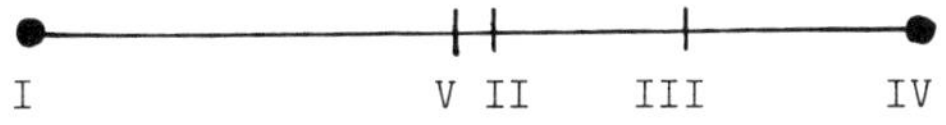

This figure shows that alternative I very clearly occupies the first position: a small change in the basic weights will not lead to a solution in which some other alternative would become more attractive than alternative I. On the contrary, the alternatives V and II are so close that their relative ranking can be expected to be highly sensitive to marginal changes in the weights: there is near indifference with respect to V and II in the optimal solution, whereas III is clearly worse than these two, and IV clearly worse than III.

It is obvious that the weights given in table 6 correspond to a specific set of preferences; other sets of preferences will, in general, produce different weight combinations which, in turn, will yield different optimal rankings. In this study a limited number of alternative (main) weight combinations were also examined; these cases are given in table 7.

Table 7. Variations in the main weights

Main weights / Description	K1	K2	K3	K4
1. Only aviation aspect is important	100	0	0	0
2. Only economic aspect is important	0	100	0	0
3. Only spatial aspect is important	0	0	100	0
4. Only environmental aspect is important	0	0	0	100
5. All aspects are equally important	25	25	25	25
6. Aviation most important; others equally important	40	20	20	20
7. Economy most important; others equally important	20	40	20	20
8. Space most important; others equally important	20	20	40	20
9. Environment most important; others equally important	20	20	20	40
10. All criteria equally important	all subweights equal			

The optimal solutions for each of these ten cases were as follows:

Case 1:

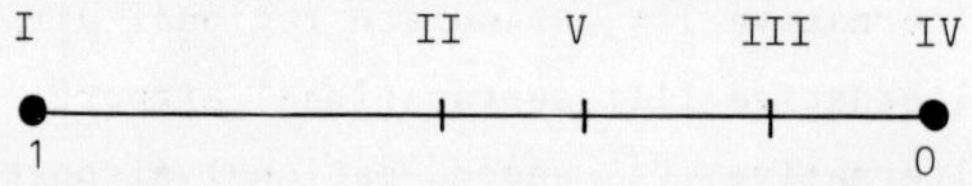

The relative positions of the alternatives are clear and the ranking is stable; with respect to the aviation aspect alternative I is the optimal solution.

Case 2:

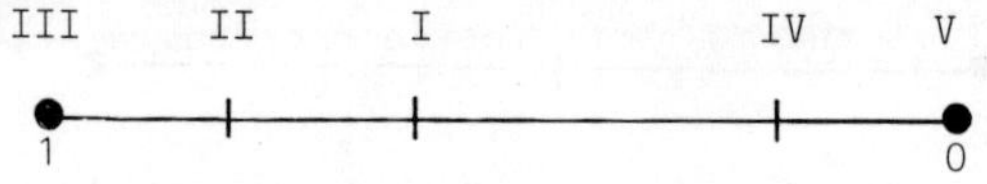

The relative positions of the alternatives are clear and the ranking is stable; with respect to the economic aspect alternative III is the optimal solution.

Case 3:

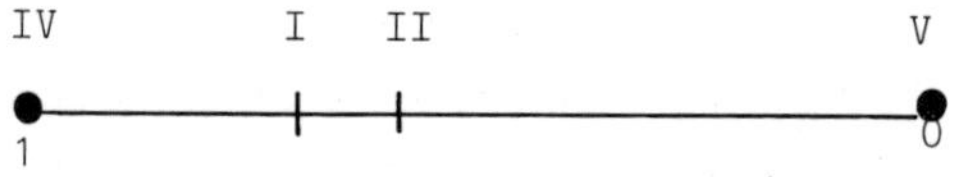

The positions of alternatives I, III and II are not clear; the ranking is unstable; alternative IV is the most attractive one from a spatial point of view.

Case 4:

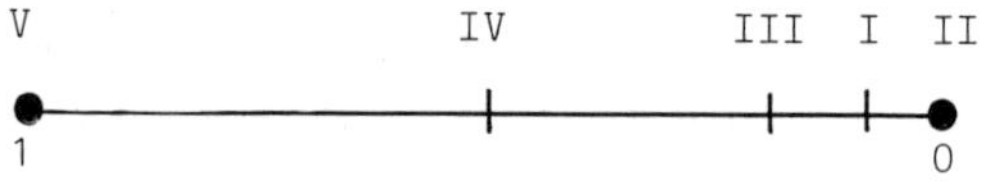

The positions of alternatives V and IV are very clear; the ranking of I, II and III is not clear; alternative V is the most attractive from an environmental point of view.

Case 5:

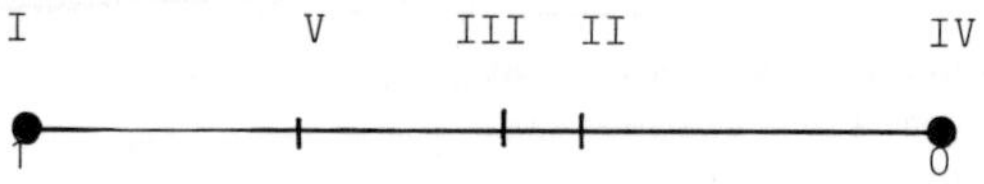

When all aspects are equally important, alternative I is the best one; the ranking of alternatives II and III is not stable.

Case 7[19]:

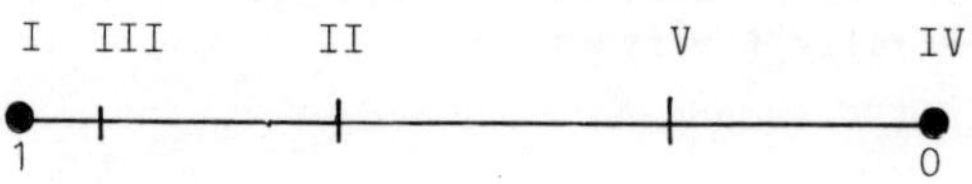

It is not clear which of the alternatives I and III is to be preferred: their ranking is not stable.

Case 8:

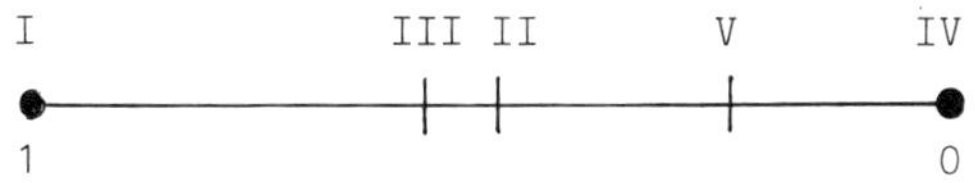

The ranking is unstable with respect to alternatives II and III; because alternative IV gets low scores on the other aspects, it takes here the last position although it is the most attractive one from a spatial point of view.

Case 9:

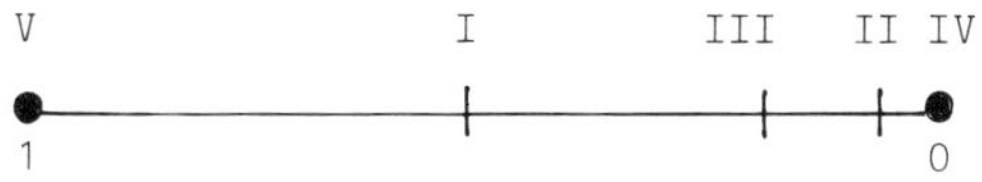

The ranking is unstable with respect to alternatives II and IV.

Case 10:

The ranking is unstable with respect to alternatives III and V.

2.2 An application to a water-management problem

In the course of the extensive C.W.G. water-management project[20] for the province Gelderland in the Netherlands it was recognised that the physical models developed in this study had to be complemented by a more integral socio-economic approach to study the relations between water demands of agriculture, households, industry, waste water control, conservation of nature reserves, etc. and the available water supply. In order to tackle these problems a case study for the region East-Gelderland was carried out in cooperation with the Netherlands Economic Institute[21].

This study can be divided into two parts. The aim of the first part is to develop a certain number of econometric models and to use these models to prepare medium-term forecast and simulation exercises to examine the (quantitative and qualitative) impact of policy instruments on water consumption; the water quality aspects, however, have been treated less extensively than the water quantity aspects. In the second part the results of these forecasts are used together with water management scenarios and management criteria to prepare the political decision process, by means of a multicriteria methodology, in a very explicit way.

First of all a relational scheme between the regional interest spheres was constructed; with the aid of this information, six alternative scenarios $P_1 \ldots P_6$ were derived and water demand predictions for the different sectors in a 10%-year in 1990 were calculated. The different scenarios $P_1 \ldots P_6$ are summarised in table 8; the following comments further characterise the six schemes:

P_1 (reference scenario): a more or less equilibrated distribution of the available water is aimed at. There is a shortage of sprinkling water of 19.10^6 m^3 in a 10% dry year;

P_2 (nature friendly scenario): the water demand is compressed by a tax of f 0.25 per m^3 on ground water abstraction by industry and by an increase of 20% of the drinking water tariff, sprinkling is restricted to 25% of the pasture land. Because of protection of wetlands, the costs of improvement works are increased by 50%;

P_3 (scenario with emphasis on agricultural and nature conservation): compensation works for nature protection lead to rises in the costs of improvements, farmers have priority over drinking water companies with respect to ground water abstractions, and, as a consequence, the water supply companies have to abstract about 19.10^6 m^3 per year surface water from the big rivers Rhine and IJssel;

P_4 (ground water economy scenario): ground water is saved by a tax on ground water abstraction (f 0,25 per m^3) to be payed by industry and farmers; sprinkling is restricted to the areas of 1976 (13% of pasture land);

P_5 (minimum scenario): minimum predictions for water demand and minimum change with respect to the existing situations;

P_6 (maximum scenario): maximum predictions for water demand and maximum change (within the feasible domain) with respect to the existing; in order to remain within the feasible constraints water prices are raised.

Table 8. Alternative Schemes

Plan / Characteristics	P_1 Reference (r)	P_2 Nature friendly (n)	P_3 Agriculture favouring (l)	P_4 Ground-water economy (g)	P_5 Minimum plan (a)	P_6 Maximum plan (z)
A. Agriculture A 1 Drainage	high & average priority regions see B	as P_1, see B	as P_1, Winterswijk is drained	as P_3	as P_1	as P_1, see B
A 2 Sprinkling	50% of pasture (10%-drought)	25% of pasture (10%-drought)	as P_1	13% of pasture (10%-drought)	as P_4	as P_1
A 3 Ground/ Surface water	ground water & paying surface water, see C_4	as P_1	ground water priority, see C_4	as P_1	ground water, see C_4	as P_1, also expensive surface water
B. Nature conservation	no works in 'nature-municipalities'*)	as P_1, in other municip. drainage costs are risen to protect nature	as P_2 plus drainage of Winterswijk	as P_3	as P_1	drainage of all nature municip. plus risen costs
C. Watersupply C 1 Quantity	mean forecast	as P_1	as P_1	as P_1	min. forecast	max. forecast
C 2 Tariff	no change	tax on ground water (industry); drinkw. tariff plus 20%	as P_1	tax on ground water (industry & agriculture)	as P_1	as P_2
C 3 Situation Pumping Stations	10-years master plan**), see B	min. damage to agriculture, see B	as P_2	as P_2	as P_1	as P_2
C 4 Ground/ Surface water	ground-water priority over agriculture	as P_1	ground water and surface water	as P_1	as P_1	as P_1
D. Environmental Hygiene D 1 Quality	plan of Water Board**) (biol. treatment)	as P_1 plus phosphate removal in Winterswijk	as P_1	as P_1	as P_1	as P_2
D 2 Situation water treatment plants	plan of Water Board**)	as P_1	as P_1	as P_1	as P_1	as P_1, plus reuse of waste water

*) Winterswijk, Vorden, Herwen-Aerdt, Pannerden, Hummelo-Keppel **) existing plans

The following six policy decision criteria emerged from discussions with the experts:

(i) the conservation of nature (N);

(ii) the interests of agriculture (L);

(iii) the satisfaction of the demand for drinking and industrial water (V);

(iv) global costs and benefits of the water management system (K);

(v) aspects of environmental hygiene (M); and

(vi) the ground water reserves (G).

Further, a certain hierarchy between these criteria obtains from the outset in the sense that the first four criteria must be considered as being relatively more important than the last two; justification for this is as follows. In the case of environmental hygiene, the different scenarios leave little scope for variations because water quality aspects have been treated less fully than water quantity aspects; as a result of this lack of detailed analysis rating this criterion higher than the first four might be misleading. As to the ground water reserve, it would be difficult to argue that this criterion could be an aim in itself in view of the very important other regional interests; it is a secondary criterion which should be used to restrain decisions implied by the first four.

Given the formulation of the alternative scenarios and the definition of the criteria, the evaluations of the six scenarios have to be made in relation to the six criteria. As far as nature and environmental hygiene are concerned, these evaluations were of an ordinal nature; with the other criteria there was in principle sufficient information available to establish cardinal or quantitative measures. Regarding the criteria agriculture and costs/benefits, these measures could in the first instance be expressed in net yields in guilders per year. The quantitative evaluations are based on published sources as well as on expert's advice; medium-term forecasts of water demands were computed by means of the demand models developed in the first part of the study and in function of the specific assumptions concerning the values of the explanatory variables and policy instruments as specified by the alternative scenarios. The results of the computations, which in certain instances correspond to fairly sophisticated evaluation processes, are summarised in table 9; all these computations were made under the restriction that the physical limit of the ground water supply does not exceed 70.10^6 m^3 per year. The evaluations with respect to the cost/benefit criterion as represented in table 9 are expressed with respect to the reference plan as a basis.

Table 9. Evaluations of the scenarios with respect to the criteria

Criteria \ Scenarios	r	n	l	g	a	z
agriculture (L)	3850	1688	3392	(-) 3027	2421	1514
nature (N)	+++	++++	++	++	+++	+
water supply (V)	52.8	34.7	52.8	38.7	40.8	46.5
environment (M)	+	++	+	+	+	++
costs (K)	0	(-)9717	(-) 458	(-)20297	2046	(-)23052
ground water (G) reserve	0	12.5	0	19.4	17.4	0

In the case of this application, the QUALIFLEX-method was developed one step further to yield a statistical-type analysis of the solution space. In this respect it is useful to introduce the concepts of decision space and decions subspaces which constitute the framework for the implementation of the method. The decision space is defined by the set of all possible combinations of weights which can be associated with the policy criteria; this decision space is then divided in subspaces corresponding to all possible weight combinations respecting a particular priority ranking of the criteria. For example, with three criteria, the decision space consists of all the points corresponding to all the possible values of the triplet (w_1, w_2, w_3) such that $w_1 + w_2 + w_3 = 1$ and w_1, w_2 and w_3 are non-negative values; a particular subspace can then be defined as the set of all points where, for example, $w_1 \geqslant w_2 \geqslant w_3$, meaning that within that subspace criterion number one is always more important than criterion number two, and that criterion number two is always more important than criterion number three. With three criteria, one obtains six (3!) such subspaces; this situation is illustrated in figure 2.

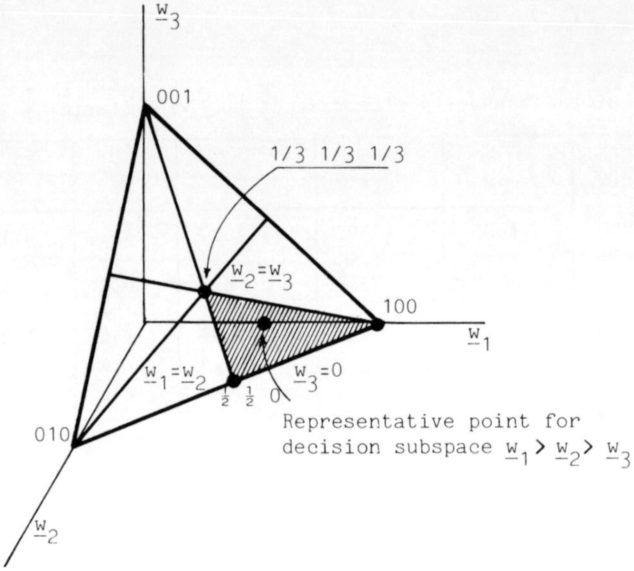

FIGURE 2. Decision space for a problem involving three criteria

This division of the decision space into subspaces is useful for the organisation of the study of the optimal solutions to the decision problems corresponding to all possible priority rankings of the policy criteria. Indeed, especially when the number of criteria increases, it may become extremely laborious to investigate in detail all possible choice situations. Although it is not the role of the researcher to determine the specific weights which should be associated with the criteria (and not even their priority rankings), he may like to make a more detailed examination of certain parts of the decision space, because they may appear to be particularly sensitive to marginal variations in the relative values of the weights or because they correspond to typical 'political' profiles. This partitioning of the decision space into subspaces leads to two types of multicriteria analyses: a general study of the whole space or of a very large part of that space to obtain a general picture of the variety and of the occurrence frequencies of the optimal decision possibilities as a function of the possible priority rankings of the criteria and a much more detailed study of the local structure of any selected subspace.

In order to illustrate the technique a fairly detailed analysis of a subspace with a simple structure will first be presented; the subspace selected corresponds to that part of the decision space in which the weights of the criteria obey the following (decreasing) priority ranking: agriculture, nature, costs, water supply, environmental hygiene and finally ground water reserves.

Figure 3 represents the results of scanning the subspace studied. A direct graphic representation of these results is not possible, because six criteria imply a five-dimensional subspace. The graph is a hexagon the corners of which represent the extreme combinations of the weights, given the ranking chosen. In point A the first criterion, agriculture, gets all the weight, the others playing no part there; in the next vertex, C, the first two criteria, agriculture and nature, get equal weights, the others being left out of considerations; in that way more criteria are gradually introduced until, in point K, all criteria play their part, all having the same weight. The other points investigated are then generated as follows. In five-dimensional space, schematically represented in figure 3 by the hexagon, every pair of successive vertices are linked by straight lines, producing the segments AC, CE, EG, etc., in the graph; of each such segment the middle is determined, which produces points B, D, F, etc. Still in five-dimensional space, these points are again connected pairwise by straightline segments, and the middles of the segments found, and so on. The procedure has several advantages: it permits simply and systematically to generate points within the five-dimensional subspace; it leads to a well-ordered and clear graphical representation, and it allows the generated points to converge to the point of gravity of the five-dimensional figure.

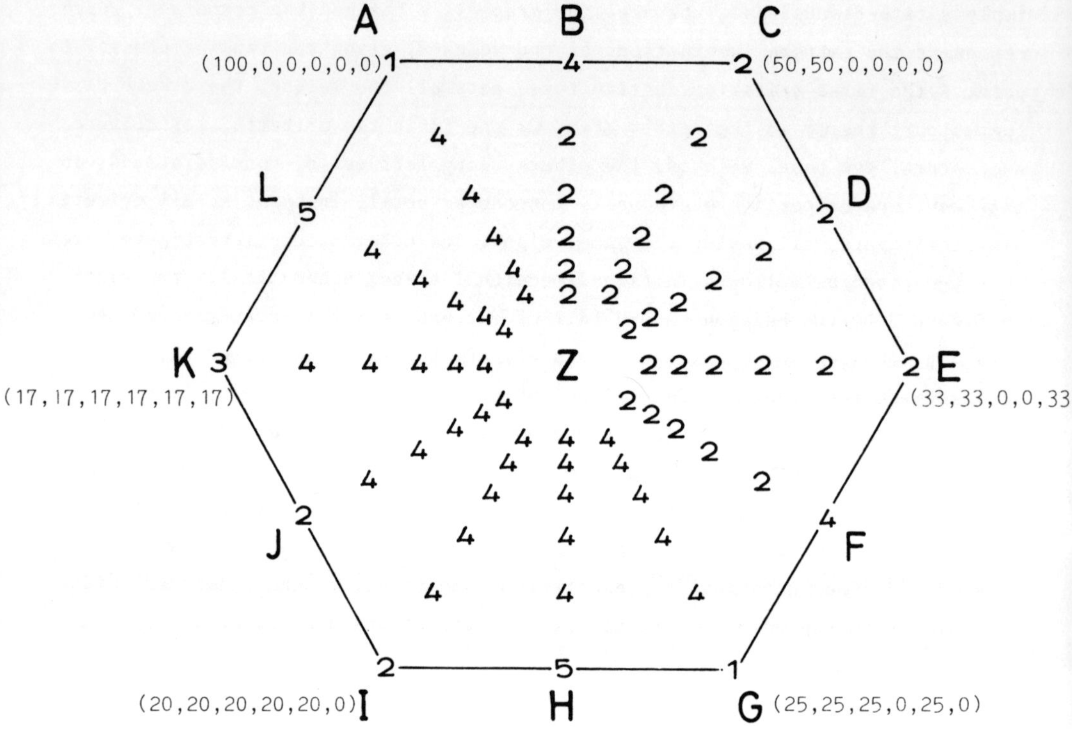

Number	Optimal ranking	Number	Optimal ranking
1	rlanzg	4	rnlazg
2	nrlazg	5	rlnazg
3	nralzg		

Legend: Alternative schemes:

r: reference plan
n: nature favouring scheme
l: agriculture favouring scheme
g: groundwater economy plan
a: minimum plan
z: maximum plan

Criteria:

N: nature
L: agriculture
V: water supply
K: costs
M: environment

FIGURE 3. AQUAFLEX. The optimum permutations in a decision subspace. Ranking of the weights L - N - K - V - M - G

For each point examined, figure 3 indicates the optimum ranking of the alternative scenarios by the integers from one to five; the corresponding rankings are defined in the accompanying table. In point A, for example, where agriculture is given weight 1 and where the other criteria are left out, the optimum ranking of the plans is ranking number 1, with the reference scenario in the lead, followed by the agriculture-favouring scenario, the minimum scenario, the nature favouring scenario, the maximum scenario, and with the ground water saving scenario bringing up the rear. In point C, where the criteria agriculture and nature both get weight ½, the nature-favouring scenario takes pride of place (as a result of bringing in the criterion nature), while the agriculture-favouring and the minimum scenario drop back in respect of the the optimum ranking of point A. In the next vertex, point E, where the third criterion, that of costs, is introduced with a weight equal to 1/3, the optimal ranking remains unchanged compared with the situation in point C. In the fourth vertex, point G, the optimal ranking is the same as in point A: introduction of the fourth criterion, water supply, with a weight equal to 1/4, has neutralized the impact of the previous two criteria.

The most important conclusion arising from the study of figure 3 is the division in about equal parts of the largest part of the subspace into two areas where rankings number two and four respectively are found to be optimal; the only difference between these two rankings is the relative ranking of the first two plans. When nature and costs are rated to be relatively important criteria, the nature-favouring scenario is the winner and in the other cases the reference scenario is the preferred alternative.

In order to illustrate the detailed analysis presented in the previous subsection figures 4 to 7 represent the results of scanning four subspaces which could correspond to relevant profiles in a policy decision situation with respect to water management. In order to preserve legibility the graphical representations which are analoguous to that of figure 3, are limited to the rankings of the three most attractive scenarios in each point studied.

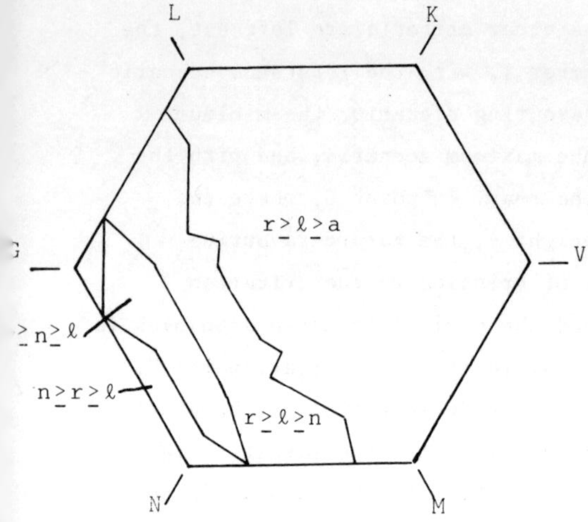

(L≥K≥V≥M≥N≥G)
FIGURE 4.
The agricultural expert

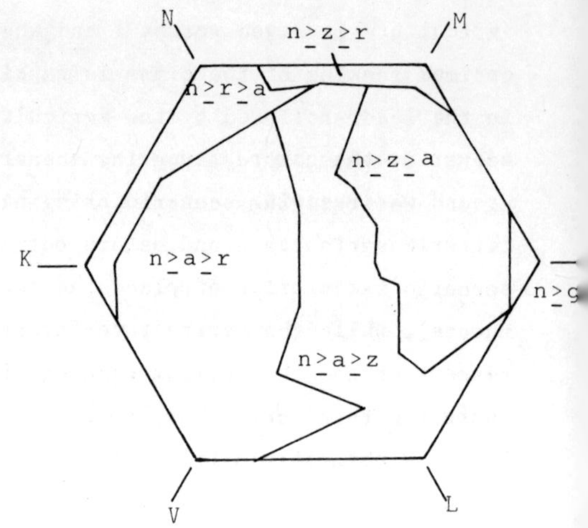

(N≥M≥G≥L≥V≥K)
FIGURE 5.
The ecologist

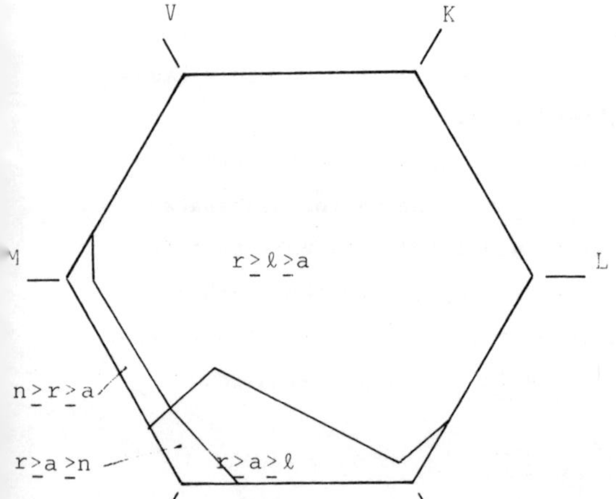

(V≥K≥L≥G≥N≥M)
FIGURE 6.
The drinking water supply companies

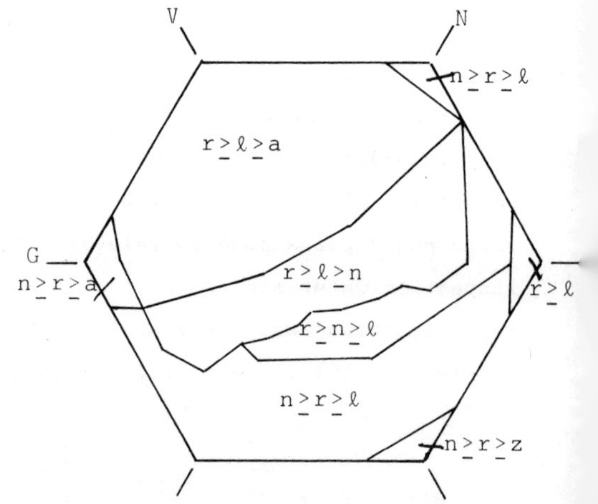

(V≥N≥L≥M≥K≥G)
FIGURE 7.
The provincial official

The first subspace (figure 4) is characterised by heavy weights for agricultural interests and cost elements; this priority ranking could be interpreted as corresponding to the preferences of the agricultural representative. From this figure it appears clearly that, as long as the first three or four criteria dominate (L, K, V and M), the optimal ranking of the scenarios is $r \geq l \geq a$; when the last two criteria, N and G, are introduced with steadily higher weights, the nature favouring scenario becomes gradually more attractive: it first takes third place ($r \geq l \geq n$), then second place ($r \geq n \geq l$) and finally first place ($n \geq r \geq a$ and $n \geq r \geq l$). The most typical ranking for this agricultural 'profile' probably corresponds to the upper right hand part of the hexagon, so that, in this case, ranking $r \geq l \geq a$ would be chosen.

The second case (figure 5) where nature, environmental hygiene and ground water reserves are the priority objectives could be typical for the ecological 'profile'. In this subspace the nature favouring scenario always takes the lead. The rankings of the other scenarios are rather variable. When M, G and L are relatively important (right hand part of the figure) the maximum and the minimum scenarios take up second and third place. In the left hand part of the figure, where criteria V, K and N carry relatively higher weights, these two scenarios lose their respective positions in favour of the reference scenario, which scores favourably with respect to these criteria.

The situation of figure 6 could be typical for the representative of the drinking water supply companies: high priorities to V, K and L. In this subspace the configuration is particularly simple: practically the whole subspace is dominated by the ranking $r \geq l \geq a$; only in the extreme lower left hand boundary some changes occur in favour of scenarios n and a.

The last case (figure 7) assumes that the satisfaction of demand for water by households and industry, agricultural interests and nature conservation are the primary objectives and that the other criteria are relatively unimportant. This 'profile' which could be representative of the preferences of the local authorities specially refers to the lower right hand part of the hexagon, where the rankings $r \geq l \geq n$, $n \geq r \geq l$ and $r \geq n \geq l$ dominate. This subspace has a more complicated structure; nevertheless the reference scenario nearly always takes up the lead often followed by the agriculture favouring scenario, especially when criterion V carries a large weight. In the lower left hand part of the hexagon the nature favouring scenario is the most attractive one as a result of the combined action of the environmental hygiene, costs and ground water reserves criteria.

From the study of these profiles it is clear that an 'aggregation' of figures 4 to 7 would in general lead to the choice of the reference scenario. Only if the ecological priorities of figure 7 were very dominant, the nature favouring scenario would be chosen. It is, however, relevant to point out in this context that, if all criteria are given equal weights (the extreme right hand vertex of the hexagon) the most attractive scenario is the nature favouring one, followed by the reference scenario.

The detailed study of a certain number of particularly relevant subspaces can be completed by a general study of the whole decision space. Indeed, as soon as the number of criteria is larger than 3 or 4, the number of subspaces increases so quickly that it becomes impractical to study all of them in detail. On the other hand some of these subspaces will be of particular interest to the researcher and to the decision maker because they correspond to weight combinations which are realistic and relevant with respect to the specific situation at hand, but other subspaces will obviously have a very much more marginal character, so that detailed analysis of these is not really required. Nevertheless, in order to get an overall picture of all possible solutions (e.g. to examine the robustness of the solutions or to arrive at a small number of synthetic statistics for the complete set of optimal solutions) one may wish to add to the detailed studies a general study, or at least a study covering a larger part of the possible sources of variations than any of the detailed studies.

This possibility is briefly illustrated hereafter. All 24 possible priority rankings of the criteria obtained when ground water and environment are always given respectively the lowest and second lowest priorities, are studied globally[22]. For each of the 24 selected subspaces 50 points or weight combinations were examined; these points were largely chosen in the more excentric parts of the subspaces (or near the boundary of the hexagon in figure 3), in order to allow for maximal variability in the corresponding rankings of the scenarios in those points.

The results of this general study can be summarized in the form of a frequency distribution; given that there are six scenarios the maximum number of different rankings is $6! = 720$. Analysis of the frequency distribution has shown that, although 1200 points were examined, only 15 different rankings were found, and that for individual subspaces that number is even lower: between 5 in the cases $L \geq N \geq V \geq K \geq M \geq G$, $L \geq N \geq K \geq V \geq M \geq G$ and $L \geq K \geq N \geq V \geq M \geq G$, and 12 in the case

K>N>V>L>M>G. Since the generation of points was concentrated in the more excentric parts of the subspaces (where, as can be seen from figure 3, the variability of the optimal permutations is much higher than in the region around the centre of gravity) one can already conclude that the results are very stable with respect to changes in the priority rankings of the criteria. This conclusion is confirmed when one studies the distribution in detail. It appears from this study that only four rankings cover 73% of the examined points: ranking rlanzg (meaning, by decreasing order of attractiveness, the reference scenario, the agriculture favouring scenario, the minimum scenario, the nature favouring scenario, the maximum scenario and the ground water saving scenario) in 24% of the points, ranking rlnazg in 18% of the points, ranking rnlazg in 16% of the points (this is ranking 4 in figure 3) and ranking nrlazg in 15% of the points (this is ranking 2 in figure 3). In a further 19% of the points two additional rankings hold: nralzg and rlazng. The main information contained in the frequency distribution is presented, in an aggregate way, in table 6; this table presents a cross-classification in percentages of the scenarios and the frequency of occurrence of their rankings (r comes in 72 of 100 cases on the first place). From table 10 an average picture emerges. The best scenario is undoubtedly the reference scenario; the second place, on average, is taken by the agriculture favouring scenario, the last but one and last places are taken, respectively, by the maximum and ground water saving scenarios. The nature favouring scenario shows a wide spread among the first four rankings; it is handicapped in several instances by the high drinking water prices it implies.

Table 10. Frequency distribution of the scenarios and the rankings for 1200 different weight combinations of the criteria

Ranking \ Scenario	r	n	l	g	a	z
1st	72	28	-	-	-	-
2nd	28	17	54	-	1	-
3rd	-	18	33	-	49	-
4th	-	25	13	-	50	12
5th	-	10	-	8	-	82
6th	-	2	-	92	-	6
Average ranking	1.28	2.78	2.59	5.92	3.49	4.94
Variance	0.20	2.07	0.50	0.01	0.47	0.18

2.3 An application to a waste disposal and - recycling study

In the case of this application[23] the method was further expanded to examine, given an optimal solution to the decision problem for a fixed cardinal priority ranking of the choice criteria, in how far the originally exogenously held variables should be modified to yield a different optimal solution. This problem can be related to the uncertainty elements characterising such variables as prices and markets for recycled products, new experimental technologies, etc. This type of use of the method leads to the so-called 'inverse' multicriteria problem which seeks to quantify the price to pay - in terms of original variables and/or weights of the criteria - when a suboptimal solution is preferred to the optimal one.

In a simple situation and in the cases where numerical or pseudo-numerical evaluations of the alternatives with respect to the criteria are used, the solution to this problem is straightforward. Suppose that for two given projects, r and s, the 'break-even' point is t, i.e. the minimum changes of their respective valuations with respect to a specific criterion necessary to induce a reversal of their rankings, when originally project r dominated project s in the optimal solution.

In terms of the notation introduced at the end of section 1, given the evaluation matrix (1.2) and a given set of weights w_i ($i=1,\ldots,I$) for the criteria, project r dominates project s in the optimal solution, according to (1.8), if

$$\bar{x}^*_r = \sum_i w_i x^*_{ir} < \bar{x}^*_s = \sum_i w_i x^*_{is} \tag{2.1}$$

or, equivalently, if

$$\sum_i w^*_i x_{ir} < \sum_i w^*_i x_{is} \tag{2.2}$$

where

$$w^*_i \triangleq \frac{w_i}{\frac{1}{2}\sum_{j,k} x_{ij} - x_{ik}} \tag{2.3}$$

Suppose γ to be the value by which the evaluation of project r with respect to criterion t must be increased and, at the same time, the value by which the evaluation of project s with respect to criterion t must be decreased, to obtain an equality in (2.1) instead of an inequality, to yield:

$$\sum_i w_i^* x_{ir} + w_t^* \gamma = \sum_i w_i^* x_{is} - w_t^* \gamma \tag{2.4}$$

It follows from (2.4) that, for equal allocation of the increments between the valuations of the two projects with respect to the same criterion, the 'break-even' point defined above obtains for

$$\gamma = \frac{\sum_i w_i^*(x_{is} - x_{ir})}{2w_t^*} = \frac{\bar{s}_{sr}}{2w_t^*} \tag{2.5}$$

This simple result (2.5) shows that, other things being equal, the sensitivity of the optimal rankings of the projects with respect to variations in the input data will be higher

(i) the 'closer' the projects are with respect to all the criteria and

(ii) the higher the weights of the criterion with respect to which sensitivity is examined.

The generalisation of this partial analysis to allow for variations in the evaluations with respect to more than one criterion, obviously offers an infinity of ways of arriving at a breaking point. In terms of variations Δx_{ir} and Δx_{is} of the original evaluations x_{ir} and x_{is}, condition (2.4) then becomes

$$\sum_i w_i^*(x_{ir} + \Delta x_{ir}) = \sum_i w_i^*(x_{is} + \Delta x_{is}) \tag{2.6}$$

Furthermore, if the condition of symmetric 'compensations' is imposed, i.e.

$$\Delta x_{ir} = -\Delta x_{is} = \Delta x_i \tag{2.7}$$

(2.6) yields

$$\sum_i w_i^* \Delta x_i = \frac{\sum_i w_i^*(x_{is} - x_{ir})}{2} = \frac{\bar{s}_{sr}}{2} \tag{2.8}$$

implying (I-1) degrees of freedom for the choice of the Δx_i's. However, it may be worth noting that the weighted sum of all these increments must equal half the total score obtained for the pair of projects (s,r).

Briefly sketched, the data for this application were the following; five different scenarios were selected: 100% sanitary landfilling, a combination of 76% incineration and 24% sanitary landfilling, a combination of 69% mechanical sorting and 31% sanitary landfilling, 100% incineration and finally 100% mechanical sorting.

Concerning the decision criteria, eight aspects were selected: three mainly economic ones, four environmental ones and a social one. These criteria are: minimum net costs of a scenario, maximum recycling of primary inputs, energy saving, minimum air, soil, surface water and ground water pollution, minimum space needed and finally the social aspects consisting of a certain number of elements referring to general working conditions within each of the scenarios.

Table 11 provides evaluations of each scenario with respect to each criterion. These evaluations refer to a basic situation where the following assumptions are made for the medium term : 'high' forecast of the refuse flow, 'global' cost estimates and 'average' prices for recycled products.

Table 11. Basic evaluations of the scenarios

Criterion \ Scenario	100% sanitary landfilling	incineration (76%) & sanit. landf. (24%)	mech. sorting (69%) & sanit. landf. (31%)	100% incineration	100% mech. sorting
Economic aspects					
Net costs[a)]	299	405	329	403	326
Recycling of primary products[b)]	0	0	48	0	70
Energy saving[c)]	0	122 - 531	114 to 423	161 - 700	166 - 613
Environmental aspects					
Air pollution[d)]	none	positive	negative	positive	negative
Surface water pollution[e)]	+	++	+++	++	+++
Soil and ground-water poll.[f)]	100	62	52	50	30
Space needed[g)]	0	58	62	90	90
Social aspects[h)]	4	2	0	4	1

Notes: a) in .000 guilders per week
b) in percentage of the quantity supplied
c) net energy saving in TJ per year (minimum and maximum assumption)
d) positive: pollution increase, negative: pollution decrease
e) the more +'s, the better
f) degree of pollution according to a combined score
g) percentage volume reduction of supplied refuse
h) combined score

As outlined above, the criteria were divided into three large groups: the economic aspects, the environmental aspects and the social aspects. The general conclusion at the level of these main groups, obtained according to the methodology outlined in the previous sections, was the great robustness of the optimal solution with respect to changes in weights for the criteria. In order to further test the outcomes for sensitivity a detailed study was conducted at the level of the subcriteria; this will be illustrated here for one example, in which the main criteria are all judged equally important and the individual subcriteria also all carry equal weights within each main group. The optimal solution for this case is given in table 12 below.

Table 12. Optimal solution in the case where all subcriteria are equally important within each group and the main groups also carry equal weights

Scenarios	100% sanitary land-filling	incineration & sanitary land-filling	mech. sorting & sanitary land-filling	100% incineration	100% mechanical sorting
optimal ranking	4	5	3	2	1
relative distances	80	100	65	29	0

From the point of view of the choice to be made the two most important alternatives are undoubtedly the 100% incineration and the 100% mechanical sorting scenarios. Indeed, the other three can be seen as subcases of these two major options. It seems therefore relevant to examine the relation between the original evaluations of the alternatives (table 11) and the optimal ranking of the scenarios (table 12) specially with respect to these two techniques. In particular, it may be of interest to compute the amounts by which the original evaluations must be altered in order to yield a reversal in the optimal ranking of these two scenarios.

The results of such an analysis are presented in table 13; they correspond to the weight combinations used in table 12. The alterations of the original evaluations are maximum changes in the sense that they all refer to changes in the evaluations with respect to only one criterion, leaving the evaluations with respect to the other criteria unchanged; furthermore, the changes have been equally allocated to the two scores. With respect to net costs, it means

Table 13. Changes in the evaluations necessary to produce an inversed optimal ranking of the main alternatives

Criterion	New evaluations		Percentage change with respect to the original evaluation
	100% incineration	100% mechanical sorting	
Costs	20.1	17.9	3.1
Recycling	27.1	31.9	27.1
Energy	41.7	16.3	11.7
Air pollution	26.4	16.6	16.4
Surface water pollution	28.1	16.9	15.1
Soil and ground water pollution	41.9	17.1	17.9
Space needed	44.8	13.2	15.8
Social aspects	41.7	4.3	5.7

that for the scenario 100% incinerations costs must be reduced from 403 thousand guilders per week to approximately 345 thousand guilders per week, whereas, at the same time, the costs of 100% mechanical sorting should rise from 326 thousand guilders per week to approximately 388 thousand guilders per week. The necessary changes with respect to the recycling criterion are infeasible because, given that recycling is impossible for the incineration scenario, the total amount of the changes should be imputed to the mechanical sorting scenario, which would make this scenario completely irrelevant. With respect to the energy criterion, the implications of the changes are that the new interval would be respectively 235 to 945 and 92 to 370 for the two alternatives. With respect to the three pollution criteria, the changes imply that the corresponding ordinal evaluations should be reversed. The percentage reduction of the quantity supplied (which was originally estimated to be of the order of 90%) would have to become maximum (100%) for the incineration alternative and nearly nihil for the mechanical sorting scenario; this would obviously produce a nonsensical situation. Finally, with respect to social aspects the relative advantage of the incineration scenario above mechanical sorting should be dramatically increased.

These changes correspond to rather extreme situations, because in each case only two elements of the evaluation matrix are modified. Such changes can, of course, also be combined. Nevertheless, it appears from this analysis that the incineration scenario practically never dominates the mechanical sorting techniques; this would only be possible if the social aspects were given a relatively very high weight or if the original evaluations would all have to change in the same direction with more than marginal amounts, exceeding by far the order of magnitude which can be expected from estimation errors, uncertainty elements and the qualitative nature of some of the evaluations.

2.4 Other applications

Two other applications of the QUALIFLEX method should be mentioned. They are of special interest because they correspond to much less obvious multi-criteria-type situations than the case-studies presented in the previous sections; nevertheless the method proved to provide a powerful tool of analysis for these cases.

In a first case QUALIFLEX was used to evaluate and compare a series of so-called level of service indicators for urban public transport. This evaluation which was part of a study commissioned by the Ministry of Transport and Public Works of the Netherlands[24] was designed to select appropriate indicators for the purposes of subsidy allocation to town councils in the area of public transport infrastructure.

Table 14 summarises the degree to wich the various indicators satisfy the various criteria selected. The qualitative evaluations (measured by the scores) of 14 level of service indicators with respect to eight criteria, summarised in table 14, can be used as the starting point for a multicriteria analysis of the indicators with respect to a given set of priority rankings of the criteria. In this context a multicriteria analysis tries to provide answers to the following questions:

(a) Are there structural rankings among the indicators which remain invariant across different weight combinations (i.e. are certain indicators consistently attractive, are other indicators consistently unattractive, independently of changes in weights associated with the criteria)?
(b) What is the sensitivity of an optimal ranking of the indicators (given a weight combination for the criteria), to marginal changes in the weights?
(c) What is the specific effect of individual criteria on the ranking of the indicators?
(d) If instability is observed in the optimal ranking across priority rankings of the criteria, where does it occur and how can it be characterised?

Table 14. Summary evaluation of level of service indicators*)

	Comparability	Coverage	Responsiveness to need	Benefit measurement	Comprehensibility	Flexibility	Efficiency	Data availability
Indicator								
(1) Supply related indicators								
a. Route density	xx	x	x	x	xxxxx	x	x	xxxx
b. Route density weighted by population	xxx	xx	xx	xx	xxx	x	xx	xxx
c. Proximity to stops	xx	x	xx	xx	xxxx	x	x	xx
d. Proximity to stops combined with route density weighted by population	xxx	xx	xxx	xx	xxx	x	xx	xx
e. Vehicle operating speed	x	x	x	xx	xxx	x	x	xxx
f. Service frequency	x	xx	x	xx	xxxx	xx	x	xxx
g. Service frequency related to population and density	xx	xx	xxx	xx	xxx	xx	xxx	xxx
(2) Generalized time-related indicators								
a. Generalized speed	xxx	xxx	xx	xxx	xxx	xx	xxx	x
b. Generalized cost	xxx	xxxx	xx	xxxx	xx	xx	xxx	x
c. All-mode competition ratio	xxx	xxx	xx	x	x	xx	xxx	x
d. Auto competiton ratio	xxx	xxx	xx	x	xx	xx	xxx	x
(3) Demand related indicators								
a. Ratio of actual to potential demand	xxx	xxxx	xxxx	xx	xx	xx	xxx	x
b. Service elasticity of demand	xx	xxx	xxx	xx	xx	x	x	xx
(4) Combined indicators								
a. Benefit-cost ratio of additional services	xxxx	xxxx	xxx	xxxx	xx	xxx	xxx	x

*) The indicators are scored under each criterion from x = lowest score to xxxx = highest score.

The results of the computations are summarised in figure 8. Twelve different weight combinations for the criteria are considered: with the exception of the last one, case E of figure 8, they are all consistent with the priority ranking of the criteria which emerged from the discussions of the contact group and which correspond to the natural order of the columns of table 14 (i.e. comparability (1) takes on higher priority, data availability (8) lowest priority).

The cases denoted I to VIII in figure 8 correspond to the gradual introduction of criteria, one by one, in the decision process, the 'active' criteria being given equal weights. In case I only the most important criterion, comparability, is used to determine the optimal ranking of the indicators and it is assigned 100 percent of the weight (this corresponds to a unicriterion situation); in case II the next most important criterion, coverage, is introduced and the total weight is equally divided between the two 'active' criteria; finally in case VIII all the criteria take part and they all have equal weights (this could be interpreted as the neutral situation, since all criteria are equally important in the classification process). The purpose of studying these eight weight combinations is to establish the impact of the introduction of individual criteria in the process on the previous optimal ranking of the indicators.

Cases G, A and B correspond to three weight combinations which can be considered to be typical for the stated ranking of the criteria. In case G, the weights are the coordinates of the 'centre of gravity' of a figure in eight-dimensional space determined by the vertices whose coordinates are the weight-sets used in cases I to VIII; the weights in case G are the averages of the weights of cases I to VIII. Cases A and B are variants on case G. In both cases comparability clearly dominates the other criteria and data availability is clearly relatively unimportant; the other criteria are given pairwise equal weights. The difference between A and B is that in the latter case the weight distribution is more even than in the former cases.

Finally, case E corresponds to an extreme perturbation of the stated priority ranking: in this case the weights take on the same numerical value as in case G but in reversed order.

In figure 8 the level of service indicators are ranked for each weight combination according to the optimal solution found, the most 'attractive' indicator appearing on the extreme left and the 'worst' alternative on the extreme right in the graphs; the relative distance between the positions

Figure 8. A multicriteria comparison of level of service indicators

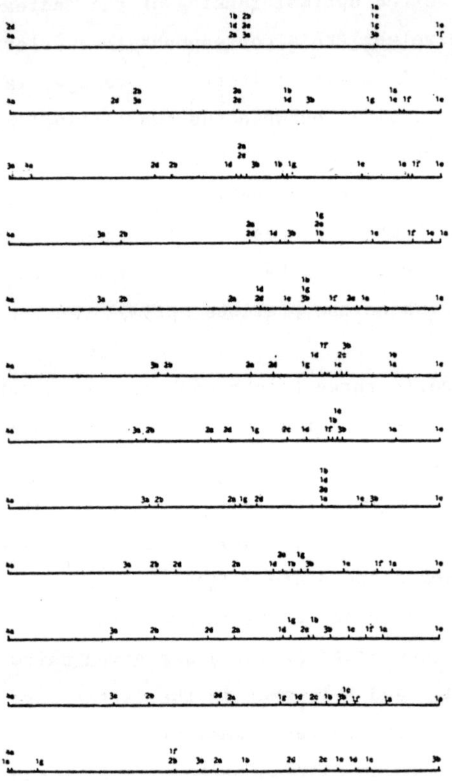

OPTIMAL RANKING OF INDICATORS	CRITERIA (1)	(2)	(3)	(4)	(5)	(6)	(7)	(8)
I	100	0	0	0	0	0	0	0
II	50	50	0	0	0	0	0	0
III	33	33	33	0	0	0	0	0
IV	25	25	25	25	0	0	0	0
V	20	20	20	20	20	0	0	0
VI	17	17	17	17	17	17	0	0
VII	14	14	14	14	14	14	14	0
VIII	12½	12½	12½	12½	12½	12½	12½	12½
G	34	21	15	11	8	5	3	2
A	24	18	18	12	12	6	6	3
B	21	17	17	13	13	8	8	4
E	2	3	5	8	11	15	21	34

occupied by the indicators in their optimal rankings are measures of the 'robustness' of the solution: the larger the distance between two indicators the more stable the corresponding relative ordering[25]. The analysis of figure 8 gives rise to the following comments:

(a) In the 'unicriterion' situation I four clusters are obtained corresponding to the evaluation of the indicators with respect to the first criterion (comparability) as given in the first column of figure 8; when one moves from situation I to situation II these clusters explode as a result of the introduction of the second criterion (coverage): this second criterion is relatively favourable for indicators 1f, 2b, 3a and 3b so that these indicators become more attractive, and relatively unfavourable for indicators 1a, 1b, 1c, 1d and 2d which become relatively less attractive; this reordering process continues until case VIII, where all criteria take part in the process with equal weights; in this 'neutral' situation one obtains five or six clusters: the combined indicator, 4a, is clearly the best one, followed by 3a and 2b; the performance of 2a, 1g and 2d can be considered to be 'average', indicator 1e is clearly the worst one, all others performing relatively poorly.

(b) Comparing cases G, A and B, which are more representative weight combinations for the stated priority ranking of the criteria, with the 'neutral' situation in case VIII, one observes that, as far as the more attractive indicators are concerned, the solutions show little change: the combined indicator definitely remains the preferred one, followed by 3a (ratio of actual to potential demand) and 2b (generalized speed) which show a tendency to move forward; in general, all supply related indicators perform poorly.

(c) The solutions are very insensitive to marginal changes in the weight combinations: this appears from a comparison of cases G, A and B; even if the priority ranking of the criteria is drastically changed, as in case E, a great degree of robustness is observed for certain indicators: the more attractive indicators 4a, 2b, 3a and 2a maintain their positions, but they are now competing with some of the supply related indicators (1a, 1g, 1f, 1b) probably as a result of the favourable rankings of the latter with respect to data availability and comprehensibility which become more important criteria.

Another - and last - illustration of the multicriteria method QUALIFLEX given here pertains to its application for the construction of an indicator of the level of urban services in regions in Europe[26].

An indicator of the level of urban services is a multi-dimensional concept. If the most obvious component of such an indicator is the population of the largest agglomeration(s) in the region, other elements also contribute to qualify the urban character of a region. Such elements are, for example, the rank occupied by the large cities of the region in the urban hierarchy (does the region contain the national capital city, large international business centres, seats of international organisations, etc.?), the accessibility of the large cities from the point of view of interregional and international transport and communications, the general urban structure of the region (mononucleus versus extensive cluster structure). Even the above mentioned obvious population component of the indicator is not a clear-cut objective data: should this element be restricted to the population of the largest city in the region, or to that of the largest agglomeration or to that of an even larger entity? These different variables will converge in certain regions, whereas in others considerable discrepancies between them will be observed.

The approach used attempts at combining these various relevant elements in order to obtain a composite indicator of the level of urban service in the 76 standard regions in the European Community; the final urbanisation variable is again based on multicriteria analysis whereby the various dimensions of the variable are interpreted as criteria with respect to each of which each region obtains a given score (at any moment in time); and these ratings can thus be combined, via the multicriteria technique, in different ways according to the priority rankings associated with the components (or criteria) to result in a comprehensive indicator.

If the resulting series can be shown to be stable with respect to variations in the weighted combinations of the components (within realistic limits), it can be used as a set of acceptable indicators of the level of urban service.

Some of the elements, such as population in large agglomerations, can be quantified and other elements, such as the presence or absence in the region of the national capital city, are of a qualitative nature. Furthermore, different units of measurement are used to measure different quantifiable components: population is measured in numbers, population density in numbers per square kilometer. This implies that a straightforward (weighted or unweighted) adding-up procedure is impractical; at least some prior transformations of the original data must be made before these can be combined into a global indicator.

An empirical way to obtain such an indicator would be to start from the most important component of the indicator - 'population in large agglomerations' - and to correct this variable, in an ad hoc fashion, in function of the perceived specific urban context of the regions; such a procedure, however, would be unsatisfactory on several accounts. Firstly, because of the arbitrary nature of the 'correction process', it is to be expected that different experts would obtain results which would be significantly different and that they would be unable to come to an agreement as their criteria would remain largely implicit. Secondly, even if these experts could agree, potential users of the resulting indicators would probably mistrust the data on the argument that they were obtained in a subjective manner and that slight changes in the weightings of the component factors might have led to totally different conclusions. This would lead to an endless 'dialogue de sourds', would leave all parties very unsatisfied and would finally be extremely counterproductive.

It is therefore necessary to adopt a more rigorous, scientific approach in order to guarantee the objectivity and the credibility of the indicator. The most important requisites of such an approach are the expliciteness of the components on which the indicator is based, the complete and exact knowledge of how the elements are combined and the possibility of testing the sensitivity of the indicator to changes in the inputs. In other words, if subjectivity cannot completely be eliminated - because a selection must be made of the components, weights must be chosen to combine them - it should be possible to provide indications about the degree of subjectivity which is present in the final results. The multicriteria methodology meets these different conditions.

It can be shown[27] that the QUALIFLEX method can be written in the form of a mathematical program consisting of a quadratic objective function to be maximised subject to a number of linear constraints; this formalisation makes it possible to go one step beyond the determination of the optimal ranking of objects (regions) for any given weight set to obtain a representation of this ranking on a numerical scale over a fixed interval (such as the interval [0,1], where, in the present context, the value 0 corresponds to the region with the lowest level of urbanisation and the value 1 corresponds to the region with the highest level of urbanisation). Indeed, the loss in value of the objective function with respect to its maximum value for a suboptimal solution generated by the permutation of two regions in the optimal solution can be interpreted as an indicator of the difference between levels of urban service offered by the two regions.

The choice of the weights to be used in the computations is of course of crucial importance. Although some hierarchy of the components immediately emerges (in the sense that, for example, the population variables are felt to be more important elements than the availability of an international airport in the region) it is extremely difficult to define a single numerical weight combination for these elements which would be universally aceptable. It is therefore necessary to study a certain number of alternative weight-sets in order to cover a sufficiently large spectrum of possibilities. If the resulting indicator shows a considerable sensitivity to changes in weights it would be dismissed as being unreliable and further investigations would be necessary to obtain more robust series; on the contrary, if stable results are obtained, one has at the same time solved the practical problem of constructing a reliable indicator and met the objection regarding the subjectivity issue.

Table 15 presents five sets of weights which have been selected to conduct this exercise. In the first weight set (W_1) the decreasing weights correspond to a typical representation of the hypothesis whereby the components as listed in the table would be of decreasing importance. The second weight set (W_2)

Table 15. The weight combinations for the components of the urban service level indicator*

Component	Weights				
	W_1	W_2	W_3	W_4	W_5
Population variables: min. and average cases	.40	.17	.30	.40	.50
Polulation variables: maximum case	.37	.14	.20	.30	.35
Population density	.23	.14	.10	.10	.15
Urban structure	.24/.16	.17/.14	.15	.20	.10
Presence of capital city	.16/.11	.17/.14	.15	.10	.10
Presence of intern. organ.	.10/.07	.17/.14	.15	.10	.10
Presence of business centre	.06/.04	.17/.14	.15	.10	.10
Intern. airtransport facilities	.03/.02	.17/.14	.10	.10	.10

* The first weight sets are functions of the number of criteria: where the notation a/b appears in the table, a corresponds to the value to be used in a six-component situation (population variables: min. and average cases) and b corresponds to the value for a seven component situation (population variable: maximum case).

corresponds to a situation where all components are combined with equal weights, they are all assumed to be equally important ingredients of the aggregate indicator; this can be considered to be an extreme hypothesis given the relatively low weight of the population variables. The other three weight sets acknowledge the relative importance of the population variables and distribute the residual weight mass more or less evenly across the other components, the last case (W_5) being the one where the population variables are allowed the strongest dominance.

These five weight sets combined with the three alternative specifications of the population variable generate a table of 15 series for each year. With the first two population variables (minimum and average cases) one deals with a six component situation; the third population variable (maximum case) gives rise to a seven component situation, as a result of the introduction in this case of the population density variable, acting as a correcting factor for the overoptimistic population measurement.

In order to test the robustness of the computed series with respect to variations in the weights used to combine the different elements, these sets of five series have been computed for the year 1960 using the weights defined in table 15. For the three sets of results corresponding to the three alternative specifications of the population variable the mean of the series varies from 0.0796 to 0.1298 and the standard deviation from 0.1393 to 0.1911; the largest part of this variation, however, occurs between tables, i.e. is due to the introduction of different population variables rather than to changing weights. In the case of the third specification of that variable, the mean and the standard deviation are both marginally higher than in the other two cases: they respectively range from 0.1117 to 0.1298 and from 0.1762 to 0.1911, illustrating the stability within the tables.

To test the relative invariance of the series with respect to changes in weights the Pearson product moment correlation coefficients have been computed for all within tables pairwise comparisons of the series. From these results it appeared immediately that the method used produces indicators which are extremely insensitive to changes in the weights of the original components: 73% of the correlation coefficients are equal to 0.99, the lowest value being 0.96 (first specification of the population variable: situations where all components get equal weights versus situations where population weights are as large as all the other elements taken together). If on the other hand one makes similar comparisons across different specifications of the population variable for given weight sets the variability increases slightly.

Finally, series have been computed for 1950 and 1970[28], using weight sets W_1 and W_5 (the most extreme combinations, as appears from table 15 and from the correlation analysis). Comparisons of these results point to a small upgrading tendency of urban service level through time (increasing mean) and a more questionable tendency to increasing dispersion of this variable through time (in most cases, increasing variances). These comparisons are also useful to provide indications about the stability of the indicator through time. If the series show no great stability through time it is necessary to incorporate this variable into models as a time-dependent variable and to pursue further data collection efforts beyond 1970. As in the previous case, this stability can be tested by analysing the appropriate correlation tables; these tables provide illustrations of the results for the second specification of the population variable (average case) respectively with weight set W_1 and weight set W_5. Inspection of these tables also points to a great stability of the series through time, so much so that it is reasonable to consider these indicators as invariant in the time span of the study. Even if small cardinal variations are observed through time, ordinal rankings of the regions are hardly likely to be affected.

In summary, it can be said that the computed series show a high degree of robustness on all counts: with respect to changes in the weights with which the basic elements are combined, with respect to time and, to a somewhat lesser extent, with respect to alternative specifications of the population variable.

A final comment is in order concerning the actual content of the series. A striking feature of the results is the logarithmic-type shape of the series: this leads to a fairly natural division of the regions into classes.

Table 16 attempts such a grouping procedure, on the basis of the series for 1960, with weight set W_5 and the second population variable (average case); these classes have finally been used to complete the regional map of Europe (figure 9).

Table 16. Distribution of regions in Europe according to the indicator of level of urban services

Value of indicator	Regions
more than .30	South-East (GB), Region Parisienne (F), Nordrhein-Westfalen (D).
.20 to .30	Lazio (I), West-Nederland (NL), North-West (GB), Brabant (B), West-Midlands (GB).
.10 to .20	Sjaelland (Dk), Hamburg (D), Scotland (GB), Yorkshire (GB), Hessen (D), Lombardia (I), Berlin (D), Baden-Würtemberg (D), Luxembourg (L), Bayern (D), Ireland (Ir).
.01 to .10	all other regions.
.00 to .01	Noord Nederland (NL), Centre (F), Bourgogne (F), Fyn (Dk), Limousin (F), Umbria (I), Marche (I), Picardie (F), Abruzzi (I), Trentino/Alto A. (I), Basse-Normandie (F), Franche-Comté (F), Corse (F), Poitou-Charentes (F), Basilicata (I), Molise (I), Valle d'Aosta (I).

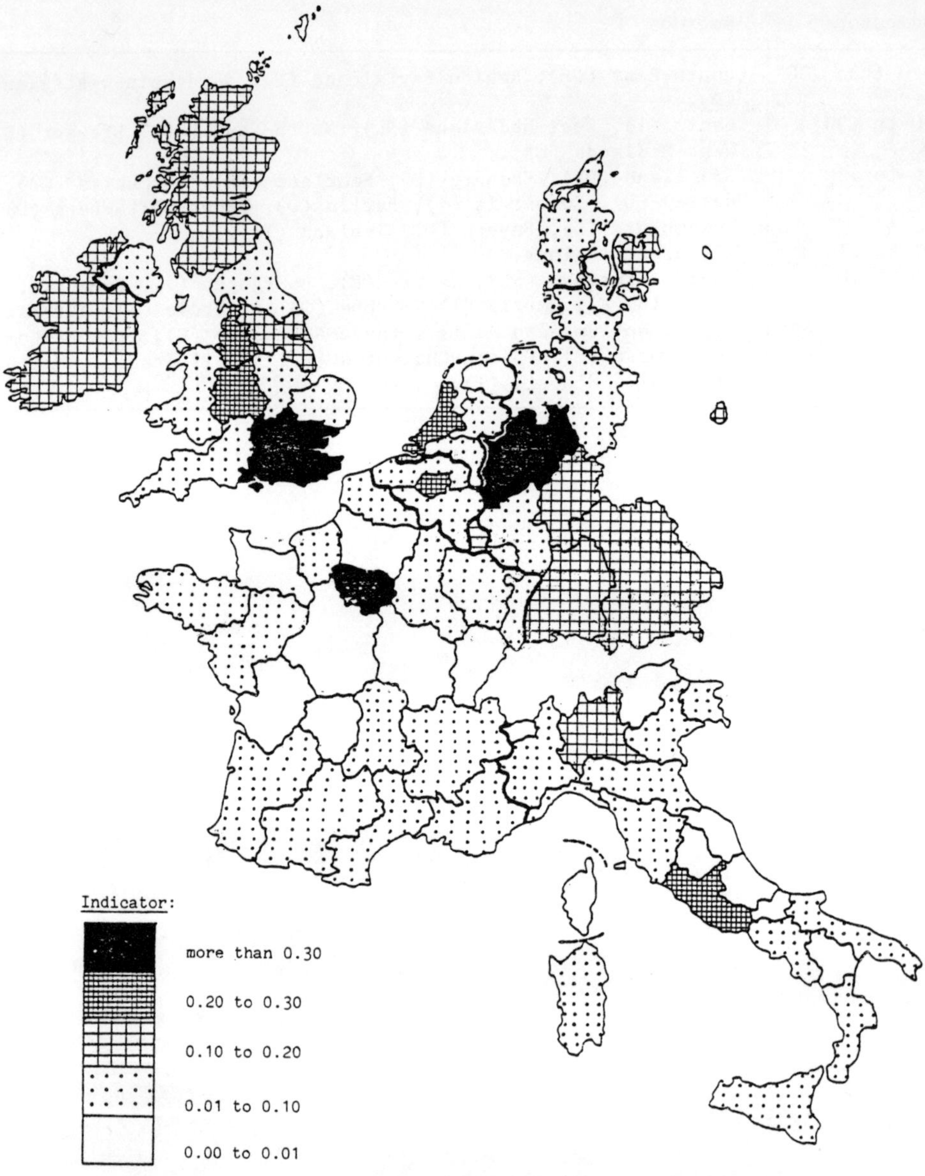

FIGURE 9. The level of urban service in regions in Europe

3. SOME MATHEMATICAL DEVELOPMENTS

In Ancot and Paelinck (1979) and Paelinck (1982, Ch. 6) it was shown that the matrix presentation problem alluded to in section 1 can be formulated as the following quadratic assignment problem

$$\max \underline{x}'H\underline{x} \tag{3.1}$$

s.t.

$$J\underline{x} = \underline{i} \tag{3.2}$$

$$\underline{x} = \hat{\underline{x}}\underline{x} \tag{3.3}$$

where $\underline{x}$ is an $(n^2 \times 1)$ 0-1 (conditions (3.3)) column vector, n being the order of the original matrix - call it A - to be permutated. H is an $(n^2 \times n^2)$ matrix constructed from the latter, J a $(2n - 1) \times n^2$ 0-1) matrix of so-called assignment conditions, guaranteeing that each row and column of A will occupy one and only one place in the final (optimal) permutation; finally $\underline{i}$ is the $(n^2 \times 1)$ unit column vector.

We first prove the following

<u>Lemma</u>: conditions (3.2) and (3.3) are equivalent to

$$J\underline{x} = \underline{i} \tag{3.4}$$

$$\underline{x}'\underline{x} = n \tag{3.5}$$

$$\underline{x} \geq \underline{0} \tag{3.6}$$

<u>Proof</u>: from (3.4) and (3.6) it follows that

$$\underline{0} \leq \underline{x} \leq \underline{i} \tag{3.7};$$

now let us suppose that for some x_{ij} (29)

$$0 < x_{ij} < 1 \tag{3.8}$$

so

$$x_{ij}(x_{ij} - 1) < 0 \tag{3.9}$$

But (3.5) together with

$$\underline{i}'\underline{x} = n \tag{3.10}$$

derived from (3.4) implies

$$\underline{x}'(\underline{x} - \underline{i}) = 0 \tag{3.11}$$

so that at least one term $x_{kl}(x_{kl} - 1)$, $l \neq i$ or $l \neq j$, should be positive, implying $x_{kl} > 1$, which contradicts (3.4). .˙.

In Paelinck (1982, Ch. 6) it has further been shown that (3.1) could be transformed into

$$\underline{x}'\tilde{H}\,\underline{x} \overset{\Delta}{=} \underline{x}'(H - \Pi H \Pi)\underline{x} \tag{3.12}$$

$$= 2n^{-1}\,\underline{\tilde{h}}'\,\underline{x} + \underline{y}\,\tilde{H}\,\underline{y} \tag{3.13}$$

$$0\underset{=}{-}1 \quad \frac{2}{n-2}\,\underline{y}'\,\hat{\tilde{h}}\,\underline{y} + \underline{y}\,\tilde{H}\,\underline{y} \tag{3.14}$$

$$\overset{\Delta}{=} \underline{y}'\,\tilde{\tilde{H}}\,\underline{y} \tag{3.15}$$

Matrix Π is a permutation matrix which corresponds to the full or complete permutation of A (i.e. row and column 1 will occupy place n, row and column 2 place n-1, etc.); furthermore

$$\underline{\tilde{h}} \overset{\Delta}{=} \tilde{H}\,\underline{i} \tag{3.16}$$

$$\underline{y} \overset{\Delta}{=} \underline{x} - n^{-1}\underline{i} \tag{3.17}$$

a cap (^) transforming $\underline{\tilde{h}}$ into a diagonal matrix [30]. The simple reason for (3.12) is that the solution to the maximum quadratic assignment (3.1) through (3.3) corresponds to A having a maximum sum of figures above the main diagonal, implying in its turn a minimum sum below that diagonal, and again a maximum difference between the sums above and below that diagonal.

Problem (3.1) through (3.3) can now be written as

$$\max \underline{y}' \tilde{\tilde{H}} \underline{y} \tag{3.18}$$

s.t. $$J\underline{y} = 0 \tag{3.19}$$

$$\underline{y}'\underline{y} = n - 1 \tag{3.20}$$

$$\underline{y} \geqslant - n^{-1}\underline{i} \tag{3.21}$$

guaranteeing that

$$\underline{y} \in \{ - n^{-1}, n-1/n\} . \tag{3.22}$$

We now prove the following

Theorem: problem (3.18) through (3.21) can canonically be solved as an eigenvalue problem.

Proof: the first-order conditions for a maximum of (3.18) are

$$\frac{\partial L}{\partial \underline{y}'} \stackrel{\Delta}{=} 2 \tilde{\tilde{H}} \underline{y} - J'\underline{\lambda} - 2\rho\underline{y} - 2 \underline{\sigma}^{-} \stackrel{o}{=} \underline{0} \tag{3.23}$$

where L is the symbol for the Lagrangean of problem (3.18) through (3.21), $\underline{\lambda}$ and ρ the Lagrangean multipliers corresponding to conditions (3.19) and (3.20), and $\underline{\sigma}-$ is a non-positive vector of dual variables belonging to conditions (3.19), with the Kuhn-Tucker product property [31]

$$\hat{\sigma}^{-} (\underline{y} + n^{-1}\underline{i}) \stackrel{o}{=} \underline{0} \tag{3.24}$$

The symbol $\stackrel{o}{=}$ stands for 'equilibrium condition'; condition (3.21) has been doubled to redefine $\underline{\sigma}-$ and ease further derivations.

Elimination of $\underline{\lambda}$ leads to

$$(P\tilde{\tilde{H}} - \rho I)\underline{y} \stackrel{o}{=} P\underline{\sigma}^{-1} \tag{3.25}$$

which from (3.24) turns into

$$[\,P(\tilde{\tilde{H}} + n\hat{\sigma}^-) - \rho I\,]\,\underline{y} \overset{o}{=} \underline{0} \tag{3.26}$$

From (3.23) there comes:

$$\underline{y}'\tilde{\tilde{H}}\,\underline{y} \overset{o}{=} (n-1)\rho + \underline{\sigma}^{-\prime}\underline{y} \tag{3.27}$$

Now supposing $\underline{\sigma}^-$ to be given, the scalar $\underline{\sigma}^{-1}\underline{y}$ is a constant as the y_{ij}'s[32] corresponding to strictly negative σ_{ij}'s are all equal to n^{-1}; so to maximise $\underline{y}'\tilde{H}\,\underline{y}$, the maximum eigenvalue of $\tilde{H} + n\hat{\sigma}^-$ and the corresponding eigenvector should be selected .˙.

The implication of the theorem is that the solution to (3.1) - (3.3) can be found via (3.18) - (3.21) from a diagonally modified $\approx$ H matrix; work is now underway to inspect the consequences of scanning over, e.g., a scalar matrix.

Some experience has been gained with non-modified $\tilde{\tilde{H}}$ - matrices[33]; in the case of an (11 x 11) matrix [34], the following result was obtained.

Table 22.

Initial ranking	Optimum ranking	Obtained ranking[35]
1	1	1
2	10	11
3	11	10
4	7	8
5	8	7
6	5	6
7	4	5
8	2	2
9	3	4
10	6	3
11	9	9

Table 23 hereafter synthesises the result.

Table 23.

Degree of shift[36]	
0	3
1	6
2	1
3	0
4	1
5 and more	0

The same result was obtained in other cases: the majority of shifts are of degree one, and can be easily located by inspecting the resulting upper and lower diagonal terms of the permutated A-matrix (the lower diagonal term being larger than the upper diagonal one). Using $\tilde{H}$ (or $\approx{H}$) instead of H[37], and despite numerical inaccuracies in computing large $\underline{y}$-vectors[38], one can obtain solutions very near to the optimum.

4. CONCLUSION

We have tried to show how logical reasoning can lead, on the one hand, to the integration of various aspects in a problem of economic decision making, and on the other hand to the discovery of new methods of solution. The latter point, especially, is illustrative of the renewal in operational thinking, and points to the dialectics between Luigi Solari's approach[39] and a possible path 'from quantitative to qualitative economics'.

NOTES

(1) European Meeting at Budapest; see J.H.P. Paelinck, (1976); the approach is part of an increasing body of literature of which we only quote A. Bailly, (1977), R.B. Banerji and M.D. Mesarovic, (1970), G. Fandel,(1972), C. Gros (1978), G. Leitmann, (1976), H. Thiriez and S. Zionts, (1976), J. Wilhelm, (1975), W.M. Wonham, (1974), M. Zeleny, (1974) and (1975), S. Zionts, (1977) and (1979), S. Zionts and D. Deshpande, (1979).

(2) See, e.g., J.H.P. Paelinck, (1976), P. Mastenbroek and J.H.P. Paelinck, (1976), J.H.P Paelinck, (1977) and (1982, Ch. 6).

(3) J.-P. Ancot and J.H.P. Paelinck, (1980), and section 3.

(4) J.-P. Ancot, (1980).

(5) J.H.P. Paelinck, (1977).

(6) Netherlands Economic Institute, (1979a).

(7) The Đ-symbol represents (strict) 'dominance' or 'preference'.

(8) P. Mastenbroek and J.H.P. Paelinck, (1976); ties can also be handled easily (in case of ties, zeroes would appear). In fact, the method is of the median ranking type; see M. Roubens, (1980) and (1981).

(9) See, e.g., L. Mimpen, (1979).

(10) R.P. Abelson and J.W. Tukey, (1963).

(11) See Schärlig, (1973).

(12) This way of approaching the problem was suggested to us by our colleague A. Rinnooy Kan.

(13) B. Korte and W. Oberhofer, (1968) and (1969).

(14) H.W. Lenstra Jr., (1973).

(15) On the general background, see N. Christofides a.o., (1977), N. Christofides, (1978), D. Hausmann, (1978), A. Kaufmann and E. Pichat, (1977), J.K. Lenstra and A.H.G. Rinnooy Kan, (1977), and T.M. Liebling and M. Rössler, (1978).

(16) See table 1 and comment; matrix X of (1.2) is a numerical and/or pseudo-numerical version of it.

(17) The authors' thanks go to W. Verstegen, who assisted in developing this programme; see J.-P. Ancot and W. Verstegen, (1979).

(18) See Ministerie van Verkeer and Waterstaat, (1979), especially Chapter VI.

(19) Case 6 has been given separate treatment above.

(20) "Commissie Bestudering Waterhuishouding Gelderland"

(21) See Netherlands Economic Institute, (1979b) and J.-P. Ancot and E.Romijn (1980), J.-P. Ancot and Th. van de Nes, (1981).

(22) The reasons why the criteria 'ground water' and 'environment' are held on the two lower rankings are the lack of variability of the scenarios with respect to waste water treatment and the nature of the ground water criteria which could be seen as a consequence of other criteria such as nature, agriculture, water supply and even costs.

(23) See Netherlands Economic Institute, (1979a).

(24) See Institute of Public Administration and Netherlands Economic Institute, (1980).

(25) These distances are proportional to the loss in the objective function incurred when the positions of the corresponding indicators are reversed in the optimal solution.

(26) This application was made in the context of the FLEUR-study on regional sectoral growth in the EEC; see Netherlands Economic Institute, (1981).

(27) See section 3 hereafter.

(28) For the first population variable (minimum case), no information is available for 1950.

(29) The notation x_{ij} is used to mean 'row and column of x_i of the original A-matrix now occupy row and column j'.

(30) The symbol $\overset{0-1}{=}$ stands for 0-1 equivalence.

(31) See J.H.P. Paelinck and P. Nijkamp, (1975), ch. 6.

(32) The notation y_{ij} is defined in the same way as the notation x_{ij}.

(33) See E. Aanen, (1981).

(34) Taken from Netherlands Economic Institute, (1979b).

(35) Using linear programming applied to $\underline{y}$ as coefficients of the objective function; see J.-P. Ancot and J.H.P. Paelinck, (1979).

(36) With regard to the optimal solution.

(37) Meaning a combination of necessary conditions.

(38) In the present case, $\underline{y}$ was (121 x 1).

(39) L. Solari, (1977).

REFERENCES

(1) Aanen, E., Verslag van onderzoek 2-B (Report on Research 2-B), Rotterdam, Faculty of Economics, Department of Mathematical Decision Theory, Erasmus University, Rotterdam, August 1981 (mimeographed).

(2) Abelson, R.P. and Tukey, J.W., Efficient Utilization of Non-Numerical Information in Quantitative Analysis: General Theory and the Case of Simple order, Annals of Mathematical Statistics, vol. 34, 1963, pp. 1349-69.
(3) Ancot, J.-P., An Econometric Spatial Demand Model for Water with an Application to the Demand for Water in East-Gelderland, Seminar on Economic Instruments for Rational Utilization of Water Resources, Committee on Water Problems of the Economic Commission for Europe, United Nations, Veldhoven, 1980.
(4) Ancot, J.-P. and van de Nes, Th.J., Integral Evaluations of Alternative Water Management Scenarios in East-Gelderland, in: Water Resources Management on a Regional Scale, Committee for Hydrological Research TNO, Proceedings and Informations, no. 27, The Hague, 1981, pp. 129-64.
(5) Ancot, J.-P. and Paelinck, J.H.P, Multicriteria Analysis, Combinatorial Mathematics and Zero-One Programming, Netherlands Economic Institute, Series: FEER, Rotterdam, 1980 (mimeographed).
(6) Ancot, J.-P. and Romijn, E., Design and Economic Evaluation of Alternative Schemes for Combined Use of Groundwater and Surface Water in Eastern Gelderland with the Use of the Multicriteria Method QUALIFLEX, Seminar on Economic Instruments for Rational Utilization of Water Resources, Committee on Water Problems of the Economic Commission for Europe, United Nations, Veldhoven, 1980.
(7) Ancot, J.-P. and Verstegen, W., Het computerprogramma QUALIF, Handleiding, (The computer programme QUALIF, Manual), Netherlands Economic Institute, Rotterdam, 1979 (mimeographed).
(8) Bailly, A., Les études d'impact, problèmes méthodologiques, Le Géomètre, no. 10, october 1977, pp. 18-30.
(9) Banerji, R.B. and Mesarovic, M.D., Theoretical Approach to Non-Numerical Problem Solving, Springer Verlag, Berlin, 1970.
(10) Christofides, N., The Quadratic Assignment Problem, Some Recent Results, paper presented at the International Symposium on Locational Decisions, Baniff (Alberta), April 1978.
(11) Christofides, N., Mingozzi, A. and Toth, P., Quadratic Assignment Problem (A Survey), Summer School in Combinatorial Optimization, Papers, Corbino, 1977 (mimeographed).
(12) Fandel, G., Optimale Entscheidung bei mehrfacher Zielsetzung, Springer Verlag, Berlin, 1972.
(13) Gros, Chr., Generalization of Fenckel's Quality Theorem for Convex Vector Optimization, European Journal of Operations Research, vol. 2, no. 5, 1978, pp. 368-76.
(14) Hausmann, D. (ed.), Integer Programming and Related Areas; Bibliography, Springer Verlag, Berlin, 1978.
(15) Institute of Public Administration and Netherlands Economic Institute, Service Levels of Urban Public Transport, A Series of documents on a study commissioned by the Ministry of Transport and Public Works of the Netherlands, III, First Interim Report, The Hague, 1980.
(16) Kaufmann, A. and Pichat, E., Méthodes mathématiques non-numériques et leurs algorithmes: 1. Algorithmes de recherche des éléments maximaux; 2. Algorithmes de recherche de chemins et problèmes associés, Masson, Paris, 1977.
(17) Korte, B. und Oberhofer, W., Zwei Algorithmen zur Lösung eines komplexen Reihenfolgeproblems, Unternehmerforschung, vol. 12, 1968, pp. 217-31.
(18) Korte, B. und Oberhofer, W., Zur Triangulation von Input-Output Matrizen, Jahrbücher für Nationalökonomie und Statistik, vol. 182, 1969, pp. 398-433.

(19) Leitmann, G., Multicriteria Decision Making and Differential Games, Plenum Press, New York and London, 1976.
(20) Lenstra Jr., H.W., The Acyclic Subgraph Problem, Mathematical Centre, Dept. of Mathematical Decision Theory, Paper, BW 26/73, Amsterdam, 1973 (mimeographed).
(21) Lenstra, J.K. and Rinnooy Kan, A.H.G., Computational Complexity of Discrete Optimization Processes, Erasmus University, Econometric Institute, Report 7727/0, Rotterdam, 1977 (mimeographed).
(22) Liebling, J.M. and Rössler, M. (eds.), Kombinatorische Entscheidungsprobleme: Methode und Analyse, Springer Verlag, Berlin, 1978.
(23) Mastenbroek, P. and Paelinck, J.H.P., Qualitative Multiple Criteria Decision-Making: Information Exhaustion, Uncertainty and Non-Linearities, International Journal of Transport Econmics, vol. III, no. 3, 1976, pp. 43-62.
(24) Mimpen, L., Multi-criteria Analyse en pseudo-metrische transformaties, (Multi-Criteria Analysis and Pseudo-Metric Transformations), Master's Thesis, Erasmus University, Faculty of Economics, Rotterdam, 1977 (mimeographed).
(25) Ministerie van Verkeer en Waterstaat, Struktuurschema Burgerluchtvaartterreinen, Deel A, Den Haag, 1979.
(26) Netherlands Economic Institute, Algemeen Rekenmodel Afvalstoffen (General Computer Model Waste Products), Verslag over een feasibility studie (intern rapport), Rotterdam, 1979a (mimeographed).
(27) Netherlands Economic Institute, AQUAFLEX, Een modelmatige Aanpak ter Voorbereiding van Beslissingen met betrekking tot de Waterhuishouding in Gelderland, Basisrapport Commissie Waterhuishouding Gelderland, Rotterdam, 1979b.
(28) Netherlands Economic Institute, Factors of Location in Europe (FLEUR), Stage V, The Explanatory Variables; Synthesis Report, Rotterdam, 1981 (mimeographed).
(29) Paelinck, J.H.P. and Nijkamp, P., Operational Theory and Method in Regional Economics, Saxon House, Farnborough, 1975.
(30) Paelinck, J.H.P., Qualitative Multiple Criteria Analysis: Environmental Protection and Multiregional Development, Papers of the Regional Science Association, vol. 36, 1976, pp. 59-74.
(31) Paelinck, J.H.P., Qualitative Multiple Criteria Analysis: an Application to Airport Location, Environment and Planning, vol. 9, 1977, pp.883-95.
(32) Paelinck, J.H.P. (with assistance of J.-P. Ancot and J.H. Kuiper),Formal Spatial Economic Analysis, Gower Publishing Company Ltd., Aldershot, 1982.
(33) Roubens, M., Analyse et agrégation des préférences: modélisation, ajustemente et résumé de données relationnelles, Revue Belge de Statistique, d'Informatique et de Recherche Op-erationnelle, 20, no.2, 1980, pp. 36-67.
(34) Roubens, M., Médiane et méthodes multicritères ordinales, Mons, Faculté Polytechnique, 1981 (mimeographed).
(35) Schärlig, A., About the Confusion between the Center of Gravity and Weber's Optimum, Regional and Urban Economics: Operational Methods,vol. 3, no. 4, 1973, pp. 371-82.
(36) Solari, L., De l'économie qualitative à l'économie quantitative, Masson, Paris, 1977.
(37) Thiriez, H. and Zionts, S. (eds.), Multiple Criteria Decision Making, Springer Verlag, Berlin, 1976.
(38) Wilhelm, J., Objective and Multi-Objective Decision Making under Uncertainty, Springer Verlag, Berlin 1975.
(39) Wonham, W.M., Linear Multivariable Control, A Geometric Approach, Springer Verlag, Berlin, 1974.

(40) Zeleny, M., Linear Multiobjective Programming, Springer Verlag, Berlin, 1974.
(41) Zeleny, M. (ed.), Multiple Criteria Decision Making, Springer Verlag, Berlin, 1975.
(42) Zionts, S. (ed.), Multiple Criteria Problem Solving, Springer Verlag, Berlin, 1977.
(43) Zionts, S., Methods for Solving Management Problems Involving Multiple Objectives, State University of New York at Buffalo, School of Business Administration, Working Paper Series, no. 400, March 1979 (mimeographed).
(44) Zionts, S. and Deshpande, D., Energy Planning Using a Multiple Criteria Decision Method, State University of New York at Buffalo, School of Business Administration, Working Paper Series, no.398, March 1979 (mimeographed)